Social Accountability and Selfhood

For my wife Ann,
and my children Mark, Laura, Emily and Jo

Social Accountability and Selfhood

JOHN SHOTTER

Basil Blackwell

© John Shotter 1984

First published 1984
Basil Blackwell Publisher Limited
108 Cowley Road, Oxford OX4 1JF, England

Basil Blackwell Inc.
432 Park Avenue South, Suite 1505
New York, NY 10016, USA

British Library Cataloguing in Publication Data

Shotter, John
    Social accountability and selfhood.
    1. Psychology, Physiological
    2. Human behavior
    I. Title
    152   QP360

    ISBN 0-631-13021-7

Typeset at The Spartan Press Ltd., Lymington, Hants
Printed in Great Britain by T.J. Press Ltd, Padstow

Contents

16418

Acknowledgements

There are many people whom I would like to thank either for help, or for encouragement, or for a willingness to listen, or for critical comments which have made me think more than twice and try to express myself more clearly (always a difficult task in the midst of all this indefiniteness). They are: Alan Gauld, whose sensibility and moderation in all things mental I have always admired; Rom Harré, who is always trying to cheer me up; Ken and Mary Gergen, John Newson, David Smail, Keith Davis, Peter Ossorio, Bill Joynson, Peter Collett and Chris Blunsdon, my word-processing mentor. The immediate irony of the choice of cover picture for this volume will not escape the families of academics who write; the deeper ironies I'll leave to Freudians.

I am very grateful to the publishers of articles which form the basis of some of the chapters of this book. Chapter 3 is based on 'What is it to be human?', in N. Armistead (ed.), *Reconstructing Social Psychology* (Harmondsworth: Penguin, 1974, copyright © Nigel Armistead and contributors, 1974, reprinted by permission of Penguin Books Ltd); chapter 4 on 'The development of personal powers', in M. P. M. Richards (ed.) *The Integration of a Child into a Social World* (London: Cambridge University Press, 1974); chapter 5 on 'The cultural context of communication studies: methodological and theoretical issues, in A. Lock (ed.), *Action, Gesture and Symbol* (London: Academic Press, 1978, copyright: Academic Press Inc. (London) Ltd.). Chapter 6 is based on 'An ecological approach to cognitive development: implicate orders, joint action, and intentionality' (written with John Newson and used here with his kind permission), in G. Butterworth and P. Light (eds), *Social Cognition: Studies of the Development of Understanding* (Sussex: The Harvester Press, 1982). Chapter 7 began as an invited paper given at the British Psychological Society, Developmental Section Annual Conference, Durham, England, in September 1983. Chapter 8 is based on 'Vico, moral worlds, accountability, and personhood', in P. Heelas and A. Lock (eds), *Indigenous Psychologies: the Anthropology of the Self* (London: Academic Press, 1981, copyright: Academic Press Inc. (London) Ltd.). Chapter 9 is based on 'Telling and reporting: prospective and retrospective uses of self-ascriptions', in C. Antaki (ed.), *The Psychology of Ordinary Explanations of Social Behaviour* (London: Academic Press, 1981, copyright: Academic Press Inc. (London) Ltd.); while chapter 11 first appeared as ' "Duality of structure" and "intentionality" in an ecological psychology', *Journal for the Theory of Social Behaviour* (1983) *13*, 1943.

Vladimir: To have lived is not enough for them.
Estragon: They have to talk about it.

(Samuel Beckett, *Waiting for Godot*)

Introduction

The different chapters in this book each, to some extent, approach the same problem – that of what it is to be an autonomous, responsible person. Taken together, I hope they present a progressive story and each constitutes a part of a whole which is implicated within them all: that whole being what I have called 'the ecology of everyday life'.

Although the book may contain many unresolved problems and indicate many as yet unexplored regions, it attempts to chart a 'space' within which to conduct a wholly new kind of psychological research: simply, research into *what* it is to be a human being, research into our 'whatness'.

Surprising though it may seem to say it, psychology has not yet addressed the question of the nature of our being directly. Indeed, currently, the character of the question it raises is not easily grasped – 'Surely that's a mystical matter. Isn't your concern with what we used to call people's souls?', I'm often asked (or told). To me, however, there is no more practical a question. Aristotle (1928, Z 1028a) attempts to clarify its nature thus:

> There are several senses in which a thing may be said to 'be' . . . in one sense the 'being' meant is 'what a thing is' or a 'this', and in another sense it means a quality or quantity or one of the other things that are predicated as these are. While 'being' has all these senses, obviously that which 'is' primarily is the 'what', which indicates the substance of the thing.

What we believe ourselves to be determines how we treat one another (and ourselves) in our practical everyday affairs. But, by operating as a theoretical science (in Aristotles's sense of the term – see Joachim, 1951, pp. 1–18), psychology forecloses upon the question as to the nature of our being simply by assuming it, by hypothesis, to be of this or that kind, i.e. as if it were only a question of it being a 'this'. But to attempt to answer the question that way, by assuming that people simply *are*, say, information-processing devices, and then by showing that on the basis of that assumption one can act to bring about a certain range of predictable results, is to misunderstand the nature of the question entirely. On the basis of other assumptions other results could no doubt be obtained, and so on. And none of all these findings would at all bear upon the question of what in fact we are.

The question cannot be answered in that way, by the use of 'theories' (as is argued at greater length below). And in the meantime, we struggle on in our daily affairs without a disciplined way of investigating what actually we are. The answer to the question lies, I shall argue, at least in part, in how we account for ourselves to ourselves in and against the background of our ordinary everyday affairs – not just in and against a few, certain selected activities, such as games or dramas used as models for all the rest, but in and against the background of everything in which we are or can be involved. For it is within that whole hurly-burly that our being is constituted – where being able to construct orderly activities within it is just a part of what it is to be the beings that we are.

> How could human behaviour be described? Surely only by showing the actions of a variety of humans, as they are all mixed up together. Not what *one* man is doing *now* but the whole hurly-burly, is the background against which we see an action, and it determines our judgement, our concepts, and our reactions. (Wittgenstein, 1980, vol. 1, no. 629)

Our accounts of ourselves must clearly be situated in the world to which we owe our being as we understand it, in the world of our everyday social life. But what is that world?

It is, I shall maintain, a world consisting not only of socially 'constructed' institutions, continually reproduced (and transformed) by the accountable activities occurring within them, but also of a larger social process out of which such institutions arise, a process which I have called our social ecology. By that I mean a complex of unaccounted for (and intrinsically unaccountable) interdependencies between people. I have called this kind of activity 'joint action'; it is unaccountable because it is productive of outcomes unintended by the individuals involved in it. But nonetheless, due to the intrinsic 'intentionality' of human action, i.e. its specificatory, structuring or form-producing nature, such outcomes always have a structure or style to them. It is in their joint action that people produce the institutions within which they make sense of their activities to one another.

The circumstances are such that people, without any awareness of having done so, constitute between themselves a common sense, common ways of making sense of whatever occurs to, in or around them. I have attempted to capture the character of this situation in what might be called, the 'social accountability' thesis: that our understanding and our experience of our reality are constituted for us very largely by the ways in which we must talk in our attempts to account for the things and events within it – where a part of that reality is, of course, ourselves. I say 'must', because our ways of accounting for things have a coercive quality to them; only if we make sense of things in certain approved of ways can we be accounted by others in our society as competent, responsible members of it.

Now, whilst human beings who are already constituted as accountable, responsible persons can go out and gather 'information' in a wholly individualistic way about the 'things' and 'events' in their 'external world', they cannot gain their knowledge of how to be such persons in that manner, i.e. persons who are able to see their surroundings as constituting an 'external world', containing 'events', 'objects', etc., as well as other 'persons' like themselves. They owe that knowledge, I shall argue, to their embedding in social activities of a particular kind in their society, to their embedding in certain 'developmental practices'. It is in this sense that the issues of selfhood and social accountability are inseparable: one cannot become the kind of person required in one's society, i.e. one able to reproduce its social order in one's actions, unless one learns its accounting practices, the authoritative ways of making sense which constitute its reality in their operation.

In Part I, I set the scene with a discussion of accounting practices and the difference between accounts and theories. As accounting goes on everywhere in life, and not just in special circumstances, some issues to do with the 'ecology' of everyday life are introduced here also: the different rights and duties of first, second and third persons regarding one another are discussed, as well as whether accounts are given retrospectively, prospectively or simultaneously with the activity to which they are applied. Part I continues with a discussion of psychology as a practical-descriptive science rather than as an empirical-theoretical one (in chapter 2), and goes on (in chapter 3) to describe in certain important respects what it is to be human.

In Part II, the question of how one comes to be the kind of person who can act accountably in one's society is discussed. First, in chapter 4, it is suggested that autonomy consists in possessing 'personal powers', i.e. the ability to act in such a way that one knows how oneself is 'placed' or 'situated' in relation to others involved in one's actions, and that these are acquired by those around one treating one as one term in a personal relationship, i.e. as if one already possessed such powers. In chapter 5, the nature of 'developmental practices' is discussed and their 'practical hermeneutical' nature described, while the 'opportunities' for development made available to one in the social ecology of one's surroundings are described in chapter 6. Chapter 7 completes Part II by showing that most current developmental theories do not face the problem of how we learn *to be* individuals, but treat us as 'developmentally self-sufficient', i.e. as already individuals from the start. Thus it is difficult to understand how, within the frameworks they provide, different modes of social accountability could ever be learned. Chapter 7 also discusses the 'political economy of developmental opportunities': the fact the opportunities required for development are scarce (as they are not freely available, but are provided only by second persons), and thus differential access to them is socially controlled.

Part III explores further the character of the social accountability thesis. In particular, Vico's remarkable account of the human 'creation' of social institutions is discussed in relation to the notion of 'joint action' and its production of (individually) unintended consequences, due to the intrinsically intentional nature of social action (in chapter 8). It is within the institutions that they construct between themselves that people can change one another: they do it, not by *reporting* 'information' about things in the 'external world', but by *telling* things to one another (in chapter 9). However, what people say to another, although it has a certain currency in certain situations, can be deeply misleading; people can be wrong in their own self-definitions. Chapter 10 explores the over-spatialized nature of our 'mind- and self-talk' and the mystification such talk can produce.

In Part IV, an alternative 'time–space' language is introduced to describe the nature of the ecology in which we are embedded, a language of regions and moments of activity – where regions are not wholly spatial, as all activities take some time to be recognizable as the activities they are, and moments are not wholly temporal, as all activities must take up some space in order to be activities. The aim of chapter 11 is to provide a language for talking about the world at large such that selfhood is a natural or physical possibility within it.

The aim of all this talk (this writing) is, as I said earlier, to attempt to introduce the notion of a practical-descriptive psychology, where (to put the matter reflexively): a practical-descriptive psychology describes (or instructs) people in the ways in which people can tell (or instruct) one another in how to do things – including the ways in which they describe themselves and their psychological states to themselves. In other words, not only is its aim practical or instructive, but it is itself an example of the activities for which it attempts to account.

Part One

Accounting Practices and Their Paradigms

1

The Social Accountability of
Human Action

The central shift of perspective exemplified in most of what follows in this book is the attention paid, not at all to the structure of behaviour itself, but to the structure and function of the accounts of behaviour that people give of themselves in their everyday social life. Accounts can be distinguished from theories in this sense: an account of an action or activity is concerned with talking about the action or activity as the activity it *is*; it works, if it works at all, to render the activity, to those who confront it or are involved in it, as something 'visibly-rational-and-reportable-for-all-practical-purposes, i.e., 'accountable', as organizations of commonplace everyday activities' (Garfinkel, 1967, p. vii). In other words, an account is an aid to perception, functioning to constitute an otherwise indeterminate flow of activity as a sequence of recognizable events, i.e. events of a kind already known about within a society's ways of making sense of things.

A theory, on the other hand, is not concerned with activities as they are; it is not simply an aid to those confronted with raw appearances, in making sense of them. It is a cognitive device in terms of which people may reshape and reproduce events which already make one kind of sense to them, and talk about them as being other than what ordinarily they seem to be. Unlike an account, which is addressed to the second persons involved in a situation with first persons, a theory is of use to third-person outsiders, to those unconcerned with the personal situation of first and second persons; rather than context-dependent and personal, a theory may thus (to an extent) be context-free and impersonal. However, a theory must always be accompanied, it would seem, by an account of how it should be understood and used – unless, that is, it can be formulated as a set of specifications for a certain pattern of result-producing activities (Stapp, 1972). Then, the distinction between theories and accounts collapses, and theories degenerate, so to speak, into accounts. In what follows, the distinction between theories and accounts will be crucial, for my main critique of psychological research will revolve around, not so much its failings as an 'experimental' science, but its attempt to be, as McGuire (1973) puts it, a 'theory relevant' enterprise.

The Psychologist's Dilemma: 'Finders' or 'Makers'?

To state a truism: as psychologists, we are also persons as well as being scientists. Thus we cannot forever stand outside of the social life of which we are a part. Although we may find it necessary to maintain a distance from those we study while studying them, we cannot permanently stand apart from them. Besides our professional colleagues, those we study must also appraise our 'findings'. As a result, the claims we make about human conduct will have an ambiguous status. Thus the dilemma we find ourselves in is this: in addition to being evaluated as claims to scientific knowledge, such claims are also open to evaluation as accounts of human conduct in everyday life terms, working to make the conduct to which they are applied what it is. And not only may these two kinds of evaluations conflict, currently they very often do conflict. If psychology is to progress, this ambiguity must be resolved; it is in our experimental manipulations that it makes itself felt most acutely.

Experimentation: Testing Procedures

When as psychologists we manipulate people's behaviour in our experiments, we must use the normal procedures and resources available to us as members of our society for so doing, procedures implicit in our society's way of life. If we do not, then we run the risk of being misunderstood, and of people not treating the experimental situation as we psychologists desire. A central resource available to us as to other people is the ordinary language of everyday life, and the ways of speaking it allows. People can and often do influence one another's behaviour merely by the use of words – for language is not just a system within which we can all describe things but is a medium within which we can 'do' things with others through communication with them (Austin, 1962; Searle, 1969). Furthermore, when we do talk about what we have done, are doing, or are about to do, i.e. describe or account for our actions, we must do that also within the ordinary language of our society. We are, in fact, inescapably embedded with it; our reality is constituted for us, whether as ordinary persons or as psychologists, by the very language we use in our attempts to describe it (Winch, 1958; Berger and Luckman, 1967; Smedslund, 1978). In other words, people are restricted in what they can intelligibly and legitimately express in their language, by the framework of concepts implicit in it. And these concepts seem to be interconnected in such a way that (1) there are severe limitations upon what are acceptable ways of talking, perceiving, acting, thinking and evaluating, and (2) given one set of utterances, acts, perceptions, thoughts or evaluations, others follow necessarily, or are necessarily excluded (Smedslund, 1978). In other words, in using ordinary language one must, apparently, make implicit reference to a system of norms or standards indicative of its proper use. As psychologists, if we want to be understood by ordinary people, we are restricted in the same kind of way; we cannot formulate any generally intelligible theories about human conduct except ultimately in its terms – or, if not in accord with its implicit standards, then at least we must take notice of them in some way. Hence, the ambiguity of any claims we might make; for we have to satisfy social as well as scientific criteria.

Much of the knowledge people have of how to do things with other people in the course of communicating with them is of course vague and unformulated, known only unreflectively in a taken-for-granted kind of way. However, few people would disagree that we do in fact know quite a number of ways in which we can influence the outcome of another persons's behaviour (in fact psychologists are always being accused of rediscovering the obvious): we can change what another person can do by making the tasks before them more difficult; by telling or showing them things; by changing their rewards; by influencing what they expect to be the outcome of an action; and so on. And people act at a practical level in anticipation of achieving such aims, not because people are naturally consistent with themselves and each other, but because they *must* be consistent. As members of a moral order, they have a duty to act in ways which are not only intelligible, but which make sense in other kinds of ways also. They must make reference to the 'vocabulary of motives' (Mills, 1940) current in their society at the time. And it is only in virtue of their ability to fulfil the duties associated with being a member of such an order – by becoming responsible adults not reliant like children upon others to judge and evaluate their behaviour – that they can qualify for the status of autonomous persons, with the right to act not under the continual surveillance of others. It is because one is a member of a moral community that one *must* act so as to fulfil in the future the commitments implicit in one's actions in the present (Winch, 1958; Shotter, 1981a and b).

Thus, if one wants to remain an intelligible, acceptable member of one's society (even if on occasions one feels it is one's society not oneself that is wrong), then one must make reference in one's actions to the standards, values, criteria, etc., embodied in its ways of speaking, in its modes of acceptable communication. All our practical conduct should be informed by the 'guidance' they give; one cannot as an individual transcend them. They cannot be 'refuted' like scientific theories: by expected outcomes, based upon them, failing to occur. For if, as ordinary persons, our interpersonal projects fail, we do not question the validity of our knowledge of the workings of social life at large, in fact we do just the opposite: we put it to use once again in attempting to discover the possible reasons for *our* failure – perhaps the task we set the person was too difficult, their ability insufficient, or the rewards too small, etc. In other words, what is at stake at a practical level is not the validity of our knowledge but the validity of our actions, whether the procedures proposed in attempting to bring off a desired outcome will work or not. Parents with their children, bosses with their workers, governments with those they rule over, even psychologists with their subjects, all attempt to influence people's behaviour by manipulating the conditions under which they expect the behaviour they desire to occur.

Hence the ambiguity of the psychologist's position: they make use of the social-psychological knowledge implicit in their common sense, not only to formulate explicit theories about the conditions conducive to certain kinds of behaviour in certain kinds of people, but also to devise conditions supposedly appropriate for their test, conditions which require social skills to establish. The ambiguity of their position is revealed if their procedures fail to produce the outcome predicted by the theory: was the theory wrong or the procedure inadequate? The results of social-psychological research thus may have not just one use, as is commonly supposed (namely in the empirical testing of theories), but two, for they may also be used as

TABLE 1   *The dual function of data*

	seen as data	as indicators
function	to confirm theory	to validate procedure
evaluated by	formal match with deduced predictions	'measured' against intuitive expectations
standard referred to in evaluation	explicitly stated, but initially uncertain principles	implicit, but already certain principles (see Schutz's account of stocks of knowledge – 1964, pp. 72–3)

indicators of the efficacy of a procedure in provoking a particular outcome. Table 1 illustrates some of the major differences between these two uses, i.e. between 'data' actually seen as data, and the results obtained being seen as indicative of a practical skill at managing action outcomes.

Although they ought to be distinct, these two uses of experimental results are completely confounded in social psychological research, at the moment – due to the insistence that social psychology exists in only one guise, as a 'theoretical-empirical' science seeking context-free principles (when it must exist primarily, but not exclusively, as a context-dependent 'practical-descriptive' science concerned with accounting for, and the criticism of, our accounting practices – see next section). Besides producing a great deal of methodological muddle into the field (e.g. over the proper place and function of experiments: as to whether they serve to test theories, or merely to provide 'hints' about the texture of our social life – see Tajfel and Fraser, 1978, p. 12), the most bewildering consequence is that the response to experimental results can be somewhat arbitrary; their empirical force as data may be accepted seemingly almost as a matter of taste or preference. Thus, as Joynson (1974, pp. 11–13) and Gergen (1980, p. 71), as well as many others have pointed out, circumstances can always be found in which many supposedly significant findings in social psychology can be completely reversed.

Take research in the area of interpersonal attraction for instance: the obvious proposition that 'like attracts like' (in some circumstances) can be matched with the equally obvious proposition that (in others) 'opposites attract'. McGuire (1973, p. 449) remarks, in discussing the dilemma raised by just such an example:

> Both the original obvious hypothesis and the obvious reversed hypothesis are reasonable and valid in the sense that if all our premises obtained, then our conclusion would pretty much have to follow.

It would have to follow, not because of the causal relations involved, operating irrespective of people's interests and desires, but because if all our premises obtained, then they would constitute the conditions under which the behaviour in question ought normally to occur (if other circumstances do not intervene); that is how normal people would choose to behave, to retain their membership of their society. If they did not, then we would seek the reasons why.

In other words, the problem here is the familiar one of knowing full well that particular modes of human being and action are real possibilities, but of not knowing the particular conditions required for their actual instantiation. Depending upon circumstances it is certainly true that both 'like attracts like' *and* 'opposites attract'; but upon what circumstances? These, of course, can be investigated. But it is an investigation of a practical kind to do with 'managing' an interpersonal situation, and not at all like that involved in testing scientific theories. Thus, as McGuire (p. 449) points out, what an experiment may test

> is not whether the hypothesis is true but rather whether the experimenter is a sufficiently ingenious stage manager to produce in the laboratory conditions which demonstrate that an obviously true hypothesis is correct.

That is, it can be simply a test of their 'management' skills. (Their 'theories' remain invulnerable in such tests, for *what* is actually claimed theoretically is never systematically and explicitly described – Harré and Secord, 1972, pp. 35–36).

Many of the 'hypothesis testing' investigations in social psychological research are in fact, McGuire maintains, of this kind, i.e. tests using hypotheses already known to be tautologically true in the context assumed by those testing them; hence, rather than 'finding' the results they obtain, psychologists can often be said to have 'made' them. This need not in itself disqualify such investigations as scientific investigations, for, as Lakatos (1970) shows, it is a benign feature of all major scientific research programmes that they are anchored in a 'hard core' set of principles which are irrefutable in principle – a point we shall be at pains to argue also. In psychology, however, the consequences seem not to be benign, for as McGuire (1973, p. 449) adds:

> Experiments on such hypotheses naturally turn out to be more like demonstrations than tests. If the experiment does not come out 'right', then the researcher does not say that the hypothesis is wrong but rather that something was wrong with the experiment, and he corrects and revises it . . . .

In other words, while the avowed aim of psychological researchers may be to make their notions of truth conform to things as they are, they in fact often work to bring things into conformity with their notions of truth. This is why the consequences of Lakatosian irrefutability cannot be looked upon as benign in psychology: people can be a source of change in one another.

Indeed, as already mentioned, it is a well-known although little codified fact of social life, probably because it is considered reprehensible, that people can manipulate one another's behaviour by establishing the conditions necessary for desired outcomes to occur. Because he did attempt to set out explicitly, as if in a 'workshop manual', the conditions in politics necessary for achieving one's desired ends, Machiavelli was called diabolical (though later the devil was called Machiavellian). In his advice to princes, Machiavelli (1961) suggests, for instance, that the wise prince should, if his authority is uncertain and he requires the faithful support of his people in time of adversity, 'devise ways by which his citizens are always and in all circumstances dependent on him and on his authority; and then they will always be faithful to him' (p. 71). However, it must be added here that establishing the conditions necessary for a particular outcome does not mean that people will necessarily produce the required outcome; whether they actually do so or not is still an empirical matter. Just as with Newton's laws of motion, other factors may intervene to modify the outcomes such principles describe. Recollect, for instance, the first law which states: 'Every body will continue in a state of rest or uniform motion (*unless acted upon by an external force*).' Nonetheless certain conditions may be necessary to the performance of an action, even if they are not always sufficient.

Researchers have attempted to escape from the 'epistemological worry', as McGuire terms it, about manipulational laboratory experiments not being adequate tests of theories, by attempting to test their theories in natural settings (e.g. Argyle's (1969) 'new look'). But as McGuire points out, the same problem arises again. Researchers failing to confirm their hypotheses may still say that they unwisely chose an inappropriate natural setting in which to test them. Thus, if this deep defect in what he terms 'theory relevant research' is to be overcome, a more fundamentally new outlook is required, he feels, than that provided by research in naturalistic settings. I agree: however I think a quite different solution is required.

I shall suggest that psychologists must turn away in large part from 'theory relevant research', at least in the sense in which such research is currently conducted, towards research of quite a different kind, towards what one might call 'practice relevant' research: an activity in which one conducts oneself primarily as a person, and only secondarily, still within a personal context, as a scientist. But psychologists cannot forget their professional status as members of academic institutions, with all the rights and duties which such a status implies. This inevitably puts constraints upon what legitimately they may undertake to do: their task as agents in a social world is not to 'make' or to 'do' (see the section below for the sense of these terms), but to *talk*: to describe what is, as well as what might be possible, and the conditions of its possibility, and thus by implication to criticize current forms of life – they do not themselves have a brief to make changes (hence the non-benign character of much psychological research in which people are 'made' to take on this or that character under the guise of 'finding' the truth about them). Only if psychologists are clear as to their role at any one moment, as to whether it is as a person, a professional academic, a professional scientist, a human engineer, etc., can the dilemmas of reflexivity be avoided.

Accounting: Evaluating Action Outcomes

I shall propose in the next chapter that we approach psychology as a 'practical science' in Aristotle's sense of that term. Primarily its stance is non-empirical in the sense of not having anything to do with the testing of theories; this does not mean, however, that it cannot support a body of research, nor that the accounts (of our accounting practices) it offers cannot be warranted or evaluated. The research activity it gives rise to is, as we shall see, very like, but crucially different from, artificial-intelligence (AI) research in cognitive psychology. As such, it is an activity which can be justified in many of the same ways as AI (Newell, 1973; Allport, 1975; Boden, 1977; Cohen, 1977; Johnson-Laird and Wason, 1977). Workers in AI claim: (1) that experimentation cannot lead to the formulation of theories, as experiments are only to test theories once they have been formulated (Johnson-Laird and Wason, 1977); and (2) there are some quite specific *a priori* criteria arising out of common-sense considerations which any psychological model should satisfy, and these must be formulated as a system of necessary relations before any rigorous empirical work can begin (Cohen, 1977, Ch. 1). However, rather than building models of 'inner' psychological processes, we shall be concerned with investigations into ways in which accounts of our actual accounting practices might be systematically formulated. The failure to recognize the necessity for such research, and the misunderstanding of its nature, arises from the fact that psychologists still conceive of themselves as studying a field of objective phenomena, similar to that studied by other sciences. Whereas the phenomena they study are not only conscious phenomena, they are phenomena which are only manifested within the confines of an everyday form of social life; rather than objects, they are activities, requiring description by verbs, not nouns. Thus the behaviour of interest to psychologists is not only unlike that of billard balls and planets, it is also unlike that of animals, for ultimately it is accountable behaviour. It is the behaviour of ordinary people in everyday life, in which it is normally necessary for those performing it to know, at least in some sense, *what* they are doing, and to be able to give an account of it or to justify it to others in some way, if called upon to do so (see Mills, 1940; Garfinkel, 1967; Scott and Lyman, 1968; Harré and Secord, 1972; McHugh *et al.*, 1974; Harré, 1979, for accounts of accounts, accounting and accountability).

Although accounts serve to render objects and events 'visibly-rational-and-reportable-for-all-practical-purposes', to repeat Garfinkel's formulation, to account for one's behaviour is not to illustrate, depict or represent it; it is not to repeat in some way the same behaviour again. It is to do something else, something different in addition to what one has already done; it is to communicate something *about* what one's behaviour was, is, or might be – for as Harré and Secord (1972, p. 159) point out, an account may be anticipatory, retrospective or contemporaneous with the sequence of things done to which it refers. As such, it stands in quite a different relation to the behaviour for which it accounts than a causal theory of that behaviour: a theory explains the behaviour in terms of events, or things existing prior to it, while an account is merely a more explicit description of what the action actually *is*. In other words, it serves to describe the action as something explainable within the familiar framework of everyday life. Often it does this by being an indicator of future action, i.e. by describing the goal at which the person was trying to aim in the future by their action at that moment. Or it may serve to justify people's behaviour by revealing the criteria or standards they applied in their 'tryings', the grounds of their action, thus to assure questioners of their action's acceptability, legitimacy, appropriateness, etc. As Ossorio (1973) shows in his 'parametric formulation of behaviour' (see Shotter & Burton, 1983), according to the context in which an account is requested, it indicates what the behaviour *is*, by mentioning whatever is necessary to distinguish it from other behaviours with which it might be confused; hence, the account may explicitly refer to any one or a number of different parameters or dimensions in terms of which actions may be individuated. This does not mean to say that, as descriptions, our accounts are formulated simply in superficial terms, referring merely to observable behaviour or private experiences. They are formulated in psychological terms; they refer to people's states of mind, to their beliefs, motives, desires, perceptions, imaginings and suchlike – and the task is not to discover what the objects are to which such terms refer, but to understand what can be done by their use (and what it is which makes such an activity possible) in everyday life.

People cannot of course account for all their conduct, nor need they be able to. In fact, it is usually immediately evident as to what they are doing. It is only normal to request them to account for it if it is not immediately obvious what they are up to. Indeed, the very existence or possibility of being motivated to request an account arises out of the fact that, rather than puzzlement, the more usual state of affairs is of understanding people's actions perfectly well. A successful account of human activity in everyday life restores that understanding. It serves to construct a relation between unusual, unanticipated, special, puzzling, untoward, suspicious or enigmatic conduct and a more familiar pattern or framework of intelligibility. And it is in this sense that accounts may be said to explain problematic conduct: by making it clear in relation to such a framework, *what* that conduct is, i.e. what part it plays within the framework. In the process, the intelligibility of such a framework, though not explicitly articulated, is taken for granted as a directly experienced reality (Ryle, 1963; Schutz, 1962, 1964, 1967).

This reliance upon a body of taken-for-granted intuitive or common-sense knowledge, or as Schutz (1964) terms it 'the stock of knowledge at hand', existing prior to any observing or theorizing that we might do, is crucial. It is the conceptual capacities we acquire during our socialization which allow us, as autonomous adults, to make sense of and account ourselves for our actions in socially acceptable terms. One cannot oneself be said to know or to be doing anything unless one already knows in some sense what it is that one is doing, saying or thinking; all such activities presuppose conceptual capacities (Gauld and Shotter, 1977), i.e. an ability to talk about or to represent one's actions in one way or another publicly. Although not always ultimately decisive (as powerful authorities may play a decisive role also in defining what it *is* one is said to be doing), such a reliance upon a body of taken-for-granted knowledge is usually sufficient for most practical purposes. Accounts (explanations) may be evaluated by reference to it, by 'measuring' them up, so to speak, against the standards provided by the tacit or intuitive knowledge they are meant to specify and describe, to check whether they do in fact succeed in explicitly specifying them appropiately (see Chomsky, 1965, for a more formal account of such evaluation or justification procedures with respect to linguistic descriptions). Thus central to the activity of giving accounts is reference to people's intuitive knowledge of the normative structure of everyday social life, and the fact that anything intelligible we say about human conduct is open to evaluation as right or wrong, accurate or inaccurate, adequate or inadequate, true or false, good or bad, etc. Such judgements are not mere expressions of prejudice, but are grounded on reasons which may themselves be evaluated as 'good' or 'bad' in their turn, and so on. In fact, such evaluations of accounts are commonplace and may be aimed at satisfying many distinct kinds of criteria (see section below).

Reflexivity and Accounting for Accounts

To repeat a number of points made earlier: as persons, psychologists know how to stage-manage the production of certain experimental outcomes because, after all, they have grown up into, and currently live within, the same system of social constraints and enablements as those they study. Thus it should come as no surprise that they can, to an extent, manipulate their subjects in the laboratory; such an ability is simply an application of the manipulational skills possessed to a degree by everyone – though some clearly have more talent at it than others. However, if they want to have their conduct as psychologists evaluated as intelligible, rational and legitimate by ordinary people, i.e. by those they study, they must also evaluate it in the same terms as they do. For, as already mentioned, everyday activities are intrinsically reflexive in the sense that they contain within themselves devices, methods or procedures for justifying, explaining, interpreting or in some way making those same activities accountable. The psychologist as a person with a particular role and status is susceptible to this kind of accountability.

This is where the psychologist's dilemma as a scientist lies. For other scientists do not have evaluations placed upon them by their own subject matter. If other scientists claim, as scientists are prone to do, that 'X is best explained by supposing that it is not really what it appears to be, namely X, but something else altogether, possibly Y,' they do not run the risk of self-refutation. For they are not a part of their own subject matter and thus do not have implicitly to include themselves in their claims. Psychologists, however, do run such a risk: they cannot deny certain 'foundation-tenets of common sense' (Koch, 1975, p. 5) – e.g. that they are acting, thinking, observing, evaluating, accountable persons – without brooking self-contradiction. They cannot, in other words, conclude from a body of evidence that X is really Y, if by ordinarily taking X to be Y the very activity of drawing such conclusions from such data is precluded by that conclusion – unless, that is, they want to claim that for some reason they really do have special access to processes of understanding, reasoning, observing, etc., unavailable to everyone else, i.e. that they are not included in their own theory. But then, were they to make such a claim, if their knowledge were communicable, their 'advantage' could soon be wiped out, and their claim nullified (Scheibe, 1978).

Psychologists' accounts of human conduct must, therefore, be reflexive, i.e. they must account for the psychologist's own conduct. Thus the whole psychological endeavour fails if, in their accounting, psychologists neglect or decline to account for their own accounting. Lacking reflexivity, their explicit accounts of human conduct will conflict with what, in everyday life at large, they do when acting as ordinary persons. In the later chapters of this book I shall offer some accounts of accounts and accounting. With this in mind, it will be useful to make some comments here of a grammatical nature, with the purpose of indicating just some of the different functions accounts may serve in ordinary, everyday affairs. For many of the issues discussed so far are recognized and marked in the structure of ordinary discourse, particularly in the person and tense of verbs.

Grammatical Categories and Accounts: Person and Tense

Accounts, in rendering phenomena explainable as events or objects within the framework of everyday life reality, may be constructed either from a second- or third-person standpoint. Being related as a second-person to a first-person is quite distinct from being related as a third-person to a first, as all texts upon grammatical categories (e.g. Lyons, 1968) will make clear. Linguistically, first and second persons, even if non-personal or in fact inanimate, are always personified, and related to one another as persons, as beings present to one another in a situation. By contrast: third persons need not be personified (they can be 'its'); nor are they 'present' in themselves, so to speak, to other beings or entities; nor are they necessarily 'in a situation'. Indeed, the category is so non-specific that it may be used to refer to absolutely anything so long as it is external to, or outside of, the agency or situation of first as well as second persons.

Arguably, the three roles are necessary to the possibility of accountable action, its existence being dependent upon people's capacities as first persons to act, as second persons to monitor their actions as to what they are and what they mean, and as third persons to judge it as acceptable or not, etc., against objective, impersonal standards. They would (all three roles) thus be mutually constitutive and reciprocally determining; i.e. none could exist except in relation to the others.

These grammatical categories may be used in accounts to mark an important distinction: that between accounts of those occasions when people are present to or immersed in a situation with things they experience as being other than but nonetheless like themselves (i.e. other agencies), and accounts of those occasions when they experience other entities as being both outside of and quite unlike themselves (i.e. as objects). Objects afford us our experience of them without taking any part in the matter themselves; our experience of them simply arises *within* us, while our experience of other agencies arises in the relation *between* them and us, with them contributing along with ourselves to the outcome. The relation is thus mutual, and its products are the joint products of those actively involved in it. Objects may be experienced in immediate perception as in some sense complete; agencies in being known only in their actions are experienced – unless there is a known prior limit upon what they can do – as boundless, as in some sense free agents. There is thus an intrinsic uncertainty as to their natures, as to whether they can be completely known or not. Thus accounts given in answer to questions of the kind 'What are you doing?' referring to second persons, will clearly have quite a different quality to them from those, such as 'What is he (it) doing?', which refer to third persons. And people's expectations regarding them will thus vary accordingly: for instance, as to whether the account supplied is open-ended or not, or refers to someone or something 'inside' one's situation or not, etc.

Another grammatical category of significance concerns the tense of verbs. As Lyons (1968, pp. 304–6) notes, it is usual but misleading to relate a verb's tense to time-relations, as to whether the action is past, present or future. For one could equally well in a 'timeless' fashion use tense to mark whether one was delivering an account as a report, an expectation, a telling or an avowal. Thus without committing ourselves with respect to the temporal location of an action, the aspect of tense of interest to us is to do with the distinction between the *perfect* and *imperfect* tenses, between completed and still ongoing action. In response to the question 'What are you doing?' (continuous action) one may reply by describing the overall goal at which one is aiming in one's current action. While in response to 'What have you done?' (completed action), on some occasions at least, one may simply point and say 'That' (referring to the objective result of one's action). As scientists, psychologists are concerned very largely with completed actions from a third-person, external-observer point of view; persons, however, are concerned very largely with ongoing, incomplete activity from a second-person standpoint, with the meaningful rather than the objective properties of people's actions. See chapter 9 for a discussion of the distinction between accounting 'for' and accounting 'in' action.

Rights and Duties: The Moral Ecology of Everyday Life

The rights and duties associated with these grammatical categories will also influence the style and function of expected accounts. In everyday life, one may be a first-person performer, a second-person 'understanderer' or recipient, or a third-person observer, judge or critic, or 'object' of another's action. As a second-person recipient one has a status quite different from those in third-person roles: one is involved in and required to maintain the action; one must attend to what is intended and ignore what just happens (what is not intended). As second-persons in everyday life, we do not have the right to step out of our 'personal involvement' with other people, and attend to aspects of their person to which they do not intend us to attend — and to ask them to account for matters for which they do not deem themselves responsible. In the ecology of daily social life, there seems to be a moral sanction against such a shifting of roles; unless, that is, one is a physician or psychotherapist, hairdresser or dentist, or suchlike, and then people do intend you to examine the unintended aspects of their behaviour and appearance. The obligation second persons are under, however, does not extend to third persons. Hence our unease when, as first-person performers attempting a tricky interpersonal encounter, we notice ourselves observed by a third-person outsider; we experience ourselves as someone else's 'object', as under surveillance, fearful that we shall be judged and questioned about something over which we have no control. The rights, duties, privileges and obligations of the different 'persons' in everyday social life are such as to give rise to two kinds of accounting: (1) that from within the flow of action, when one clarifies one's action as a first person to a second person in some way by further action (see chapter 9, and Shotter, 1981a); and (2) that in which one breaks off, or is uninvolved in the flow of action, and delivers one's account as a third-person outsider (Harré and Secord, 1972).

A theory of accounts and accounting must make clear the relations between these two kinds of account from these two different standpoints, for currently they are confounded, and this leaves psychologists unclear as to their own role and status: are they finders or makers? If they are to be just finders, that does not preclude them from finding out, of course, about how making is done. And my point in making these distinctions is this: the conduct of social life is based upon a right we assign to first-persons to *tell* us about themselves and their experiences, and to have what they say taken seriously as meaning what they intend it to mean (Cavell, 1969) — as long as we feel they can observe a duty both to distinguish in their conduct those activities for which they are responsible from those for which they are not, and to execute the former in an intelligible and legitimate manner. All our valid forms of inquiry are based upon such a right, and it is this right which I aim to reassert. For it seems to me the authority of first-persons has been usurped in recent times by the third-person, external observer position. Thus, if this book is read as a treatise aimed at increasing the authority of *that* position yet further, it will be misunderstood.

2

A Science of Psychology: Theoretical or Practical?

As the 'practice relevant' approach I want to discuss can be characterized in terms of distinctions already drawn between different kinds of 'science' by Aristotle in his *Metaphysics*, it will be worthwhile at this point to describe his classification of the 'sciences' (see Joachim, 1951, upon whom I rely heavily for this account; and A. E. Taylor, 1955). This will allow us to see the important differences between 'theory relevant' research and a 'practical-descriptive' alternative to it. As my position has been strongly influenced by Harré's (1970a) account of powers and agency, and as he and particularly Bhaskar (1975, 1979) have extended the 'realist' position to which it gives rise in the natural sciences to apply to the human and social sciences, it will be also worthwhile at this point to examine Bhaskar's views in the light of Aristotle's distinction between theoretical and practical sciences. We shall find that, although there is a case to be made out for the unity of the natural and social sciences, in that both involve a hermeneutical, interpretive component,[1] the fact that they remain 'theoretical' sciences, satisfying a requirement for exper-ience-independent knowledge, precludes them from using the form of understanding required to understand the practical actions of particular individuals. In short, I reject Bhaskar's 'transcendental realism' and sub-stitute for it a 'mundane realism'.

Artistotle's Classification of the Sciences: Theoretical, Practical and Productive

Artistotle distinguishes three different kinds of 'science': the theoretical (speculative), practical and productive sciences. Now, we would only apply the term 'science' to an activity if a body of theoretical knowledge is involved in it (such that different sciences would involve different bodies of theory), so such a threefold distinction for us would involve three different kinds of theory or modes of theorizing. Aristotle's distinction works, however, in quite a different way; our way of distinguishing would for him only distinguish between three 'theoretical' sciences. He, however, is concerned in his classification to cover the whole sphere of people's intelligent activity, their doings and makings, as well as their contemplating and speculating.

The concept of knowledge he inherited from Socrates and Plato was of knowledge as being inseparable from the power of doing and making. In modern philosophy, by contrast, we have, as Anscombe (1957, p. 57) puts it:

> An incorrigibly contemplative concept of knowledge. Knowledge must be something that is judged as such by being in accordance with the facts. The facts, reality, are prior, and dictate what is to be said, if it is to be knowledge. And this is the explanation of the utter darkness in which we f[ind] ourselves. For if there are two knowledges – one by observation, the other in intention – then it looks as if there must be two objects of knowledge; but if one says the objects are the same, one looks hopelessly for the different *mode of contemplative knowledge* in acting, as if there were a very queer and special sort of seeing eye in the middle of the acting.

This Cartesian view of knowledge – as if it were like an inner object requiring an inner eye to read its characteristics off, so to speak – renders practical action incomprehensible; but it was not Aristotle's view. Neither, for Aristotle, was being thoughtful something one did by withdrawing from action into thought. For thought (i.e. intelligence, reasoning – as the distinguishing characteristic of human beings – permeated all of people's being and doing; and they could just as easily conduct themselves thoughtfully in social life, as craft an object thoughtfully, or thoughtfully ponder and speculate upon the nature of the universe. Thus for Aristotle, any department of human activity – speculation, conduct, production – could be called a 'science' as long as it was alive with true thinking (see also Macmurray, 1957). What Aristotle covers with his classification, then, are the ways in which people can exercise their intelligence, and the different goals that they can achieve in so doing. To slightly adapt Searle's (1979a) useful 'intentional' terminology: people can be said to be aiming at achieving in their activities mind-to-world directions of fit (in speculation); mind-to-mind (in conduct) and world-to-mind (in production).

The accounts he provides of the different attitudes of mind and different procedures involved in the different 'sciences' can be specified in more detail: (1) In a theoretical science, one's attitude of mind is contemplative. The 'scientific person', in this restricted sense of the term, is entirely concerned with knowing or understanding, in a way which leaves them untouched in their *being* by such experiences. Socially and developmentally, they must already be accounted as individuals who know their way around, so to speak, within their society's accounting practices; they already understand its ways of making sense of things. Thus they can play the part of spectators of what there *is* in it – and is there independently of their individual wishes or opinions. Persons adopting such a stance neither desire, nor are they able, to alter the truth of things. Their object is not to bring things into harmony with their notions, but as already mentioned, to achieve a mind-to-world direction of fit in their accounts of things. If such persons experiment and manipulate things, their purpose is still to observe a process, not to modify it. It is the expression of a thing's own nature, independent of any impositions they may make upon it, which they wish to understand.

(2) In the practical (doing) and productive (making) 'sciences' – the art of life or conduct, and the crafts and fine arts respectively – people's object is either to live or to act in certain ways, or to make or to do certain things: it is not to understand them, except as a means of action or production – and then they require the help of 'practical-theory', of images, metaphors or paradigm cases (see below). In these 'sciences', people are concerned with the sphere of process or change: not with the unalterable nature of things. They are concerned not with how things *are*, but with how they might be other than what they are, with how they might change them. Thus the source of the change in the people or the objects dealt with or encountered in such 'sciences' is not seen as being in them, but as being in the actions of the persons acting upon them. It is their will, their deliberate decision or purpose, which produces the *changes* in the entities 'outside' them which are called 'their' acts, for they are acts for which they can be held responsible. Hence Aristotle speaks of the practical and the productive 'sciences' as powers or faculties in the sense that their possession works as 'a source of change in others' (see Harré on 'powers' below and in chapter 4). And this is the point of such 'sciences': in relation to them, people should not be seen as already socially or developmentally (completely) knowledgeable about their society's methods or ways of sense-making. There must still be various phenomena which puzzle them, at which they do not know how to be spectators, phenomena which they have not yet learned how to 'see' (i.e. perceive) in a properly accountable manner. It is the function of

practical-theory to change them in their *being*, to indicate to them such ways or methods of 'seeing'.

In psychology, we are of course interested in doing and making, as well as in understanding. And the distinctions Aristotle produces will be found relevant in all that follows. However, as I pointed out above, as professional academics our task is not ourselves to do or to make, but to talk: to produce accounts of how persons account to themselves for themselves. And although it is clear that one might argue for three different modes of psychology, exemplifying Aristotle's three kinds of 'science', in what follows I shall be arguing primarily just for one, the practical-descriptive mode – a mode which elsewhere (Shotter, 1975) I have called a 'moral science of action'. To argue otherwise would seem to me to be suggesting that the arena of public discourse should be bypassed, and changes produced in society without public consent.

Transcendental Realism: Agencies as the Subject-Matter of a Science

Recently, Bhaskar (1975, 1979), following Harré (1970a and b), has set out a whole philosophy of science in which he describes the properties that people and societies must possess if they are to be possible 'objects' of scientific knowledge for us. Essentially, he suggests, they must be understood as causal agencies, or generative mechanisms with causal powers, which can only be known as such, in their actions, and which cannot be shown merely by the observation of regularities to exist, i.e. they are to be known by their powers, their capacities to bring about material changes in other things. As Bhaskar's approach takes the problem of agency seriously, and claims to establish the possibility of studying social 'objects' in the same way as natural ones, discussion of his position here will serve to clarify further the issues at stake in still approaching psychology as a 'theory-relevant' enterprise, rather being content to conduct it as merely a practical-descriptive activity.

As 'experimental' sciences, individual, social and developmental psychology modelled themselves essentially upon a positivist view of the natural sciences. Many (e.g. Koch, 1959; Harré, 1970b; Harré and Secord, 1972; Bhaskar, 1975, 1979) now regard such a move as mistaken: not only because it results in a science inadequate to the facts of human being and action, but because it also is based upon an incorrect view of the natural sciences. In criticizing positivist doctrines – as well as their hermeneutical rivals, which he claims also accepted uncritically the same mistaken account of the natural sciences – Bhaskar suggests (1) that, rather than discovering constant conjunctions of events, the goal of *all* sciences, whether natural or social, is to discover intelligible connections between real things at a deeper level. Thus, he claims, the proper subject-matter of all the sciences is not observable regularities, but the things which work, under the appropriate conditions, to produce or generate them. Such things are best thought of as active causal agencies with causal powers which exist and endure as the things they are, whether their powers are exercised or not; and which, when they do act, always act in their normal fashion, whether the appropriate (closed) conditions obtain for their lawful behaviour to be immediately perceptible or not. So, although neither their regular effects nor the things themselves may be directly observable as such, they may still be 'accounted' real objects – transcendentally real in the Kantian sense of being the conditions of possibility for the phenomena observed – and treated as existing on the ground of their capacity to bring about material changes in the world. On this criterion, as Bhaskar puts it, 'to be is not to be perceived, but (in the last instance) just to be able to do' (1979 p. 16); and it is in their doings that such agencies may be known. Such a position is a 'realist' one in the sense that, as we shall see, such agencies must be accounted as actually existing, in some sense at least, independently of our attempts to investigate and describe them – although in what sense that is, is the most difficult aspect of Bhaskar's position to characterize.

Another of his claims is implicit in his statement that 'to be is to do'; to state it explicitly: (2) Epistemological questions should be clearly distinguished from ontological ones. To claim that the aim of science is to discover observable regularities is, he suggests, to confuse epistemological questions with ontological ones; such an aim leaves the material of the world undescribed. Furthermore, in the collection of data, it covers up what he calls an 'ontological gap' between actual causal laws on the one hand, and the evidence for them in empirical observations on the other: for in fact, (*a*) as products, surface regularities need not reflect in any simple way the operation of the processes producing them; and (*b*) a natural order of things may endure, and the laws describing their individual operations continue to hold even though conditions are such (i.e. open rather than closed) that their regular and orderly conduct is unobservable in their combined operation.

Only under certain special conditions – i.e. closed, experimental conditions – can that 'ontological gap' be closed, and, with all else held constant, just the operation of the thing in question observed.

Otherwise, its functioning is immersed in and intermingled with the functioning of many other things. 'In an experiment,' says Bhaskar (1979, pp. 11–12),

> scientists produce a pattern of events. There is nothing in itself special about this. For, as causal agents, we are co-responsible for events all the time . . . . What distinguishes the phenomena the scientist *actually* produces out of the totality of the phenomena he *could* produce is that, when his experiment is successful, it is an index of what he does *not* produce. A *real* distinction between the objects of experimental investigation, such as causal laws, and patterns of events is thus a condition of the intelligibility of experimental activity. And it can be seen that the Humean account depends upon a misidentification of causal laws with their empirical grounds . . . . The objects of experimental activity are not events and their conjunctions, but structures, generative mechanisms and the like (forming the real basis of causal laws), which are normally out of phase with them.
>
> But of course we not only experimentally establish, we practically *apply* our knowledge – in systems, which may be characterized as *open*, where no constant conjunctions of events obtain.

It follows from this that causal laws must be analysed as tendencies which only manifest themselves as empirical invariances under the relatively special, closed conditions of an experiment. Can appropriate conditions be set up to investigate social phenomena in the same way as natural ones? Yes and no.

In Bhaskar's view, as we have seen, there is no difference between the natural and the social sciences regarding the nature of their subject matter. But what does distinguish them is that it is much more difficult to study social things – people and societies – under closed conditions. Such conditions distort their normal mode of being, the only mode of being in which they remain the things they are. For example, adults in a society have a duty to act intelligibly and responsibly, in ways which relate to other people's concerns and make sense to them. But as long as they observe that duty, they are free to act as they please. To put limitations upon them is to deny them that right; it is to damage their status as persons. Similarly, one can show that a society under closed conditions is a different kind of object than when open. Under closed conditions, both people and societies cease to be what they are normally. Thus as a consequence, Bhaskar asserts, (3) the social sciences are denied, in principle, decisive test situations for their theories. They thus cannot be experimental sciences. As the criteria for the rational confirmation of theories *cannot be predictive*, it must be *exclusively explanatory*, i.e. theoretical entities are justified (*a*) by the way in which they make observed phenomena intelligible, and (*b*) by the way in which absurd, incoherent, counterintuitive, or counterfactual results follow if such entities are denied. For example, a child otherwise seemingly normal fails to learn to talk. An explanatory theory as to the cause might be that in order to learn to talk, the child requires certain social conditions, conditions which constitute the required 'developmental opportunities'. A theory of 'developmental opportunities' is confirmed when it is found (*a*) that, indeed, all those in his immediate surroundings are dumb, and are unable to provide such opportunities, and (*b*) it makes no sense to argue that he or she could still learn in the absence of such opportunities. The assumption of his normality is confirmed by his beginning to learn to talk when placed amongst people who can talk. (Note that the possibility of explanation rests upon prior knowledge as to what is normal here; this will be a feature in all the explanatory processes I shall discuss below.) As Bhaskar stresses, although confirmation by explanation may influence the subjective confidence with which we hold scientific theories, it has no ontological significance at all: our theories are not produced from the superficial effects we observe. But what about the relation between such things and our theories of them?

Distinguishing between ontological and epistemological questions, besides leading Bhaskar to clarify the proper conditions required for experimentation, also leads him to distinguish between what he calls the real objects of science and the cognitive objects known to us in our theories of them. Thus (4) scientific knowledge is, he claims, knowledge of real objects which exist and can act independently of our knowledge of them – these are what he calls the 'intransitive' objects of such knowledge. But if we are to avoid the absurdity of such knowledge being produced *ex nihilo*, then it must depend upon the use of pre-existing cognitive materials – what he calls the 'transitive' objects of knowledge. Although the objects of our knowledge exist and act independently of our individual wishes, beliefs, opinions and desires, they can nonetheless only be known to us in historically specific social forms. In Bhaskar's view, then, no science can be solely an individual, third-person enterprise. While it may entail the use of third-person standpoints (from which to observe forms and patterns), and reference to third-person 'intransitive' objects, as a social process it inevitably contains first- and second-person positions as well, along with, he claims, their associated 'transitive' objects. The knowledge it produces must be, as he puts it, 'a produced means of prodcution with transitive objects existing independently of it' (1979, p. 19).

It is at this point that the difference between Bhaskar's position and the one which I have adopted begins to become clear. His concerns, clearly, are with the social sciences as *theoretical* sciences, in Aristotle's sense of that term. He is concerned to produce, as a result of his scientific activity, theoretical objects, the 'transitive' changing objects, which give access to the unchanging experience-independent 'intransitive' objects he thinks of as constituting social reality. But recall here briefly Anscombe's dilemma quoted earlier. Clearly Bhaskar accepts two knowledges: one known to us transcendentally (in intention), gained by us in our practical but socially accountable encounters with the phenomena in question, and the other in our theoretical accounts, gained by us making scientific observations – the first gained, I would say, as an unintended consequence of the 'joint action' (see chapter 8) in which we are involved, the second as an intended consequence of our own individual actions. With Bhaskar's formulation, we again find ourselves in the darkness of which Anscombe speaks, for (*a*) the relation between the two is unclear, and (*b*) as Anscombe points out, a 'queer and special sort of seeing eye in the middle of the acting' seems to be required if knowledge of Bhaskar's 'intransitive' experience-independent objects is to inform our actions, and to inform them, of course, in a socially accountable way. For in psychology (as I discuss in the next section) our talk of such things as our emotions, etc., itself works to constitute what our emotions *are*, and as such, as an accounting practice, works as a real determinant in our actions. In other words, the idea of experience-independent objects is difficult to uphold in psychology.

To avoid this dilemma, a more appropriate account of intentionality is required than that given by Bhaskar (1979, p. 44), merely in terms of people's ability, not only to control and monitor their performances, but to monitor their monitoring. For, as we shall see, an ability to report on and to account for one's performances need play no part in their initial shaping. The intentionality of action is itself such that – in being directed upon an object (or as Searle would say, in being 'fitted' to one), whether any such object exists or not – it is intrinsically informed by the context into which it is directed; no reference to any objective things is necessary at all, whether 'inner' or 'outer' (see chapters 8 and 11).

Mundane Realism and Practical-Theory in a Psychology of Everyday Life

Bhaskar argues for the possibility of naturalism, for an essential unity of method in the natural and social or human sciences. Whether he does so successfully or not, in the social accountability view I am proposing here he fails to account rationally for its adoption; in C. Taylor's (1980) terms, which I will elucidate below, he fails to make explicit its 'desirability characteristics'. Clearly, the 'scientific' mode of accountability Bhaskar outlines is not the only mode there is; others exist and have other aims, other implicit intentions; and we choose between them in terms of what we find significant for ourselves at the time of our choosing. While claiming, essentially, that sciences create in their own traditions and practices their own criteria by which they evaluate the theoretical entities which they propose as real, he seems to adduce only historical and pragmatic ones in justification of the overall stance he proposes. However, if our reality is constituted for us by the ways we commit ourselves to talking about it in our attempts to account for it, what kind of reality is it which Bhaskar's way of talking would lead us to constitute?

As C. Taylor (1980) argues, one of the requirements which has traditionally been seen as central to science being science, is the 'requirement of absoluteness', a criterion realism satisfies:

> that the task of science is to give an account of the world as it is, independent of the meanings it might have for human subjects, or how it figures in their experience. (1980, p. 31)

An adequate scientific account cannot be about things which exist only in people's experience. Thus: since Galileo said in a famous passage of *The Assayer* in 1629, 'tastes, odours, colours and so on are no more than mere names . . . they reside only in consciousness,' such things have been denied a place in a proper science of real objects. But are not tastes, odours, colours and so on, real determinants in how we act in the world? At least, is it not the case that it is perfectly legitimate in everyday life to account for some of our actions in these terms? Similarly: in accounting for others, we talk of our emotions, intuitions, understandings, aspirations, values, etc. These words may not 'stand for' things, but they are clearly an effective currency in the conduct of social exchanges (Mills, 1940; Wittgenstein, 1953, 1980). They may not denote any entities 'in' an individual, but they can nonetheless 'indicate' or 'index' (Bar-Hillel, 1954) an individual's real commitments, their powers and tendencies, the real point of their actions for them, in terms accountable to others. Hence, in our attempts to understand someone, these are the real things we want to know about.

The realism being proposed here might, to contrast with Bhaskar's transcendental realism, be called simply a 'mundane realism', for it suggests that the ways of making sense of things indexed by the terms people use in their accounting practices, or which are otherwise indicated 'in' their actions (see chapter 9), really *are* the terms in which they are trying to conduct their affairs. They 'point to'[2] the things which make an action desirable for them (or what makes it undesirable); to understand it, we need to grasp the appropriate 'desirability characterizations', as Taylor calls them. For a person, we need:

> to understand [what we call] his emotions, his aspirations, what he finds admirable and contemptible, what he loathes, what he yearns for, and so on. Understanding doesn't mean sharing these emotions, aspirations, loathings, etc., but it does mean seeing the point of them, seeing what is here which could be aspired to, loathed, etc. Seeing the point means grasping the objects concerned under their desirability characterizations.
>
> To use the language made familiar by phenomenology, understanding another person is understanding his world; it is grasping the significance of things for him. (1980, p. 32)

A science which must meet the requirement of absoluteness, claims Taylor, precludes this kind of understanding.

Thus, to claim that there is no essential difference between the social and human sciences on the one hand, and the natural sciences on the other, on the grounds that both possess an interpretative (i.e. hermeneutical) component and that both have unobservable (if not necessarily imperceptible) real objects as their subject matter, is to forget that as theoretical sciences (in Aristotle's terms) the aim of the natural sciences is to account for things in experience-independent terms. This is achieved (Shotter and Burton, 1983) by the use of idealizations and formal systems of interpretation which determine, prior to any empirical investigations, the basic kinds of things being sought, from which the 'world' being investigated is composed. In other words, the mode of accountability pursued in a theoretical science constitutes reality as a 'unity of homogeneity' (see chapter 11), as a 'world' composed from a small number of different kinds of *already existing* 'fundamental elements'. The human sciences cannot, however, so limit themselves; they cannot afford, by the use of idealizations and systematic formulations to prejudge their discoveries, determining prior to any investigation the 'whatness' of their subject matter (see Introduction). Their task, if they are to be adequate to people's experience, is to understand what different people's 'world's' contain, and what their relation to their 'world' is. Thus they must discover a way of talking which allows for such a possibility, which constitutes a 'unity of heterogeneity' (see chapter 11), a 'world' in which the elements composing it are all true individuals, all distinguishable from one another while all, nonetheless, a part of the same unity, and having an essentially indeterminate nature.

How then can we proceed? Our initial task is simply (to put it ironically) to describe our human ways of living: the activities, procedures, methods, discourses, behaviours, nonbehavours, doings, makings, thinkings, speakings, and so on, in terms of which we come to be as we are, and to do and to talk as we do. Yet how, exactly, should such goings-on and states of affairs be described? The fact is that with the world of everyday social life we are always dealing with a pre-interpreted, a pre-understood reality, a reality already seen as being a reality of a particular kind by the social actors involved in it. Although unformulated and only vaguely conceived, although indefinite and amenable to a multitude of descriptions (Goodman, 1972, 1978), this pre-understood grasp of reality is nonetheless sufficient at a practical level to render social action intelligible to those involved in it, and to mediate interpersonal relations. Thus, if we are to account for human behaviour in everyday life, as the accountable behaviour it is, we must account for it in at least some of the same terms as those in which it is conducted – for irrespective of their inadequacy, their incompleteness, their indirection, their misleading and perhaps downright mistaken nature, such terms serve to determine its nature.

Thus while we might want to criticize certain ways of talking – claims, for instance, that our 'outer' expressions are caused by prior events 'within' us; that we possess 'selves' conceptually separable from ourselves as persons; or that mental events are contained 'in our minds' (see chapter 10) – we can do so by appealing, not to any particular method or special source of knowledge, but simply to other forms of usage, to other ways of talking readily available in our everyday accounting practices. For our accounting practices seem to revolve around 'images', 'pictures', 'paradigm cases' (Wittgenstein, 1953; Rosch, 1973; Ossorio, in Davis, 1981[3]), or 'metaphors' (Lakoff and Johnson, 1980; and see chapter 10); and the mistakes we make often arise from extending a way of talking beyond the form of life, beyond the activity within which it originally had its currency.

Sometimes, however, criticism will not be sufficient; alternative images or paradigm cases will be required to replace those currently being used. Occasionally, even, new images will have to be introduced *de novo*, to indicate a form of order, a way of human being, an activity or relationship previously unrecognized. Such terms will have the *form* of 'theoretical' terms (as if denoting the real things at a deeper level investigated in a theoretical science), but they do not have the same functions at all. As they serve the purposes of practice, I shall call what they provide 'practical-theory'; but there is no need to use special terms for individual practical-theories other than those already at hand: for they are images, metaphors, paradigm cases, etc. Their primary function, to repeat Garfinkel's dictum, is to work to render unreported and in fact as yet unreportable human phenomena, 'rationally-visible-and-reportable-for-all-practical-purposes, i.e., 'accountable', as organizations of commonplace everyday activities'. Their purpose is not to help people, who are already clear as to what and who they are, simply to gather further information relevant to decisions as to how to act: but to help change people in their *being*, in their mode of relationship both to themselves and to others. Thus they are not to be evaluated as theoretical terms in a theoretical science, in terms of their correspondence to reality. Their task is not to provide a ground-plan for a mechanism working independently of human consciousness or experience; nor is it their function to finalize a decision, to achieve a universal consensus within a group of individuals who already know their way around in the world, so to speak. Indeed, just the opposite is the case: their function is to promote a form of understanding which, as Wittgenstein (1953, no. 154) suggests, is best described not as the occasioning of a mental process but as the provision of circumstances in which individuals say 'now I know how to go on.' And those circumstances are provided by 'paradigms', etc., which work as instruments in the 'making' of accounting practices (in, as Wittgenstein would put it, the setting up of 'language-games').

As an example of what he means here, he discusses the use of hermetically sealed colour samples as standards in the definition of colour names. The example itself is not a particularly good one, for we already know how to 'see' (perceive) colours, and thus it is not obvious that that *is* the problem towards which it is directed. But his account of the function of paradigms in the process is instructive. He describes the status of the activity of naming a particular standard colour sample thus:

> [It] is an instrument of the language used in ascriptions of colour. In this language-game it is not something that is represented, but is a *means of representation* . . . . It is a paradigm in our language-game; something with which comparison is made . . . . (1953, no. 50, my emphasis)

As a 'means of representation', paradigm forms of accountability suggest to us ways of 'going on' with certain kinds of phenomena which otherwise, at a practical level, would leave us bewildered; they suggest ways of 'seeing' them as being of this or that kind of thing; they indicate or 'point to' a stance we might adopt regarding them. Their function is thus rhetorical or instructive; they are aimed at changing us. But as 'transitive' objects of knowledge, their function cannot be to 'stand for' or indicate 'intransitive', experience-independent objects, for their function is not to create new practices *de novo*, but simply to render 'rationally visible' what already we do, to provide us with a way of accounting for it[4] – thus to account more adequately for our 'whatness'.

And our aim in our attempts to find a form of talk appropriate to our 'whatness'? It is simply a practical one, a question of increasing our own powers and competencies by, so to speak, understanding how better to find our way about inside our own human accounting practices: 'A philosophical problem has the form: "I don't know my way about"' (Wittgenstein, 1953, no. 123). But if the aim is simply to make clear to ourselves the character of what we already have 'on hand', so to speak, what has prevented us from discovering the appropriate 'principles of navigation', so to speak, before? 'A *picture* held us captive. And we could not get outside it, for it lay in our language and seemed to repeat it to us inexorably,' Wittgenstein suggests (1953, no. 115), a picture which came from Descartes (see chapter 3). It led us to believe that the paradigmatic way in which we gained knowledge was by the empirical testing of systematic theories. But such theories were only aimed at helping us, not to find our way about 'inside' our own social practices, 'inside' ourselves, but to give us mastery over our 'external world'. And what we want to know now is different: we want to know not what might be *made* to be the case, but what *is* the case. Thus:

> It is not our aim to refine or complete the system of rules for the use of rules in unheard-of ways.
>   For the clarity that we are aiming at is *complete* clarity. But this simply means that the philosophical problems should *completely* disappear . . . . (1953, no. 133)

Yet one is still tempted to say that there must be a system, a complete pattern to be found, for otherwise one's powers are incomplete, partial and uncertain; one seems to lack mastery, and a theoretical system seems to promise it. Yet isn't one's lack of complete mastery one's true ecological state? One is not powerless, but neither is one successful in everything one does. One has powers, but is not omnipotent; one survives just as much because of others as *in spite of* them; one lives in fact in interdependence with them. It is that state of affairs in which no one has total mastery which has to be described. But such mere description is difficult because:

one believes that one needs to fill out the facts in order to understand them. It is as if one saw a screen with scattered colour-patches, and said: the way they are here, they are unintelligible; they only make sense when one completes them into a shape. — Whereas I want to say: Here *is* the whole. (If you complete it, you falsify it.) (Wittgenstein, 1980, vol. 1, no. 257)

Thus: '*Not* to explain, but to *accept* the psychological phenomena — that is what is difficult' (1980, vol. 1, no. 509). Yet it is only by such an acceptance, and an attempt to describe things simply as they are, that we can begin to clarify, at least for ourselves if not in any absolute experience-independent terms, the question of 'what is it to be human?'

3

What is it to be Human?

In chapter 2 I suggested that from a practical point of view, our thinking seems to work in terms of 'images', 'metaphors' or 'paradigms', and that often, when our thinking goes wrong, it is because we have extended the use of an image or metaphor into domains where it ceases to apply. Here I want to examine (1) the image of human being which seems to have informed psychological discourse during its attempts to function as a natural science; and (2) to begin to set out an alternative image, derived from a consideration of what must be the nature of human beings, to live as we know they do from our ways of accounting to ourselves for ourselves in our daily lives: i.e. as individual persons, within a society, with a culture and a history to it, and with the ability to talk about such things.

The Domination of Nature

The Cartesian Legacy

Modern philosophy begins with Descartes (1596–1650), and it is largely from his proposals that modern science emerged – but with it came all the problems we face in psychology today. It would be wrong to lay the blame for the confusion in which we currently find ourselves wholly at Descartes' door, for clearly, in attempting 'never to accept anything as true that I did not know to be evidently so' (Descartes, 1968, p. 41), he merely succeeded in giving explicit codification to the implicit ethos of his times (see chapter 10). But nevertheless, it is not to do him an injustice to take his codifications as paradigms for the many others produced at that time. Yet of Descartes' formulations concerning the nature of mental activities, Ryle (1963, p. 10) in his *Concept of Mind* says:

> it is a part of the thesis of this book that during the three centuries of
> the epoch of natural science the logical categories in terms of which

the concepts of mental powers and operations have been co-ordinated have been wrongly selected. Descartes left as one of his main philosophical legacies a myth which continues to distort the continental geography of the subject.

And that is the thesis of this book also.

With equal justice, or injustice, one could have made the same claim about the legacy of, say, Bacon, Hobbes or Locke, or a host of other writers and polemicists at the time. For it was between 1500 and 1700 that the whole western world began to take on the features which, in the dominant opinion of today, would make it 'modern' and 'progressive'. But, as Merchant (1980) has shown, those changes were not all caused by philosophical writings, far from it. Nonetheless, if I had to choose just one statement by which to characterize the ethos of our modern age, it would be this one from Descartes' sixth discourse:

> instead of the speculative philosophy taught in the Schools, a practical philosophy can be found by which, knowing the power and the effects of fire, water, air, the stars, the heavens. . . we might put them. . . to all the uses for which they are appropriate, and thereby make ourselves, as it were, masters and possessors of nature. (1968, p. 78)

I would choose this rather than a passage from Bacon, Hobbes or Locke because it seems to me to state in a clear, simple and frank manner the interests and intentions implicit in our current 'scientific' ways of knowing and valuing: mastery and possession.[1] These, I think, are the key concepts in terms of which we can understand, not only the character of our major activities in the world these last three hundred years, but also our relation to and treatment of ourselves. Promising a deep and effective knowledge of the natural world, Descartes' practical philosophy held out the great hope that, instead of victims, we may become masters and possessors, not only of nature, but of our own natures also. And, implicit now in our psychology, in our conception of ourselves, our interests, capacities, motives, etc., is that same intent, but directed towards ourselves; except that now it becomes both ambiguous – for is it our own nature or that of others we wish to master and possess? – and problematic – for what is one's (or another's) nature such that one could be said to master or possess it? And indeed these are some of the confusions we have wrestled with in our attempts to understand ourselves.

Nonetheless, the fact remains that our modern conception of people, psychologically, is as 'possessors' of their own selves and their capacities; a possession they gain by virtue of their mastery or control over them, by virtue of their competence in their exercise. Indeed, in the next chapter, in discussing the growth of children's abilities, as persons, to act deliberately and autonomously, as they themselves desire, I myself conceive of the matter in just these terms: as a process of appropriation from nature, in which children are helped by adults to bring the 'natural powers' available to them, by virtue of their birth as human beings into a human society, under their own control, thus transforming them into 'personal powers' (see chapter 4; Shotter, 1974b). One can see the same image (metaphor) at work also informing Freud's battle cry: 'Where Id was, there shall Ego be.' But is the image of nature in these views that of something external to ourselves, existing as an unlimited resource, or is it of something limited, within which we ourselves are embedded?

The Medieval Cosmos: An Organic, Ecological Conception

Prior to Descartes, everything in the medieval, Aristotelian cosmos was characterized by greater or lesser degrees of value or perfection according to an interconnected hierarchical scheme, with matter at its foot and God at its summit, and with the world at its centre, with people (men!), also hierarchically arranged, centred in the world. As essentially an organic totality, people were linked to the animals below them, with which they shared sensation, and the angels above, with whom they shared rationality. Human society was also conceived of as an organic whole, stratified according to status, with peasants at the bottom, the king and pope at the apex, and women (Merchant, 1980) below the men of their particular status group.[2] Conceived of as a living unity, an injury to a part was seen as an injury to the whole; and it was this apparent interconnectedness of things which inhibited the drive towards the exploitation and domination of nature.

By excluding values and reducing everything tangible to matter in motion according to mathematically expressible laws, Descartes, among others, helped to destroy that older notion of the cosmos. His practical philosophy had the effect of displacing people, from a position of immersion and interplay within it – within which people were depicted as having only very partial and equivocal powers requiring a great deal of care in their exercise – and of transporting them to a place beyond it, thus making what then became their 'external world' (Russell, 1914) available to them (or at least to some of them) for their appropriation and use. God was no longer present in the world, nor for that matter were men, in the sense of having any obvious place assigned to them there for themselves. As a mind, quite separate from the world as matter, the role of man himself could only be that of dominating his surroundings and becoming master and possessor of them, putting them to all the uses to which they are appropriate. And the world itself, containing as it does only matter in lawful and orderly motion, becomes, as we shall see, both a timeless and lifeless place; its organic unity is lost. And it becomes impossible to explain how a world, filled with essentially dead and passive matter, could ever contain within its workings the possibility of personhood.

If we are ever to study ourselves without disempowering ourselves in the process – without destroying our own abilities to be self-determining – it is Descartes' account of our being in the world (his ontology) and the accounts of how we came to know its nature (his epistemology) that we must replace.

The Cartesian World and its Investigation

To an extent, while deploring its hierarchical social structure, I intend to return to the medieval image of the cosmos, in which people's powers were only partial, and in which they lived immersed in their surroundings. Two properties of such a scheme of things are important: (1) people's surroundings, instead of being considered inorganic, as being full of dead and passive matter, must be considered as consisting of living material – as in fact made up of at least other human beings (although the nature of the world must be such that personhood is a real possibility within essentially its physical nature); thus, in such a scheme of things, not only people but the environments in which they develop and grow must be considered as intelligent also; and this, as we shall see, has important consequences for the understanding of our social ecology and the resources it provides for our personal development. And (2) such a scheme of things is indeterministic in the sense of being open to new possibilities, thus allowing people the power of action, the power to do and to make, not just to be spectators and thinkers. I would like to introduce the idea of an indeterministic growing world of form-producing processes by contrasting it with the classical picture of the world psychology inherited in large part from Descartes.

The publication in 1637 of Descartes' *Discours de la methode* (the full title of which in translation is 'Discourse on the method of properly conducting one's reason and of seeking the truth in the sciences') engendered, as I have said, the great belief that it was possible to translate methodically all that is unknown into the realm of indisputable common knowledge. The method consisted in the four rules: (1) never to accept any thing as true that was not known to be self-evidently so (that is, to start from 'clear and distinct ideas'); (2) analyse, divide the difficulties into as many parts as possible; (3) reconstruct the parts into a system, supposing the parts to have an order amongst themselves which accounts for the events observed; and then (4) to check one's deductions from the system against omissions, etc.:

> These long chains of reasonings, quite simple and easy, which geometers are accustomed to using to teach their most difficult demonstrations, had given me cause to imagine that everything which can be encompassed by man's knowledge is linked in the same way . . . . (1968 p. 41)

Thus, via the unity of mathematics – remember Descartes had shown how in co-ordinate geometry, geometry could be translated into algebra – such a method promised a new unification of the cosmos, an artificial, 'man-made' one (literally – see note 2), to replace the old, living unity of the medieval cosmos. And the nature of this 'new world', as Descartes called it, is such that with this method, Descartes said: 'there can be nothing so distant that one does not reach it eventually, or so hidden that one cannot discover it' (p. 41). It is a world in which all that there is of it already exists; a causal place; best characterized by number; a place in which everything of importance can be measured and quantified; a deterministic world in which the nature of one's object of study remains fixed, unchanged by the methods used to study it; with all the data relevant to its understanding being gained from the position of an external observer; a world only of third persons.

Thus, when we speak of 'the method of the natural sciences', we can trace part of it back to the *Discours*; it was to this emphasis on mathematically expressible laws that Newton added the experimental method. In a latter to the secretary of the Royal Society of 1672 he wrote:

> The best and safest method of philosophizing seems to be, first, to inquire diligently into the properties of things and to establish those properties by experiments, and to proceed later to hypotheses for the explanation of things themselves. For hypotheses ought only to be applied in the explanation of the properties of things, and not made use of in determining them.

But actually, it was only possible for him to assert this, given the way in which Descartes had idealized the subject-matter of Natural Philosophy –hypotheses *did* enter into the determination of 'things', for Descartes had written:

> I resolved . . . to speak only of what would happen in *a new world*, if God were to create, somewhere in *imaginary space*, enough matter to compose it, and if he were to agitate diversely and confusedly the

different parts of this matter, so that he created *a chaos as disordered as the poets could ever imagine*, and afterwards did no more than to lend his usual preserving action to nature, and let her act according to his *established laws*. (1968, p. 62, my emphases)

Thus scientists must study the abstract stuff, matter, which is to be known only in terms of its measurable properties, spatial extent and motion, and whose behaviour is to be investigated to yield God's established laws. All 'things' in the world, except, Descartes thought, people's rational souls, could be brought into the confines of such an investigation, for they could all be treated as identical in terms of the motion of matter moving according to mathematical laws – its evident living unity was to be ignored; indeed, it was thought an atavistic animism by later generations of scientists to take such a view.

Thus it was primarily from Descartes' metaphysics, his entirely speculative picture of the fundamental nature of the world, that the modern natural sciences, with their powerful methods for dominating nature, emerged. And as 'scientific' thought grew to be the ideal for all thought, it became imperative to bring within its confines what Descartes had left out: people's rational souls – for there was no other realm in which they could exist, except in the world of matter in motion. People's actions must be reduced to the motions of their matter.

This then is the Cartesian world: an essentially chaotic, lifeless world, from which people have been excluded. It is a world which must be investigated for the laws regulating the motions of its elementary parts. It is an already existing world in which the only changes are changes of rearrangement. Nothing in it passes into existence and out of it again; it is a world of being, not becoming. If at any moment we are unable to predict its future in it, that is not because it is in principle impossible – quite the contrary: it is because we are still too ignorant; we have not yet amassed enough knowledge; yet more research is needed. In such a world, as Laplace (1886) appreciated:

An intellect which at a given instant knew all the forces acting in nature, and the position of all things of which the world consists – supposing the said intellect were vast enough to subject these data to analysis – would embrace in the same formula the motions of the greatest bodies in the universe and those of the slightest atoms; nothing would be uncertain for it, and the future, like the past, would be present to its eyes.

It is a world in which the future is merely hidden like distant regions of space (for time is spatialized); and it seems possible, ultimately to know everything!

Such hopes and beliefs as these still motivate, I feel, much of what is called scientific psychology today. It is surely possible, isn't it, to discover completely people's 'inner' workings?

Being a Person

Our Sense of Our Own Responsibility: Its Fundamental Nature

While such a view as that above may capture all our significant experiences of what we now call, as a result of our Cartesian displacement, our 'external world', the world which we can make yield to our manipulations of it, it utterly fails to capture our experience of our own functioning in such a world. Because of this and also its frankly speculative character, I would like to suggest an alternative basis for our investigations in psychology: a basis in the sense of responsibility which we all, as first-persons, can have for our own actions.

We all distinguish, and indeed if we are to be accounted reasonable human beings we all *must* be able to distinguish, between that for which we as individual personalities are responsible and that which merely happens, irrespective of our agency. This distinction is fundamental not only in everyday life but also in science, where it is absolutely fundamental: it is only because we can sense, when acting in accord with theories of what the world might be like, whether the results of our actions accord with or depart from the expectations engendered by those theories, that we can ever put such theories to empirical test. No more fundamental basis for deciding the truth of empirical matters exists, nor will another ever be found – in the organizational complexity of matter, say, as some such as Sutherland (1970) have suggested – for how could it ever be established as a true basis? It would still rest upon the basis of our ability to recognize the consequences of our own actions. Our sense of responsibility as first-persons is, then, at the very basis of science itself; lacking any sense of their own functioning scientists would be unable to do experiments.

Responsible Action

The distinction I have been making above is the distinction between actions and events, doings and happenings which has been explored extensively of late in the philosophy of human action (for example, Winch, 1958; Peters, 1958; Hampshire, 1959; R. Taylor, 1966; R. J. Bernstein, 1972). If, when we are acting alone, we want others to say that we are acting not just intelligently, nor even intelligibly, but also responsibly and legitimately, then we must both make our actions intelligible to ourselves as we perform them, in other people's terms, and understand how they relate to other people's needs and interests. In other words, if we are to be accepted by other members of our society as reasonable people we are expected to show not just awareness (i.e. consciousness) of our circumstances, but *self*-awareness (i.e. self-consciousness); that is, we are expected not just to act in a manner appropriate to our circumstances but also to act in a manner appropriate to our 'place', our status in some larger social scheme of things; we must be aware of the relation of our actions to interests other than our own immediate and idiosyncratic ones. Actions judged as responsible actions within a group are related not to individuals but to interests shared by other members of the group. We thus arrive at what may seem to some a paradox; as an individual personality, I can only be truly responsible for my own actions to the extent that I know how to respond to them as others do – the criterion George Mead proposed for such conduct:

> Such is the difference between intelligent conduct on the part of animals and what we call a reflective individual. We say the animal does not think. He does not put himself in a position for which he is responsible; he does not put himself in the place of the other person and say in effect, 'He will act in such a way and I will act in this way'. (1934, p. 73)

The paradox is resolved by realizing the inherently social nature of everyone's self-conscious activity (all the activities in which people themselves know what they are doing, even if the action is as trivial as raising an eyebrow or waving a hand). I can only be self-conscious in my actions – i.e. know who I am, by knowing how I am 'placed' or 'situated' – by acting in the knowledge of my relation to others.

Now in explaining our actions to others, we have, ideally, to give our reasons, tell of our aims or intentions, to say what we expect to result and why. In practice, however, our intentions are often as obscure to ourselves as to others, and this is where further investigations of a psychological kind have their point: to elucidate further reasons for people's actions when required – because the reasons already given are suspect; because they are still insufficient to explain an action; because we are interested in the action's historical origins, and wonder about alternatives to it; etc., etc. Unlike actions, however, events just happen, they are no one's responsibility; and they are not, of course, to be explained by seeking their reasons. To explain them, we must seek collectively their causal principles, what we call 'the laws of nature' which seem to underlie the structure of their appearances – the traditional task of the natural sciences. So we must be clear when investigating psychological phenomena whether it is reasons (or something having the logical structure of reasons) or causal principles that we seek; the two belong to two quite distinct spheres of thought and investigation (to different paradigms).

To sum up so far then: while classical science demands that we study everything as if, ultimately, it could be considered as disconnected elements of matter in motion according to so-called 'natural' (or to Descartes' absent God's pre-established) laws, people seem able to act according to beliefs or interests, according to mere conceptions of laws or rules, thus exempting themselves from this demand. But in acting thus, according to what others can recognize as rules or laws, people must make their own actions intelligible to themselves as they perform them in terms of their relations to other people – they can monitor their actions (Harré and Secord, 1972). But even more than this, and this is what makes psychology as the reflexive study of ourselves possible, people are aware that they are aware of what they are doing; they are capable of monitoring their own self-monitoring, and of criticizing the account they give of themselves, and of finding that what accounts for their actions in one sphere of their lives doesn't in another. Here, and in the rest of this book, I am interested (1) in the sphere of responsible or accountable action, in which we ourselves act; and also (2) in what it is we must do in other spheres of our activity to make such a kind of action possible.

Now in attempting to act responsibly, people may fail; they may act rightly or wrongly, appropriately or inappropriately, legitimately or illegitimately. So besides being essentially a developmental social science in dealing with affairs of this sort – i.e. attempting to understand people acting responsibly in relation to shared rules or criteria – psychology also becomes, as I suggested above, a practical, moral science. And its goal? To the extent that, from a practical point of view, human nature is essentially incomplete, it can only be concerned with discovering our next possible stages of development; it must be, as Bruner (1972) has termed it, a 'policy' science. Thus at its heart we shall not find, as in the natural sciences calculation to do with the one true view, but forms of negotiation to do with possible alternatives to the current view – and to the extent that the social conditions do not yet exist in society for the appropriate forms of negotiation to take place, the appropriate forms of 'undistorted communication' (Habermas, 1970 a and b), it becomes unavoidably a politically sensitive enterprise, a science critical of current social forms.

The Need for 'Practical-Theory'

In its guise as a practical,[3] moral science, psychology cannot be, as I said above, solely the study of individual, responsible action. For while there are some things we as individual personalities clearly do *do*, there are others which just as clearly we do not *do*. These distinctly different kinds of activity belong to two different but clearly related spheres of study, and later I shall distinguish between individual action, in which individuals act all alone in terms of 'plans', 'scripts', 'ideas', 'inner representations', etc., and 'joint action', in which people interlace their activities in with one another's, and in which what one person does is determined just as much by what another does as by their own 'ideas'. And it is in explaining joint action that new terms must be introduced: 'joint action' is itself just such a term, while others such as 'intentionality', 'duality of structure', and so on will be introduced also; furthermore, it must be noted that terms like 'social structure' and 'social order' also designate entities only understood initially by use of metaphors and images, for they also do not appear in immediate perception as objects. Most of our important concepts we shall find only appear 'in' people's actions.

I would like to continue here by introducing a number of other distinctions to do with the difference between artificial or constructed things and the so-called natural world. Though we must be careful of the sense in which the word 'natural' is taken, for sometimes it means (*a*) what is done by people spontaneously, without individual deliberation (the sense in which I shall mostly use it); or (*b*) the world of the 'natural sciences'; or (*c*) as meaning a 'world of nature' which exists beyond all the accounts we might give of it.

In Chapter 4, I shall explore the distinction between the individually constructed and the socially 'constructed', between what individual personalities with their personal powers can do planfully and deliberately (using the term powers there in Harré's (1970a) sense, to do with the causal powers of an agency), and what people as unselfconscious agents with their natural powers can do; and with how the transition from this second form of activity to the first can be accomplished. This will bear upon a distinction I would like to make between the cultural and the 'natural' (in the first sense above), i.e. between social orders and institutions, and the social ecology within which they are embedded.

The Socially 'Constructed' nature of the Social Context

The Intended and the Unintended

A distinction between the natural and the cultural world has recently been drawn by Popper (1972) also, and it will be useful here to examine the terms he uses as they raise the most important issue of the unintended consequences of (intrinsically intentional – see chapters 8 and 11) social action. He distinguishes between: (1) the natural world, (2) the world of people's psychological states, and (3) those parts of the natural world which are products of the human mind – such as works of art, ethical values, social institutions, libraries, scientific problems and scientific theories – he calls them worlds 1, 2 and 3 respectively, in the order, he thinks, of their emergence into existence. It is the all-but-complete autonomy of world 3 which interests him. It is partially autonomous because, once we have produced it, it becomes an object seemingly 'outside' ourselves, and as such is then open to investigation and intersubjective criticism; and quite often we may discover in it unintended consequences, thus increasing our powers in unexpected ways. It is the introduction of world 3 into his philosophy that Popper thinks of as revolutionary, for in its autonomy and its unintended consequences it can, so to speak, work to act back upon us to determine our conduct and our experience of ourselves. Thus he suggests that:

> One day we will have to revolutionize psychology by looking at the human mind as an organ for interacting with the objects of the third world; for understanding them, contributing to them, participating in them; and for bringing them to bear on the first world. (1972, p. 156)

The 'Natural' and the 'man-made'

Within a cultural perspective, we view people as individual personalities, responsible for their actions to others, and as monitoring or interpreting their own and one another's actions in relation to shared aims and interests, whose forms are in themselves humanly constructed – and it is worth remarking in this context that no other beings construct their own goals in such a way. An action can have its meaning in terms of the part it plays in furthering a society's aims or in modifying its interests. It is being responsible for their own actions in this way that gives the structure of their behaviour a manufactured or 'man-made' aspect – it is also this 'constructed' aspect of their behaviour which, spuriously, makes it seem amenable to mechanistic explanation.

Alternatively, within a 'natural' (ecological) perspective, in contrast to people as children of culture, we can see them as children of nature, just as much a part of the natural order of things as the trees and the stars. Here we must view them as being aware of their circumstances in the sense of responding appropriately to them, but as not yet being self-consciously aware of them, in the sense that 'they' themselves could be said to be responsible for their actions; they act as they must, in relation only to their own immediate states of being – as if continually in a 'passion' (see Shotter, 1982, and chapter 11, as well as Jaynes, 1979, for a most interesting description of what he calls the 'bicameral mind'). As people themselves are not responsible for their actions in this sphere, the structure of their behaviour does not have a constructed aspect to it. It has a distinctly different structure, one which does not render it amenable to ready explanation mechanistically at all. And what it is for persons to bring sets of circumstances under their own self-control is, I shall maintain, to impose upon the 'natural' order of their behaviour in these circumstances, one way or another, an artificial structure.

In the 'man-made' and the 'natural' (or ecological), we have two distinct but related spheres of study needing two distinct but related modes of thought and methods of investigation. But this distinction is not in any sense new or original. It was proposed long ago by Giambattista Vico in his *Scienza Nuova* of 1744; for him it was

> a truth beyond all question: that the world of civil society has certainly been made by men, and that its principles are to be found within the modifications of our own human mind. Whoever reflects on this cannot but marvel that philosophers should have bent all their energies to the study of the world of nature, which, since God made it, He alone knows; and that they should have neglected the study of the world of nations, or civil world, which, since men had made it, men could come to know. (Vico, 1975, para 331)

While people make culture, it is 'nature' (or what I want now to call people's social ecology) which, as an agency, makes people; and, as we shall see, as there is an essential contingency always in the action of an agency, it is only in those spheres where people can reduce 'nature' by their manipulations to the form of a machine, thus depriving it of its agency, that they gain any degree of control over it at all.

As this distinction between the 'man-made' and the ecological is so fundamental it is worthwhile at this point going a little more deeply into the structures of the two different kinds of system: even the most complex of 'man-made' systems, machines for instance, are constructed piece-by-piece from objective parts; that is, from parts which retain their character unchanged irrespective of whether they are parts of the system or not. (And just as people may construct mechanisms for use in the affairs of their external world, so it is not inconceivable that they may construct mechanisms 'within' themselves for use in the regulation of their personal affairs – see chapters 3 and 4 for a discussion of how mothers may help their infants in the execution of this task.)

But whole people as natural systems are certainly not constructed piece by piece; on the contrary, they *grow*. They develop from simple individuals into richly structured ones in such a way that their 'parts' at any one moment in time owe not just their character but their very existence both to one another *and* to their relations with the 'parts' of the system at some earlier point in time – their history is just as important as their logic in their growth, and because of this it is impossible to picture natural systems in spatial diagrams. As Čapek (1965, p. 162) remarks, 'any spatial symbol contemplated at a given moment is *complete*, i.e., all its parts are given *at once*, simultaneously, in contrast with the temporal reality which is by its own nature *incomplete* and whose 'parts' – if we are justified in using such a thoroughly inadequate term – are by definition successive, i.e., nonsimultaneous.' There is always more to come of natural systems because as well as existing in space they realize themselves through time; true, if they contain reversible processes (see Piaget, 1971, 1972), it may be more of the same, but then again, if they contain irreversible processes (see the account of Prigogine's views in chapter 11) – which they must if they are to be in any sense growing systems – then they may manifest genuine novelty.

The Individually Constructed and the Socially 'Constructed'

Now it is clearly tempting, lacking any clear 'picture' of natural systems, to assimilate them to ones which we can picture, to assume in fact that they manifest the same 'constructional' properties as familiar man-made systems – we then know what we are all talking about. But the two systems, the natural and the 'man-made', can only be equated if the natural systems do not contain 'structure-dependent' parts (Chomsky, 1968, 1972), i.e. interdependent 'parts', and are in fact made up of objective parts: a feature which natural systems in their entirety clearly do not possess – as pointed out above, they are growing systems with successive as well as simultaneous parts. While such systems must contain some objective parts, and even something like mechanisms as they grow older, their 'parts' in general at some moment in time must only be perceptually distinguishable but not in any genuine sense physically separable – that is, if the system is to remain alive. For separation would destroy just that precise set of mutual influences by which a living system's 'parts' determine one another's functioning (and those in touch with its environment have their response determined) in relation to the whole. The analytic method, while appropriate to understanding 'man-made' systems, destroys natural ones irretrievably.

In discussing the 'man-made' world I have chosen to concentrate attention on the machine rather than upon rules and maxims, upon institutions and the socially constructed world in general, as one of my purposes is to attack mechanistic psychology and to show that there can be a warrantable alternative to it. But I would not want it to be thought that in discussing mechanistic forms of order I meant only physically constructed systems; I mean socially constructed ones too. But as Mumford (1967) argues, there is often not much of a distinction, for machines can be constructed from people, the megamachines constituting much of modern society being a case in point; people can easily experience their lives as if 'ruled' by 'mechanisms' invisible to them. Berger and Luckman (1967, p. 77–8) state the charcter of our experience of an institutional world very well:

> [It] is experienced as an objective reality. It has a history that antedates the individual's birth and is not accessible to his biographical recollection. It was there before he was born, and it will be there after his death . . . . Since institutions exist as external reality, the individual cannot understand them by introspection. He must 'go out' and learn about them, just as he must learn about nature . . . . The paradox that man is capable of producing a world that he then experiences as something other than a human product will concern us later on. At the moment, it is important to emphasize that the relationship between man, the producer, and the social world, his product, is and remains a dialectical one . . . . The product acts back on the producer.

And, they continue, it is 'only with the transmission of the social world to a new generation [that] the fundamental social dialectic appears in its totality'; each new generation is a social product.

Indeterminacy and Time

The Reality of Time and the Contingency of Action

The intention in modern thought has always been to seek the timeless and the fixed. Little thought has been given to the idea of form-producing processes, to the idea of a growing world, or growing systems, or of irreversible changes and the occurrence of genuine novelty (see chapter 11). Indeed, within Descartes' world running on pre-established principles, genuine novelty would be unthinkable: it would seem to come out of nowhere, to be unprincipled and thus uncaused. In such a world, only regularities, only reversible changes qualify for a rational (i.e. logical) explanation. But as a growing system, I myself both live in space and through time. At this moment, I myself am manifesting a particular spatial configuration *here*; then, I was manifesting another state of being *there*; next, I may or may not *be* here, I may or may be not *be* there, it all depends. Through time I can, if I try, realize different possible states of my being in space – and recognizing and recollecting them all together as mine is what gives me my own special sense of personal unity (a unity which can, of course, be lost by some deeply disturbed people). Possessing many possible modes of being, I can project myself in living from one to another – although sometimes I find myself being projected by agencies other than my own. Thus my life can have a directed quality to it, directed by myself or by others. My actions, in being directed from a past towards a future, can express an intention. I cannot, however, intend a novel action. Although I can *find* myself expressing an intention in a truly novel way, novelty is something which I simply find *happening* to me; it is not something *I* can do. But having it once happen to me, I may, under certain conditions (see Dreyfus, 1965, and chapter 11, for discussions on the determination of intentions), make it, as something which now is not of course novel, happen again.

Within the classical deterministic scheme of things a present state of affairs necessitates one and only one future state; thus the future has the same sort of unknown character to it as distant regions of space: it is simply hidden from human knowledge. If we were all not so ignorant, we could know all our future as Laplace once promised. Thus in this scheme of things, time loses its unique reality and becomes like a fourth dimension of space, and in a sense past and future coexist with the present. But the reality of time implies the reality of irreversible processes and the emergence of novelty, which is incompatible with the pre-existence of the future. In a world existing through real time, the only status the future can have is that of ambiguity, of real possibility. It is contingent not necessary; not because of our ignorance but because of a genuine ambiguity in events not yet realized.

Such a world, to contrast it with the deterministic world of classical thought, may be called indeterministic. And for genuine human action to exist, this must be the character of the world in which we live: for in acting we do something; we make something take on a form other than that which it would have had if we had not acted; thus we determine the world. For this to be possible the world must be capable of being given a form which it did not already possess, that is, the world must be essentially indeterminate. Except that his 'sea of possibilities' metaphor again spatializes time, William James (1956, pp. 150–1) has produced one of the best characterizations of indeterminism of which I know. 'Indeterminism', he said:

> admits that possibilities may be in excess of actualities, and that things not yet revealed to our knowledge may in themselves really be ambiguous. Of two alternative futures which we conceive, both may now be really possible; and the one becomes impossible only at the very moment when the other excludes it by becoming real itself. Indeterminism thus denies the world to be one unbending unit of fact. It says there is a certain ultimate pluralism in it; and, so saying, it corroborates our unsophisticated view of things. To that view, actualities seem to float in a sea of possibilities from out of which they are chosen; and, *somewhere*, indeterminism says, such possibilities exist, and form a part of truth.

Usually we do seem able to intervene in ongoing processes and to make something happen in one way rather than another, as if both possibilities had been intrinsically available in the process. In a growing world, although each present event is not necessitated by its own past, it is undoubtedly caused; it is made to happen by an act of selection or choice. What had been an uncertain future is specifically realized now, by the exclusion of other possibilities. Thus to do anything in such a world is to do this and not that. This does not mean that action in such a world is preceded by choice, that some mysterious mental act of choosing precedes all our actual choosing. While reflection may precede action, it is only a theoretical, a possible choosing, as is clear from the fact that the 'action' so chosen need not be performed. Actual choosing is intrinsic to the performance of human actions whether preceded by reflection or not (Macmurray, 1957).

The Unnecessary Nature of Plans and Rules
for Intelligent Action

Now by insisting upon the reality of time, upon a growing world full of form-producing processes and real possibilities, we have implied a distinctly different image of human being in the world than in the classical image of people as isolated contemplatives. Instead of thinking before they act, people must in general act before they think, in order later to think before they act – if this is not to be dangerous, there must be 'safe' areas in which they can play (Shotter, 1973a). This is, of course, the image of people, of children, embodied in Piaget's slogan, 'thought is internalized action', but what Piaget needs to add to this is that in order to be intelligible the structure of such thought and action must be socially negotiated (Harré and Secord, 1972; Berger and Luckman, 1967).

Although this view – that action is primary and thought derived from it – is now becoming common, it is not usually realized what such a view implies. In speaking, for instance, we can and usually do speak grammatically without it first being necessary for us to think about how to do it; it does not imply that our actions are all necessarily produced by an inner reference to a 'plan', 'script' or 'representation'. Reflecting upon possible grammatical continuations while speaking requires a high level of skill and usually leads to hesitancy (cf. B. Bernstein's (1972) 'elaborated code'); it is the exception rather than the rule. Rather than speaking as if one were a computer operating according to a pre-formed programme, one can structure one's speech by monitoring it for its meaning in relation to one's intention in the course of its production – and there are many ways of doing this (see chapters 4 and 11, and Shotter, 1982). In general we speak with feeling not with thought, and it is only as our intentions issue in performance that we are able to tell whether we are successfully executing them or not. While I usually (but not always) know what I intend, I am in no better position than anyone else for observing my own performances. They must be judged as they occur, both in space *and time* – it being the temporal sequencing of spatial possibilities that reveals a person's choice and thus manifests his intention. Lashley (1951) has been one of the few behaviourist psychologists to see in the temporal sequencing of behaviour any major problem.

Time, then, is the essential psychological medium; it is through time that we express ourselves. In the classical scheme, in which time has been spatialized, this possibility has been lost. There, if contingency was allowed to exist at all it would seem to destroy the possibility of necessity (but this is not necessarily so: see Piaget's (1971, 1972) discussions of this point). Treating time realistically suggests that our thought and feelings need not remain private, but that it is possible for us to *show* our thoughts, feelings, moods, beliefs, intentions, etc., in our actions, in our temporal trajectory through sets of contingencies. However, in our attempts to make sense of such expressions, in deciding into which public or trans-subjective category they should be assigned in order to specify them, we must refer not only to objective, to spatial criteria, but also to temporal ones. Such temporal criteria, however, would be essentially contingent; that is, they would be essentially incomplete, and determining them (i.e. making them complete) one way or another is itself a matter of choice. Thus, if they are to be made 'logically adequate', then negotiation with others is necessarily involved.

Further discussion of this issue can be found in Berger and Luckman (1967), Harré and Secord (1972) and in chapter 4 below. Suffice it to say this here: to structure our perceptions of a person we must specify a set of both spatial and temporal categories, and place him or her in relation to them. In categorizing persons spatially we can determine their objective structure and locate it, outside ourselves, in space; in categorizing them temporally we can determine their subjective structures (their mental states) . . . but where in space should we locate them? This is what has always puzzled us about mental states: because there is nowhere precisely in space to locate them, neither in the observer nor the observed, they seem to float ethereally somewhere in between, and lacking any substantiality seem to have no real existence. In the classical world of matter in motion, they have no matter. But in an indeterministic world moving through real time, they can have a location: in a person's history, and it is that which is amenable to specification. It is by the structuring of our history that we can determine our future; but if we are concerned to act always responsibly, in a way intelligible to other people, how we do in fact structure it is not a matter entirely up to us – it must be negotiated with them.

We have now begun to move into deep waters, and it will be convenient to continue discussion of these issues in later chapters. The discussion above will suffice if it conveys some of the unique properties of time, and shows that it may be quite incorrect to think of it as simply a fourth dimension of space. While the past is what has been determined (and determined by people in some degree), the future has not yet been so, and thus must be considered not as a single, fourth dimension, but multi-dimensional. It is the future, not this or that hidden region of space, which holds promise of rich possibilities.

By discussing time in this way, I have attempted to indicate that the fact that people are 'growing systems', and can by their actions give something a form that it did not previously possess, is all of a piece with the fact that they can learn, express their intentions, pay attention, communicate, pursue goals, create novelty, and so on. In other words, I hope that by realizing in broad outline how it is that we live through time, it will be possible to see that the mental categories which we have called 'fictions' in the past are truly real. And that psychology can be seen as the science which, by operating in an indeterministic world in which both logic *and* our history can function to determine our future, helps us make clear in detail the possibilities from which we may choose our next step.

Conclusions

What is it then, in the new psychology, to be human? It is to be a growing system which can, in interaction with other growing systems, increasingly localize within itself the power of responsible action. And this would be the goal of a new psychology: to increase people's personal powers of responsible action; not to increase people's mastery over other people but their mastery over their own possible ways of life. It would have nothing to do with how we as 'mechanisms' *work*, for as growing systems we are not in fact mechanisms even though we may produce them within ourselves, and be interested in so doing. As time, and thus contingency and choice are central to the new psychology, its tasks will be essentially prospective ones, for our powers will always remain incomplete. As a result of this, the scientific process will itself involve a negotiated form of interaction with the subjects of its study. Vygotsky (1962) has discussed one such form of negotiated interaction as instruction: it is by instruction that spontaneous actions can be raised into the realm of the deliberate, and it is this process which will be discussed in the next few chapters. But as Vygotsky (1962, p. 90) says, 'in order to subject a function to intellectual and volitional control, we must first possess it.' This point is of the utmost importance, for it suggests people can only gain their personal powers from 'nature', from the social ecology within which they are embedded, if their circumstances are appropriate to such spontaneous activity. Then, suggests Vygotsky, what at first they only do spontaneously in response to such circumstances, they can through another person's agency, come to do later, as they themselves please, irrespective of their circumstances. But: (1) the provision of the appropriate initial ecological conditions is vital, and (2) so is the participation of another person in the process. Only by attending closely to another's spontaneous actions, and selecting socially relevant aspects of them, can they construct a socially accountable ideal self, an image of genuine personal being, which can be held out to the other as a challenge to be attained; one person can help another to become more of a person. By instruction individuals can become responsible themselves for actions which initially arose in the context of their interaction with others.

In the past, people have invented for themselves many forms of expression, forms of language, writing, mathematics, forms of art, forms of war, forms of family and community organization; in short, they have invented for themselves 'forms of life'. And there is no reason to suppose that the process by which we transformed ourselves from cave-dwellers in the past to what we are today is now at an end. Cultural progress is surely still possible, and a science called psychology can surely assist in making our future transformations of ourselves more responsible ones, so that we can *all* in the future (not just a few select groups) enhance each other's growth. In the task ahead, the dignity, the self-respect, the confidence to believe that by acting freely people can, out of themselves, fashion new and higher forms are essential features. Beyond our freedom and our dignity in our personhood (Skinner, 1972) is the human termite colony – if, indeed, people's nature could really cease to be a growing one as some behaviourist and mechanistic visions seem to suppose.

Part Two

The Development of Selfhood

4

The Development of Personal Powers

Human babies are not born into any direct relation with nature, but into a home, not into a natural habitat but into a humanly created setting, an institution designed in advance through artifice and foresight to provide for human needs, both biological and personal. Sometimes this foresight and artifice may be defective in one way or another, and the appropriate 'developmental opportunities' lacking (see chapters 6 and 7). However, to represent the process of human development even at its earliest stages as an organic process, a process of development towards a predetermined final goal, would be to exclude all reference to these and to other exclusively human aspects of the process.[1] As babies cannot think or act for themselves their survival depends upon the thought and actions of others. It is only within this process of development, a process in which the intentions of others are of crucial significance, that they achieve a relative independence and autonomy by acquiring their own powers of responsible action (Macmurray, 1957).

Intended Development

Babies are not machines, although they may be said to possess mechanisms and appear to function mechanistically in using them; nor are they animals, although in some respects they may be said to appear to function organically; if they are to develop as individual personalities they must be treated as full terms in a personal relationship, i.e. as beings who are amenable to rationality. If nobody intends their survival and acts with the intention to secure it, they do not survive. Thus a mother's reasons for her actions (which usually follow from her beliefs about the nature of people and things), no matter how inarticulate and vague, play an important part in the upbringing of her child. And this highlights an important methodological point, an error in much developmental and social psychological research. Personal relationships and other human groupings do not exist and function as matters of fact, but are maintained by the intention, whether explicitly appreciated or not, of their members to maintain them. Without such an intention they would collapse (see chapter 8). Thus they cannot simply be observed and described from the standpoint of an external observer, for it is the projected, intended or prospective ends which structure people's actions, not those which are actually attained. Personal relationships need to be described in a way exclusively human; in terms of what the people involved in them are *trying* to do. This cannot be done without making use of the concept of intentionality (see chapter 11).[2]

Briefly: in a growing world of form-producing processes, intentionality is intrinsic to the nature of human action. 'Cognitive' theories currently suggest that all actions are informed by reference to an 'inner' 'script', 'plan' or 'representation' of some kind (see note 3, chapter 6, for a discussion of modes of representation), and it is this which gives actions their relevance or reference to the situation in which they occur. I shall not adopt this view here at all. Instead, I shall claim that the 'intrinsic interrelatedness', or 'interfittedness', or 'appropriateness' of an action to the situation of its performance arises out of its intentionality; what is said to be its 'directedness'. Human action in its intentional nature can be said to work to articulate better, or further to specify, already partially specified forms (see Shotter, 1980a, and chapter 11). I shall not explore the nature of the intentionality of human activity further here, except to say that, although intrinsically it has a creative, form-producing function, not all human activity need be directed towards explicitly determinate ends or systems of ends (although it often is); some may be involved in the determination or 'construction' of such ends. Intentionality has thus both a rule-using *and* a rule-making or creating aspect to it.

To say this is not to say that people possess some mysterious 'elan vital' or 'soul', but simply to say, but that they 'direct' their conduct in relation not to their own immediate bodily interests and needs, but to actual or potential socially constructed ones – they are thus not just 'information processing' devices; or if they are, they are ones which must incorporate a unique social identity into their operations in some way. In other words, people are aware of themselves in their actions, in the sense of being aware of their 'place' or 'position' in the larger social scheme of things as they act. And it is in this sense that intentionality is central to this chapter. For I want to suggest that to the extent that mothers interact with their babies with the intention of brining them up to be responsible adults, their development is not a 'natural' process but an intentional one. Such an intention is perhaps one of the most general and indeterminate that there is, but no less real for all that. For, in one form or another, 'to make persons of them' is the reason mothers would give for much of what they do in interaction with their children. And it is in their attempts to make their intentions determinate to themselves, in deciding upon some definite practical activity regarding the appropriate instruction of their children, where their commonsense intuitions are inadequate (see chapter 8), that the child-care literature and other sources of social influence can take their effect.

Powers

Implicitly, an entirely new image of physical reality, to replace the old classical billiard-ball universe, has been introduced above; and it includes a radically different principle of causality. Central to this new image is the idea that things or substances have powers. This is related to the old Aristotelian nation of an efficient cause (as that which initiates change), and has recently been reintroduced into science and philosophy by such writers as R. Taylor (1966), Ayers (1968), Harré (1970a), Harré and Secord (1972), and Harré and Madden (1975). An efficient cause used to be thought of, not simply as a state or event which preceded another state or event in a principled manner, but as a definite thing or substance which had an *intrinsic* power to make something happen. I have discussed this idea at length elsewhere (see chapter 2 and Shotter, 1973a and b), and so will only mention aspects of it relevant to my purpose here.

The concept of powers is related to that of agencies acting within a field of possibilities, to the idea of an indeterminate determinable world. If we say that people's pasts do not determine just one possibly real future for them but a number, then we must say that at a certain moment in time they possess intrinsic powers or potentialities to express themselves in a whole range of different ways, the way they choose depending upon their circumstances at the time. To quote Harré (1970a, p. 85):

> To ascribe a power to a thing asserts only that it can do what it does in virtue of its nature, whatever that is. It leaves open the question of the exact specification of the nature or constitution in virtue of which it has the power. Perhaps that can be discovered by empirical investigation later.

But fully describing the powers of things is to give, Harré says, at least a schematic explanation of their intrinsic nature, an explanation which, with the growth of knowledge, would not need to be changed in outline, merely filled in with detail.

So far, I have discussed the application of the concept of powers in general; I now want to go on to discuss its special application here. In chapter 3, I introduced the fundamental distinction which we can make in our experience of our own behaviour: between what I as an individual personality can make happen and what simply happens, a distinction between actions and events, reasons and causes – our social being has a duality to it in this respect (Shotter, 1980b). Now clearly, much of what goes on between and within people merely happens; they do not as people make it happen – it happens naturally or spontaneously I shall say. For when individually I decide to do anything, the nervous and muscular co-ordinations required to express the intention happen automatically without me as such intending them; they are included or implicated (see chapters 5 and 6) in the doing of what I intend. As an individual personality *I* merely seem to modulate ongoing natural processes. Similarly, in freely occurring social interaction, the outcome is a joint product of the individuals involved, unintended by any of them. I shall, thus, distinguish two aspects of people: as individual personalities with personal powers and as natural agents with access to the 'natural' powers available to them in the context of their intentional relations with that which, or those whom, are other than themselves[3] – powers which are available to them either in their personal relationships, or in their relations to the rest of 'their' surroundings.

Having distinguished these different spheres of activity, we must now seek their relation to one another. Below I shall suggest that children derive their personal powers from the 'natural' powers made available to them in the social relations in which they are involved in the course of their upbringing. But that it is not something which they can (at first, if ever) do on their own; the help of someone who already possesses them is required, and usually that help is supplied by mothers – not necessarily the biological mother, but someone who is in what I can only call a *love*-relation to them, someone who cares sufficiently to reflect them back to themselves in an *ideal* way, i.e. in a way which indicates to them which of all the things 'they' do are the things highly valued in their society. Specifically then, I want to discuss what goes on between and within mothers and their children during that part of their early development which results in the children being transformed from almost wholly 'natural' agents into individual personalities. In other words, I want to discuss the process which results in their acquisition of their personal powers.

'Psychological Symbiosis'

The Initial Stages

The most obvious fact about human babies is their total helplessness. As Macmurray (1961) puts it, they seem to be 'adapted', to speak paradoxically, to being unadapted; they are adapted to a complete dependence upon an adult human being. They are born into a love-relationship which is inherently personal; they must be treated as if they are already persons who can intend purposes; they cannot think for themselves, yet they cannot live without thought, so some way must be found of having their thinking done for them. Until they have 'constructed' their own thought 'mechanisms', I shall propose that, by their mother's courtesy, they *use* their mothers as 'mechanisms' to do the thinking required in the realization of their intentions for them.

Very young babies *do* very little; while most of the essential physiological rhythms are established (Condon and Sander, 1974; Schaffer, 1977), and a few automatic reflexes, they have no power of action as such. Around the end of the first week of life they do, however, begin to respond to some cues. One such cue is said to be change of equilibrium. If, after the eighth day, breast-fed babies are lifted from the crib and held in a nursing position, they turn their head towards the breast. In contrast, if they are held in a vertical position they do not (Spitz, 1965). In general, however, for the first two months of life children could not be said to 'perceive' their surroundings at all. After that time an approaching adult begins to acquire a unique place in a child's environment. At this stage, hungry, crying children begin to perceive, in their sense of the term, an approaching adult visually: they will become quiet, open their mouths or make sucking movements. But this is said (Spitz, 1965) to take place only when the child is hungry; the response is to a totality of both internal and external factors. Two or three weeks later there is further progress: when the infants 'perceive' a human face, they follow it with concentrated attention. Later, at three months, they will smile, and this smile is, Spitz maintains, the first manifestation of active, directed (and, he says, 'intentional'[4]) behaviour on the child's part. This is the end of what Spitz calls the 'objective stage' (the stage of no active relationship[5] with the mother) and the beginning of what he calls 'psychological symbiosis'.

This is a very interesting and important stage, a true love-relationship, for total attention to one another is required. During this period of 'psychological symbiosis' the formative processes which terminate in the children seem to have their source in the mothers, and their influence is transmitted to their children very largely in the course of affective exchanges with them. That is, they are transmitted to them in the course of exchanges in which one individual responds in an immediate, unconsidered or spontaneous manner as a result of the way they apprehend the immediate and unconsidered reaction of the other individual to them. M. P. M. Richards (1974b) mentions a number of these kinds of exchange; it is often the mother's timing of what she does that is all-important. For instance, while breastfeeding her infant she times her talking and smiling to him or her to occur in the pauses between sucking. And as Mead (1934) points out, such interlaced but spontaneous activities are a form of communication, even if they cannot be said to constitute a language – as they are not of the form in which a stimulus affects the individual who makes it in the same way as the one who receives it. It is the communication of natural agents (or, as he would say, 'biological individuals'). The sort of perception involved in these exchanges – of the expression of feeling or affect – is very primitive, and all writers on the child's early development (Schaffer, 1971; Spitz, 1965; Koffka, 1921) note that distinctive reactions to different forms of human expression appear a few months before differential reactions to 'things' or 'thing-qualities'. As such affective or unreflective exchanges between human beings as natural agents are central to my whole thesis, I must break off here for a brief discussion of this form of perception.

The Perception of Expression and the Perception of Objects

A classical problem of perception is at issue here: (1) do we perceive people's psychological states in some direct way; or (2) do we perceive them indirectly, by, say, a process of 'unconscious inference' (Helmholtz) from data about the objective characteristics of their expression (see discussions in chapters 6, 7 and 11 of 'direct' perception). As the child reacts differentially to human expressions of joy and anger, friendliness and hostility *before* he reacts differentially to colours and other thing-characteristics (Koffka, 1921), it would seem to be the former. But this suggests that ostensively more complex judgements are made at an earlier age than apparently more simple ones – simpler, that is, if one holds to the classical image of people in which cognition is primary. The resolution of this issue involved a matter of (1) access to the relevant data; (2) the determination of its significance; and (3) the determination of its source, so I will discuss each of these in turn.

(1) Take joy, for instance: anyone can, in principle, report on whether a person is behaving joyfully or not, but only the person herself can say whether she is aware of being joyful. Thus it seems that two distinct kinds of criteria are involved here, one private and the other public. And in the

past both philosophers and psychologists have supposed that, as the seemingly private criteria are not open to scrutiny, only the public ones can be used as a basis for ascribing psychological predicates to people. But this, Harré and Secord (1972, p. 121) point out, is mistaken; both criteria are necessary and *are* available for scrutiny: 'There are always some situations for any state-of-mind predicate where others have some degree of access to that state of mind, even in another person.' Our feelings, moods, beliefs, intentions, etc., are, due to their intentional nature, shown in our actions, and although they may not involve reference to objective criteria, they do nonetheless involve readily observable criteria which can be made 'logically adequate' (Harré and Secord, 1972, pp. 14–123) as required, i.e. they are negotiable. What has misled philosophers and psychologists, Harré and Secord argue, is their failure to distinguish between access and authority, although a person is often (but not always) the best authority on what she is doing – for she is, after all, her own closest observer – *she is not the only one to have access to the relevant data.* One way or another that is made available in her behaviour for all to grasp, and indeed, when it comes to her assessing the nature of her own behaviour, i.e. satisfying Mead's criterion, she is in no better position than anyone else. Only as her intentions issue in performance is she able to judge whether she is successfully executing them or not – a point we shall take up again when later we discuss talking – and she may, as they occur, realize that they require correction, amplification, etc. While people usually (but not always) know what they intend, they can only judge the adequacy of their own performances as others do, i.e. as they occur. For it is only in their actions that agents' intentions are revealed and completed as the intentions they are. And it is 'in' the ability of agents to specify, in a moment-by-moment fashion, regions of the world beyond their actions, that their 'direction' of their actions is revealed, and thus both their intentions and their personalities made manifest (Shotter, 1980a).

(2) Now, if the criteria involved in the assessment of psychological states are not private, and people do show their psychological states 'in' the temporal organization of their behaviour, how do we determine these states? Consider for a moment a related situation. We distinguish a joyful person outside us from the feelings (of joy or otherwise) which he occasions within us. If, however, we accept that all our experiences originate from 'outside' us,[6] this distinction can only be a function of the way in which we determine these categories. One aspect of our experience is determined as 'outer' and ascribed or attributed to an object (in space), the other is determined as 'inner', and ascribed as a feeling to ourselves (in time) – space and time being, respectively, the forms of 'outer' and 'inner' perception (Kant) in this 'manner of speaking' (see chapter 10). Returning

now to our problem, I want to suggest that when confronted by a person it is open to us to determine the aspects of his behaviour similarly.

Now when attempting to determine the nature of a real object it does not, so to speak, answer back; it neither acts nor reacts. Thus, in this case, the categories of 'outer' perception can be made as determinate as an investigator pleases (and his categories of 'inner' perception are idiosyncratic and irrelevant to all except himself). However, a non-object, a source of expression, cannot be determined as one pleases, for it does answer back. So there is an essential indeterminacy associated with the categories of perception in this case which can only be resolved by negotiation and agreement with the source being investigated – to approach a point about negotiation made by Harré and Secord (1972, p. 161) from another direction.

So the essential difference between the processes involved in the perception of expression and the perception of things seems more to do with the way in which these categories are made determinate than anything to do with the perceptual process itself. The criteria of 'inner' perception involve negotiation and agreement with the source (or are otherwise left indeterminate, and people do not know exactly their feelings), while those of 'outer' perception, at least in their objective paradigm form, do not involve such negotiation.

(3) Now if the process of 'inner' perception works on expressions and determines them irrespective of whose expressions they are, the classical theories of our experience of other minds are quite redundant (if not quite wrong – see chapter 10). It is unnecessary, usually, even unconsciously to infer people's beliefs, intentions, etc., from sequences of behavioural events objectively perceived in 'outer' perception. We can perceive or apprehend mental activity directly in what I have called here our 'inner' sense.[7] But, if this is the case, as in our interactions with other people, there must be a continuous flux of activity within us, undifferentiated as to theirs or ours, the problem becomes one, not of appreciating the nature of mental activity in others, but of distinguishing that which has its source in us from that which has its source in them. And this, I think, is the problem young infants face in their period of 'psychological symbiosis'. They have to discover for which, of all things happening, they are or can be responsible, and which originate in sources beyond themselves.

The Continuation of the
'Psychological Symbiosis' Period

As Spitz said, the smile is the first directed expression of affect on the child's part. At first (at three months) the individuals to whom the infant responds with a smile are freely interchangeable. This is because three-month-olds do not perceive the human face as such at all, as Spitz has established experimentally; they perceive only a 'sign Gestalt': a specific configuration within the face as a totality, consisting of just the forehead–eyes–nose sector, triggers the infant's smile response after the manner of an 'innate releaser mechanism' (an IRM – Tinbergen, 1951). But as Spitz (p. 95) remarks:

> This sounds quite mechanical: sign Gestalten, releaser mechanisms triggering innate responses. The reader may well ask: couldn't a mechanical doll, fitted with the sign Gestalt rear our children just as well? No, it could not . . . . Only a reciprocal relation can provide the experiential factor in the infant's development, consisting as it does of an ongoing circular exchange, in which affects play the major role. When the infant experiences a need, it will provoke in him an affect that will lead to behavioural changes, which in their turn provoke an affective response and its concomitant attitude in the mother; she behaves 'as if she understood' what particular need of the infant causes his affective manifestation.

Although the relationship between a mother and her child is clearly an unequal one, they do have the power in some sense to complete or fulfil one another's intentions. And the situation cannot be simply as Ainsworth (in M. P. M. Richards, 1974a) states it: that the baby 'becomes attached to the figure or figures with whom he has had most interaction'. It is the specific quality not the quantity of interaction which must be significant. To the extent that mothers can interpret their babies' behaviour as having a mental content or intentional structure – and the extent to which mothers can do that is up to them – they can attempt to complete its intention and 'negotiate' with them a satisfaction of their children's needs, e.g. to alleviate their states of discomfort, restlessness or hunger, etc. But mothers pursue their own intentions within the interactive scheme also: they want their babies to suck, to stop crying, to acknowledge them by looking into their eyes, to grasp one of their fingers, etc. And thus mothers discover strategies and tactics by the use of which they can elicit these responses from their children. So both mothers and children gain a great deal of idiosyncratic knowledge about one another as individuals, which makes it very difficult for others to substitute for children's 'proper' mothers at this stage in children's development (Bowlby, 1953).

Now within the totality of child-and-mother, she constitutes a 'mechanism' or 'set of mechanisms' by means of which the child can execute actions in the world. (That even very young children, of four to eighteen weeks, will execute 'actions' if given access to the appropriate mechanisms has been strikingly demonstrated by Bruner, 1969.) It is only by a mother's instrumentality that her child comes to differentiate the forehead–eyes –nose sign Gestalt as a meaningful entity. She appreciates in her child's movements, in the manifestations of feeling or affect, the nature of her child's mental state and responds to them in such a way that she presents the characteristic Gestalt just at the time she is gratifying her child's needs. It thus only appears and functions within the ongoing circular affective exchange which has its source and its terminus in the child, but which is mediated via the 'mechanisms' the mother provides. The child could not have distinguished the sign Gestalt entirely by his or her own devices. Currently, they can only act because their mother acts 'as if she understood' them, and it is in this sense that children of three months or so are in 'psychological symbiosis' with their mothers. They can only differentiate themselves from her by constituting within themselves some of the same 'mechanisms' the mother now provides, by gaining a degree of social competence in being a person like her, able to act as they themselves desire. We shall be concerned with what is involved in acquiring that competence in the next section.

The Constitution of 'Mental' Totalities: A Hermeneutical Model

'A central problem of interpreting the world is determining how, in fact, human beings proceed to do so,' says Chomsky (1972, p. 13). Now we can only surmize about the processes going on within the child responsible for constituting the forehead–eyes–nose sign Gestalt. But there is no doubt at all that we must postulate the existence of something like, to use Chomsky's (1972) term, 'intrinsic principles of mental organization', which, as he puts it, 'permit the construction of rich systems of knowledge and belief on the basis of scattered evidence' (p. 45). But can we follow him when he goes on to speak of an organism as possessing a 'schematism that it applies to the data of sense in its effort to organize experience and construct cognitive systems' (i.e. abstract underlying mental represen- tations) (p. 29)? For clearly the primary task of human beings at least (if not organisms) is to learn, not *of* events in their 'external world', but how *to be* such that: (*a*) they experience themselves *as* themselves, as being who and what they are in relation to all the others with whom they share their lives, i.e. as beings with a social identity; *and* (*b*) as beings who experience their surroundings *as* an 'external world', i.e. as a world existing independently of their individual wishes, desires and opinions, etc., containing other people who, in fact, have access to its contents and can confirm or deny their reality. Chomsky's account assumes all too readily the simple division of the world into 'mental' and 'physical' phenomena: when the task is in fact to explain how it is that, currently, we experience the world, and ourselves, as divided in that way – for clearly, we haven't always done so (M. Douglas, 1966; Levi-Strauss, 1966).

The model for the requisite intrinsic principles of mental organization I shall propose is *not* based upon the procedures used in the natural sciences. On that model, one must assume, as does Chomsky (1965, p. 32), that 'the child possesses an innate theory of potential structural descriptions that is sufficiently rich and fully developed' for the child to be viewed as acquiring language in the same way that a scientist tests theories. Instead, it is based upon the procedures used in 'hermeneutics': the discipline to do with the interpretation (originally) of biblical texts for their meaning (see the section on 'the hermeneutical approach' in chapter 5, as well as Palmer, 1969, and Shotter, in press). There, one's understanding of *what* something is, is clarified by 'constructing' (or reconstructing) a larger whole into which it is or can be fitted; essentially the hermeneutical procedure involves a 'constructive' or specificatory process in which something, which is already partly specified, is specified further, thus rendering what was strange, alien or unfamiliar, *as* something familiar, as something with a comprehensible part to play in the whole in which it has its being. Thus the process does not begin with a pre-established order (or orders) of things to which puzzling facts must be assimilated, allowing them to be explained, as in Chomsky's model, as particular instances of general rules (or laws), with all their uniqueness lost. It begins with one's immersion within a chaotic whole in its full individuality, as the whole it *is* – known globally to be of a certain kind (sound, movement, etc.) – and it then proceeds to specify or articulate, in a back-and-forth movement, an order adapted to the undistorted accommodation of the original chaotic whole. *What* it is, is understood by it now having a part to play, a function, a 'place' within the larger order 'constructed' to accommodate it. At a trite level, of course, we can say that as a matter of 'practical hermeneutics', people understand practically what there is in their surroundings, simply by accommodating to them; they are changed by their encounters with their circumstances.

Bohm (1965) has elucidated other aspects of this process in a way which illuminates its practical nature. He points out that nothing is seen, for instance, as the thing it is, without movements and variations on the retina of the eye, and the characteristics of these variations must play some part in determining the structure of what is seen. The relevant data must be extracted from the relations between the 'outgoing' movements, i.e. those so 'directed', and their 'incoming' consequences. So we do not at any level perceive just what is in front of our eyes; what we perceive contains 'structural features which are not even on the retina of the eye at a given moment, but which are detected with the aid of relationships observed over some period of time' (Bohm, 1965, p. 203). In fact, Bohm goes on to argue, the attempt to base our idea of perceptual processes upon some physical time-order of events can only lead to confusion for 'the order of signals is not essentially related to the order of time' (p. 210) – as, for instance, in the constitution of images in a television picture. It is the way persons relate their actions and their consequents that matter, and to some extent, that is up to them, i.e. it is an intentional process. Perceiving is a skill:

> A person must actively meet his environment in such a way that he co-ordinates his outgoing nervous impulses with those that are coming in. As a result the structure of his environment is, as it were, gradually incorporated into his outgoing impulses, so that he learns how to meet his environment with the right kind of response. (Bohm, 1965, p. 211)

In other words, the relations we detect can work to change us practically.

To sum up: (1) the hermeneutical model suggests that the forehead – eyes–nose sign Gestalt only functions within the totality of the human face, that such configurations only have their significance in relation to some mentally constituted larger totality of possible configurations. Whilst (2) Bohm's arguments suggest that the sign Gestalt (and later the mother herself, personally) is singled out only because the mother co-ordinates her activities in closely with her child's. She is the only one who can be incorporated in the circuit of activities which has its source and terminus in the child. Thus it is not by their own actions, but by the mother's instrumentality or agency in them, that children single out the sign Gestalt (and will later single out her); but it is through their own activities that they will eventually differentiate themselves from her, and end the period of 'psychological symbiosis'.

The End of the Period of 'Psychological Symbiosis'

The notional end of the period of psychological symbiosis is indicated by the development of children's ability (around fifteen months) actively to deny their mothers the option of influencing them, in other words, by their learning in effect to say 'No'. They are now beginning to move around; until this time it was simply the mother's task to gratify or not the needs and wishes of her infant, now she has to curb and prevent some of his or her initiatives. And apparently, when acting as agents in their own right, autonomously, babies will not easily tolerate being forced back into a purely reactive role; they attempt to sever the links by which mothers exert their control over them. Thus the period of social games now begins. For, if one is to play one's part in a game properly, that is, be solely responsible for what happens, one must be able to cut oneself off from the influence of others while doing it; however, only if one is open to the influence of others does one know *when* to play it. Thus children, if they are to be able to play social games, must first develop a clear distinction between people and things (animate and inanimate), and then learn as their first social skill how to open and close the social link at will. And a part of being able to do that is being able to acknowledge the humanity, the autonomy and cognitive status of the other by some form of greeting – even if only a smile. Self-conscious beings 'recognize themselves as mutually recognizing one another' (Hegel, 1966).

The Exercise of Natural Powers in Play and Their Regulation According to Rules in Social Exchanges

Three-year-olds still react to adults affectively but in contrast to early childhood these affective reactions are directed and regulated in a generalized manner, e.g. children act as if they sense an adult's authority, friendliness, etc. Their behaviour manifests the influences of their past exchanges with adults and the physical world and is, presumably, regulated by some internally constituted structures as a result.

Now, in Vygotsky's (1966a) view, the child's play at this stage is essentially a generalized expression of affect: an expression of the child's basic needs and desires, structured as a result of the child's earlier action exchanges with adults and the world. Thus children when they play do not explicitly understand (in the sense of being able to account for it) *what* they play, they simply play in accord with some internal structure, what Vygotsky calls an 'imaginary situation'. It would be wrong then to say that they play 'according to rules'; they do not. The establishment of rules or rule-systems is, as we shall see, a final consequence of this process, not an essential part of it. So, although the children's play may seem to be regulated by rules, and someone may extract rules from it, and use them to re-enact their play, to extract the rules is not to reconstitute its original basis. The rules would only characterize the possibilities realized by children in the situations in which they were observed; they would not necessarily capture the whole field of both realizable and unrealizable[8] tendencies within the children's 'imaginary situations'. Any rules there might be in the child's play are not formulated in advance, but issue in the course of playing with others in a co-ordinated way, i.e. they issue in the invention of a game (Shotter, 1973b). It is at this point that I think the capacity for ceremonial emerges, which Harré (1974) so rightly emphasizes as being of crucial significance in the child's life. Of particular interest here are the rituals and comfort habits of the young child (Newson and Newson, 1968) and his linguistic incantations (Weir, 1962); these phenomena both occur on the child going to bed, at a time free of external demands. One could go on at this point to investigate the relation between ritual, myth and ceremonial in child and primitive thought as indeed Cassirer (1957) has done partially, but it would be out of place here to do so.

Now, most importantly, playing in accord with an 'imaginary situation' involves meanings. Usually, the entities in young children's environments dictate themselves how they must be used, but in play in an 'imaginary situation' this is not the case. Here, children regulate their own behaviour not by reference to the 'things' actually present in their own environment at all. In that sense, they are detached from it, and are acting in a cognitive or mental realm. The 'things' in their environment may be incorporated into their play, not for what they are in themselves, but for their meanings. That is, they may be incorporated into it to the extent that they fall in with or offer no resistance to those aspects of their play regulated by their 'ideas'. Their behaviour has ceased to be wholly context-dependent and begun to be structure-dependent, in Chomsky's (1972) sense of the term; that is, its elements come to have their significance in terms of the part they play in relation to the field of possibilities inherent in children's image of their 'play-world'. And the most unlikely things may enter into their play in all sorts of guises. All that matters is that whatever 'thing' is used it must allow for the execution of at least some of the same actions as the imaginary thing in an imaginary situation. (And in this sense, of course, a child's mother can be the best 'play-thing' he or she has.) Now we are not at the stage of symbolism involving rules yet, such play still essentially operates in affective terms, but now the affective meanings children assign to 'things' dominate and determine their behaviour towards them. But as long as such images are used as enactive representations (Bruner, 1966), as long as 'things' can mean almost anything in play, how can meanings and 'things' ever become linked in any determinate fashion? The role of other people in this process seems to be crucial.

Vygotsky (1966a, p. 9) discusses a situation in which two sisters (five and seven years) play at being 'sisters'. The vital difference between simply being sisters and playing at it is that, in play, they intend to be sisters and are conscious of one another's aim. They thus distinguish and discuss what it is to be a sister; they enact whatever emphasizes their relationship as sisters *vis-à-vis* other people: they are dressed alike, they walk about holding hands, the elder keeps telling the younger about other people – 'That is theirs not ours.' Everything associated with the children's intuitions of what it is to be a sister is expressed on one way or another and emphasized, and presumably on occasions discussed amongst themselves and accepted, modified or rejected accordingly. Thus, to quote Vygotsky, 'What passes unnoticed by the child in real life becomes a rule of behaviour in play.' Now this situation is most interesting for the sisters are, in fact, playing at reality. They are interacting with one another not in terms of what they are to one another in any immediate sense, but in terms of how they imagine one another to be; they are interacting in terms of what they *mean* to one another in their roles as sisters. Each is playing their proper part in a social game. Clear criteria have been adduced, some in action others in discussion, and what it is to be a sister has, for the moment at least, been decided between them. They have laid down the rules for their 'sisters-game'; they thus know what criteria they must meet in order to be sisters; they can thus now be self-directing in sisterly activities.

But the function one sister performs for the other here is the function children's mothers continually perform for them: in their play with them, mothers get their children to co-ordinate their activity with theirs in relation to definite criteria which are important to them in some way. Mothers cannot in this situation instigate their children's own activities for them, but they can nonetheless exert powerful controlling influences. They can do this because they know their children intimately from their earlier inarticulate and affective relationships, and they are still the means of their children's gratification. Thus they make use of this relationship time and again to draw their children into involvements which, if left to their own devices, they would never otherwise undertake.

It is thus, in the course of these informal involvements, that 'language games' (Wittgenstein, 1953) are established. Now there is nothing absolute about the rules or criteria functioning as the reference points in such exchanges. As Wittgenstein (1965, p. 25) remarks:

> remember that in general we don't use language according to strict rules – it hasn't been taught us by means of strict rules, either. We are unable to clearly circumscribe the concepts we use; not because we don't know their real definition, but because there is no real 'definition' to them. To suppose that there *must* be would be like supposing that whenever children play with a ball they play a game according to strict rules.

Clearly, they do not. What they do is to negotiate rules as required. And clearly, this is the one most important skill children acquire in the course of their 'games' with their mothers, the skill the sisters manifest in their 'sisters-game': the skill to make the meanings of their otherwise indeterminate actions *determinate* as required, by co-ordinating their behaviour with others, and by making implicit or explicit agreements with them one way or another.

This then is the nature of people's activity in social exchanges: it is as if one were making moves in a great political game such as 'Diplomacy' – for in fact one is! But the relationships that people have to one another, besides having an aspect of mutual use, also provide a reciprocated access to being – people help one another to be themselves. Now it is a common assumption that the social world is the product of emotional bonds; but, to quote Harré (1974, p. 247), 'a much more accurate response is to stand back in astonishment in the face of the maintenance in existence of forms of social cohesion in actual situations of emotional flux.' The exchanges in the mother–child world are most certainly mediated by affect, but mother and child become just as separated from, as bound to, one another in their early affective exchanges.

Natural Agents Determine Forms: Individual Personalities Monitor Them for Their Meanings

We have arrived now at the stage when social games are possible, and we can begin to touch upon the nature of personal powers, the powers whose exercise is monitored by the individuals exercising them. These, I have suggested, are derived from the 'natural' powers only made available to one in one's surroundings, in the regions of the world beyond oneself – and in particular, of course, in one's surroundings when one is one of the terms in a personal relationship.

In discussing the development of personal powers it will be convenient to concentrate our attention upon the activity of speaking. Clearly, no explicit agreements making meanings determinate are possible until children have learnt the skill of making agreements verbally, and they must first learn 'language-games', and the agreements they involve, implicitly, by participating in the appropriate 'forms of life' (Wittgenstein, 1953). It is in the course of interlaced social action that they co-ordinate their activities, including their vocal aspect, with the activities of others. The processes discussed above suggest how this might be done; thus there is no necessity and indeed no warrant to assume that, at first, they vocalize according to rules. Their vocalizations are not, of course, always intelligible; the constitution of their natural powers of vocalization allow for the expression of a whole field of possibilities appropriate in some tenuous way to the current situation. Their vocalizations are thus regulated but not yet rule-regulated.[9] It is by instruction that these skills are acquired (Vygotsky, 1962); it is by such interventions by others that spontaneous actions can become transformed into deliberate ones, that personal powers can be derived from natural ones.

'In order to subject a function to intellectual and volitional control, we must first possess it,' says Vygotsky (p. 90). And he goes on to discuss (pp. 100–1), as an example, a situation in which although a child cannot say 'sk' deliberately, out of any sort of context, he can say 'Moscow', when asked, with ease. It is only later thanks to instruction in grammar and writing that he becomes aware of what he is doing in such speech performances and learns to use his skills consciously, and realizes that 'sk' is a part of 'Moscow'. But, in being instructed in grammar, someone other than the children themselves – who must monitor their own speech for its meaning – must observe their speech forms and draw their attention to them. It is attending to the forms of behaviour within a performance, while at the same time monitoring the behaviour for its meaning, that even the most highly practised performers find difficult. Reflecting back to one the form of one's action – treating it as a sequence of named events rather than as the action it is – is a service that only another person can provide; a service that is essential if one's perform-ance is to be structured into components or episodes which can then, as a set of named episodes, be arranged and rearranged as one pleases, i.e. planned and deliberated upon in theory before being performed in practice.

Consider now the speech of children at a much later stage, when they have begun to construct lengthy utterances: while it may be correct to assume that they are aiming at definite articulatory 'targets' in their determination of word-forms, and definite syntactic criteria in their determination of sentence-forms, it is still not necessary to assume that they are using words and sentences according to any definite criteria at all. To suppose that there must be strict rules for using words and sentences 'would be like supposing that whenever children play with a ball they play a game according to strict rules'. A sentence is something one uses to express one's meaning; it is not an expression of a meaning itself. Its meaning is a logical construction to be completed both by oneself and one's listener out of the influences exerted by one's utterance. And one may find, just as one's listener does, that the sentence just uttered was inadequate to the purpose intended; one may find even in the course of uttering it that it is inadequate – one hesitates and begins again.

The construction of a sentence (as an instrument) is thus to be distinguished from the uses to which it can be put. And, although sentences are clearly constructed for precise and special functions, it would still be a mistake to think that its use was completely specified by its construction. Rather than specifying a single actual use, its construction seems to specify a field of possible uses. And as I said earlier, only if necessary, for particular practical purposes, are the criteria making its use determinate established and agreed upon, and there are all sorts of strategies for doing that, some drawing on agreements made before the use of the sentence, some made during, and some after its use.

What then is the relation between personal powers and rules? Do we speak in accordance with rules? While speaking we obviously remain sensitive to our listener's nods of comprehension and grimaces of bafflement, and modify our talk accordingly. It is just not the case, empirically, that we turn our eyes inward, shut ourselves off from our environment, and refer to some pre-established inner plan to determine what we say. We can in some cases, but usually we do not. Face-to-face conversations are not mediated solely by linguistic 'rules'. In any case, such rules are couched in terms of idealizations; the assignment of utterances and their constituents to linguistic categories depends upon a prior grasp of their meaning, and idealized linguistic categories need play no part in the understanding of spontaneous speech. Rather, what seems to be the case is that we continually monitor the construction of our expressions in relation to our intended purposes. And we do this by constructing as we utter them our meanings – in just the same way as our listener must construct them. Thus we can say that the natural powers made available to us in 'our' situation present us with possible forms of expression, while our personal powers allow us to select from among them the expressions whose meanings are appropriate to our purposes. In other words, we as individual personalities perceive the possibilities open to us as if presented to us from 'outside' ourselves. Merleau-Ponty (1962, p. 215) describes the situation thus:

> I am a sentient subject, a repository stocked with natural powers at which I am the first to be filled with wonder . . . .
> Every perception takes place anoymously. I cannot say that *I* see the blue of the sky in the sense in which I say that I understand a book or again in which I devote my life to mathematics . . . . So, if I wanted to render precisely the perceptual experience, I ought to say that one perceives in me, not that I perceive . . . .

Similarly, something within me constitutes for me the linguistic forms I require in my speaking; I do not have *myself* to determine them; although originally, as a child, I myself might have been present in their initial acquisition.

So, while the determination of linguistic forms need not be *self*-directed and intended, but simply directed or intentional in quality, the use of linguistic forms in a purposeful manner *is* a self-directed activity. And besides being self-directed, potentially at least, their use may also be rule-regulated – but I say 'potentially' for it may very well be that the agreements which will actually make the meanings of one's utterances determinate may only be reached *after* one's utterance, in the course of subsequent exchanges. So what people seem to be aware of while they talk are not regulations determining the possible forms of their talk, but the possible social criteria (and thus the possible procedures or methods) necessary in determining what is meant by their talk. And these are in no way fundamental. They reflect just as much aspects of one's experience as 'the general character of one's capacity to acquire knowledge' (Chomsky, 1965, p. 59) – for they may be methods or procedures, or ways of doing things, invented in the history of our culture.

Child Development as a Concept-Informed Process

The theme of this chapter has been that the human child does not develop psychologically according to 'laws of nature', but in an intentional manner; that is, the concepts in terms of which we interact with our children play an important part in determining the form of their psychological development. It is the idea of intentionality which has been central; the idea that action is essentially a matter of the specification or determination of something which is open to such determination. Now the goal of an action, being a conceptual matter, a matter of intention rather than fact, is in itself indeterminate before the action is performed; it is determined or not as the case may be by the agent in action. If the important aspects of children's psychological development are concept-ual, that is, if they depend upon the intentions we pursue in our interactions with them, how can empirical investigations be conducted in this sphere? Well first, let us be clear as to what the aim of such investigations might be. Surely, they can only be aimed at understanding how to increase people's powers of responsible action, i.e. the understand-ing of 'ontological skills' – how to be this or that kind of person. With this aim in mind, empirical investigations take the form of experimental attempts at instruction, with personal knowledge of one's pupil playing a crucial role in such attempts.

Here, then, I have tried to construct a conceptual framework within which we can conduct and make sense of empirical findings in this area of research. It has been concerned with the concept of personal powers and their development, i.e. with what empirically is involved in developing into an individual personality. I have attempted to give the general form of some of the criteria involved in distinguishing persons from things, actions from movements, etc., in the hope of establishing a way of recognizing human action when we see it. But I have not been able to detail the actual criteria relevant to all such practical situations, for to satisfy the criteria to be a person in one situation is not to satisfy them in general, and in any case the criteria are not general but negotiable – we have to intend personhood continually and discover empirically in each practical situation how to fulfil it. And this is not a natural scientific but a moral task – a choice that is ever present for us.

5

Developmental Practices: Practical Hermeneutics and Implication

To qualify as an autonomous person, not reliant like a child upon others to complete and give meaning to one's acts, having them decree *what* it is one is doing, one must develop the ability to be able at some point in one's acting to stop and to deliberate, and, as a result, make clear to oneself (and/or to others) one's reasons for one's actions. That is, one must be able to make clear in terms intelligible to other members of one's society the rational connections between what one is doing, its antecedents, and to what one hopes it might lead (and perhaps even the grounds for so hoping). It is proposed here that the developmental process in question is not only embedded in the communications which take place between infants and those others in their society who are already (relatively) autonomous individuals, but that these communications have a special form to them, such that they may be called 'developmental practices': for their concern is not with communicating 'information' about events in the 'external world' of those who are already constituted as autonomous persons in their society, but with instructing children in how to *be* the kind of person required by their society – if their society's social order is to be self-reproducing (see chapter 8).

The developmental thesis I want to explore here is one drawn, primarily, from Vygotsky (1962, ch. 6): simply, that the activity which issues from one spontaneously, in the course of acting as one's circumstances require, may be transformed into deliberate action if one can learn from others some reasons for so acting; or, to put it another way: such activity may be transformed if one can learn from the way in which others 'reply' to it, to what in the social world one's actions may lead. Thus later, one may act in the knowledge of the social consequences of one's actions. And what is special about the 'developmental practices' in which this occurs, is that mothers interpret (in a practical hermeneutical way) the activities of their babies – which often they (the mothers) have 'invited' – as if the meaning of their babies' activity was, in fact, a meaning their babies intended.

The Concern with Social Practices

In recent years, microanalytic studies of all forms of social interaction have burgeoned (more under the aegis of sociology than psychology; see Cicourel, 1973; Goffman, 1971), and with their burgeoning, implicitly rather than explicitly, a new way of doing psychology is beginning to develop. But now, rather than theory preceding practice as with the initial attempt to institutionalize psychological inquiry (see Koch, 1959, p. 783), practice is preceding theory. And this, as we shall see, is just how it should be if institutions appropriate to the conditions in which they must operate are to be established: they should merely institute what seem to be the effective aspects of the practices people are already performing in the circumstances spontaneously.

Now learning how to mean, how to make-sense-to-others, is not just a matter of learning how to make certain well-defined patterns of responses, that is, learning something objective. It is a matter of learning how to adapt and modify one's actions in the face of continually changing external circumstances while maintaining their relation to some internally held principle, standard or goal shared by those with whom one lives; that is, one must learn a practical skill. And in fact one must learn many different practical skills if one is to relate one's behaviour intelligibly to the behaviour of others in one's social life (whether those others happen to be present at the time or not): one must learn, for instance, how to take one's turn, to agree, to request, to name, to describe, to command, to promise, to negotiate, to love, to hate, to rationalize, to theorize, to carry out in fact a whole host of different practical accomplishments in ways which are both appropriate to one's own circumstances, and which make sense to those others. This is what it is to be a social agent. And the whole point about the nature of such activities is that they are only differentiated from one another in terms of the different ways of meaning something to others, the social practices, the use of language, involved in conducting them; the knowledge embodied in such practices need not first exist as ideas-in-people's-heads before being put into practice. Practice may precede, and exist, quite independently of theory. Thus, for children to acquire the concepts embodied in our everyday 'ways' of acting meaningfully, they do not have to acquire any ideas about the reality in which they live, nor any cognitive structures, or such-like; they simply have to learn appropriate practical skills – at least, in the first instance: the advantages of sooner or later having some 'ideas' is discussed in the next section.

Social Institutions and Selfhood

By constructing the appropriate laboratory (i.e. social) settings, it has been shown that one may elicit all kinds of characteristically human actions from infants at a very early age (Fantz, 1961; Bower, 1966, 1974) – a point to which we shall return when we discuss the role of mothers as the motivators of their infants' activity. But nothing in the results of such experiments would seem to indicate that the infant him- or herself had detected and identified, or in other words 'monitored' (Harré and Secord, 1972) their own differential responding in the same way as those experimenting upon them; still less would they indicate that they themselves had 'directed' it, and that they knew what their own activity 'meant' for how they might go on to act in the 'situation' in a socially intelligible manner (in contrast to merely responding to it).

If one is going to be a person, an autonomous individual, acting in the knowledge of who and what one is, and what one is trying to do in relation to all the others with whom one is sharing one's life, then something more than merely behaving in ways that others can recognize is involved – one must be able to recognize what one is doing, oneself.

Now while the child as an organism may seem to be provided innately with the capacities to act in many different ways, 'where' might the source of knowledge be located about the different particular uses to which these otherwise rather indeterminate capacities may be put? It must be located, I have argued (in chapter 3), in the social ecology in which the child is embedded. In other words, the knowledge which children must acquire if they are to learn how to put their innate capacities to use, intelligibly and responsibly, to do the 'done things' in their society, is 'out there', in their society, encoded not as ideas in people's heads but, as was said before, spread out in the practical activities of everyday life. Thus, in the view I am taking, practice precedes theory.

Ryle (1963), p. 31), in discussing the relation between theory and practice, puts the matter thus:

> Efficient practice precedes the theory of it; methodologies presuppose the application of the methods, of the critical investigation of which they are the products. It was because Aristotle found himself and others reasoning now intelligently and now stupidly, and it was because Izaak Walton found himself and others angling sometimes

effectively and sometimes ineffectively that both were able to give to their pupils the maxims and prescriptions of their art.

And this is how we must proceed if we are to establish institutions which are appropriate to the circumstances in which they must operate; we must study and describe the practices already existing, rather than simply seeking to institute our own theories.

But this does not mean that there is no advantage in having, so to speak, 'ideas' about what it is one is doing: in fact there is considerable point to the attempt to formulate, once practices prove effective, the 'theory' of them (Shotter and Burton, 1983). Ryle's comments suggest two reasons: (1) accounts, if their application is understood, may serve to indicate intelligent rather than stupid, effective rather than ineffective action, and thus serve to institute standards of correct and incorrect conduct; and (2) they may also be used as aids in the instruction of others into the practice. But there are other, even more important reasons: (3) by using one's theoretical accounts to formulate a plan, one may extend one's practices, deliberately, into areas other than those in which they were initially developed. And this is most important. For if people are ever to be self-determining, and act as they themselves require rather than as their circumstances require, they must develope the ability to deliberate before they act. That is, they must develop the ability to decide courses of action in theory before executing their choice in action (Winch, 1958; Macmurray, 1957; R. Taylor, 1966) – learning how to 'direct' one's own thought appropriately, in order to 'do theorizing', being itself, of course, a practical accomplishment situated within, or implying, its own form of life (Blum, 1974). And finally, of course, (4) when the 'theory', the rules, maxims or prescriptions of a practice have been learned, and can be stated (when requested), the practitioner can claim to be socially autonomous. For one acknowledges rules, not on authority, but as authoritative; pupils who can refer their actions to rules are thus freed from the authority of their teachers.

The advantages of having some 'idea', then, of what it is that one is trying to do in one's action is that one can be more than just a passably competent member of one's society, one may become a free individual within it; one may project oneself into the future and attempt to bring into existence new situations, ones which may never before have existed, but which would still be ones intelligible and relevant to other members of one's society. If one is to act as one desires, rather than as one must, in 'reply' to one's circumstances, then thought of a certain organized kind must of necessity inform one's actions. The production or 'manufacture' of a person's ability so to organize their thought in relation to their action in such a way has been called by Giddens (1976) 'the progressive rationalization of action or experience', and this is our concern below.

The Hermeneutical Approach: Practical Hermeneutics

The study of developmental practices, of learning how to mean, requires an approach of a kind altogether different from that hitherto used by professional psychologists in their studies of behaviour. It is an approach which at first may seem utterly subjective to the majority of psychologists, trained as we all have been in an approach to the study of behaviour which allows the use only of 'objective' methods. For, rather than the testing of theories by experimentation, it abandons the search for that kind of knowledge altogether. Instead, its central activity is that of seeking, in the course of something like 'dialogues' with them, interpretations of the meaning of people's actions – thus to discover their grounds, and towards what they may be directed. In short, it is just the kind of science needed to find the reasons for people's actions. It is called by some (C. Taylor, 1971; Habermas, 1972; Giddens, 1976; Gauld and Shotter, 1977) a hermeneutical approach,[1] for its task is not unlike that which originated in the seventeenth century with the problem of interpreting the meaning of biblical texts (Palmer, 1969), i.e. the task of transforming a superficial, global and perhaps misunderstood grasp of what a text is about, into an accurate, well-articulated account of its actual meaning (perhaps even goins so far as to seek its meaning not at the time of its production, but its meaning for us today!). The search for 'objective knowledge' is irrelevant to such an endeavour; understandings from within a frame of reference, a social practice, a tradition, or a society are what are required – hence the relevance of this approach to the title of this chapter. And hence, also, the mistake in any claim that it is a purely 'subjective' approach, for like any claims in a science, claims about meanings, about interpretations, can be 'warranted': not by their origins (they are unimportant), but by the procedures used in checking their correctness or truth. And in a practical hermeneutics, as we shall see, interpretations are checked out as to their correctness, or not, by the extent to which they work to promote certain kinds of concerted social action.

As a science of interpretation, then, the hermeneutical approach does not attempt to predict, control or otherwise to explain the causes of people's behaviour, as one does – by using the special standpoint of the disinterested, external observer, and referring to theories about the underlying nature of what one is observing – in the attempt to gain an intellectual grasp of natural phenomena. Instead, it takes it as given that we all have as human beings a certain special 'insider's' view of human behaviour, and concerns itself with the task of transforming the vague and perhaps mistaken understandings of human phenomena we already possess from that insider's point of view, into more precise and effective ones. It thus makes a number of major distinctions ignored by those taking a behaviourist approach to the study of such human phenomena.

(1) It distinguishes between those entities (usually, other people) which can be understood directly by communicating with them, and those which cannot, and which can only be studied indirectly by reference to a theory. In studying things indirectly, in terms of a theory, one must proceed as if they were logically structured in one way or another, and then continually check to see whether one's logical expectations are confirmed or not. Whereas in communication, one's investigations are not guided by a theoretical structure, but, due to the intrinsic intentionality of human action, by the implications of the 'replies' received from one's investigations of an entity so far (see the discussion of Smedlund's views on implication below); we find 'it' can play just as much a part in structuring the exchange as ourselves, and in so doing, reveal itself to us. For instance, suppose one day someone seizes a piece of material and is about to attempt to mould it to their purpose, when it seems to wriggle in their hands. Given the sense of responsibility that people can have for at least some of their actions, we may presume that in this instance the person senses that they were not responsible in any direct manner for the motions of the matter they experienced. Hence, they immediately drop it. Their whole attitude to it changes. Initially, they had committed themselves to treating it as inanimate matter, moulding it to one's purposes being one of the things one can do with such matter; but they then discover, as a result of their own direct contact with it, that it is not. While such a 'reply' closes off one general mode of conduct to them, it still leaves open, say whether they then deal with the material as if it were organic, or personal, or one of a number of more differentiated categories of things within these broad categories. And the point here is this: in finding that they cannot now treat the material as inanimate, they do not need to formulate *a theory* of what might now be its nature in order to be able to go on dealing with it; their idea as to its actual nature may remain utterly vague. All they must do is to switch their mode of conduct from one form of practical activity to another, their investigations being guided (because they do not yet know in any detail the nature of what they are dealing with) only vaguely by the differentiated notions (of inanimate, organic or personal) mentioned above. Thus to come to an understanding of things in communication, it is possible to begin with only a vague commitment to a particular mode of conduct, and to move in the course of the exchange to a more precisely

differentiated one. However, the opposite of vagueness is the order of the day in understanding things from the 'outside', via theories: only if one begins with a very well-defined logical structure is it possible at all to be certain about the relation between one's predictions and one's observations, if one is not going to be continually fudging the issue, and seeing all kinds of results as fitting one's theory.

It is worth adding here a comment about the nature of *commitments* in human relationships: if, for instance, we meet a stranger, even a slight smile (what other things might there be to which we 'give' slight smiles of recognition on encountering them – computers?) is sufficient for us to indicate to them that we have acknowledged their humanness, i.e. recognized them as distinct in a special way from the rest of our surroundings, and this commits us, potentially at least, to going on with them as a human being. We cannot, at least not without breaking that commitment, change to treating them as an animal, or as an inanimate thing. But our commitment here is unsystematic, indeterminate, and knowing that we are dealing with a human being, still leaves it open to us as to how to go on to make more sense of them; or to them. Rather than face ourselves with such tasks unnecessarily, we are thus careful to whom we 'give' such smiles.

(2) The next important distinction made by those taking an hermeneutical approach, but ignored by behaviorists, is this: as mentioned before, there is a sense of knowing something from the 'inside' which is quite different from that knowledge we may have of things from the outside. Hence there is a sense in which it is possible to understand human phenomena (because we are 'inside' the processes of their production) in a way not possible with nautral happenings. This kind of knowledge, the knowledge posessed by actors involved in human affairs, as opposed to those who merely observe them, is knowledge of quite a unique kind, irreducible to any other; the English language unfortunately, however, possesses no precise term for it. Possessing it, as Gauld and Shotter (1977) point out, we can 'understand', for instance, that people who have intentions will do what they believe will be most likely to fulfil them, for we know 'from the inside' that this is a part of what it is to have an intention (see Smedslund, 1978, 1979, 1980, and Shotter and Burton, 1983, for explorations of the 'logic' in the common sense knowledge we have of such psychological phenomena). And there is no other way of knowing what is involved in having an intention; certainly it is not possible in any simple sense to observe people consulting their beliefs. So here again, as above, we meet the divorce between explaining a particular event by relating its occurrence to a general law or principle, and understanding it, not by subsuming it under a generalization, but as arising from one particular

intention rather than another. It is understood when we know what *in particular* a person was trying to do, and what *in particular* were their beliefs in trying to do it.

(3) Implicit in the above is the distinction between natural and human processes that behaviourists also ignore to their cost. It is a distinction, for instance, de Saussure (1960) makes when he distinguishes between language and speech. 'Language, once its boundaries have been marked off within the speech data', he says (1960, p. 15), 'can be classified among human phenomena, whereas speech cannot.' Speaking is a many-sided natural, temporal process, a wilful act on the part of the individual, requiring many different disciplines (physics, physiology, psychology) in its study; language, on the other hand, is a human product, and, as a 'man-made' entity may be treated as if merely a spatial object – hence the possibility of (synchronic) linguistics as an (almost) autonomous discipline. If Vico is right, and we can only understand that which we ourselves make (see chapter 8), then language, law, etc., and indeed all social institutions, are understandable in a way quite impossible with natural processes (which we have not, of course, created). And this was de Saussure's point: by assigning to linguistics just the task of analysing language (as a human product), but not speech (as a natural process), linguistics has been able to make great progress while psychology, failing to distinguish human from natural phenomena, has languished.

The hermeneutical approach is concerned, then, not with explaining natural phenomena but with interpreting human ones; with the task not of prediction and control, but of helping people to increase their own self-awareness: to understand, for instance, that to treat many forces of society as 'natural' processes is radically to misinterpret them, and that another interpretation may be possible in which different people's different parts in them are made much more clear to us. In psychology, however, we are not at all clear into which category our phenomena fall. But this is not because we are muddled (which we are) and in any case do not bother with the distinction; but because, as we shall see, the distinction is, in a most interesting and important way, an intrinsically vague one; and it is a fundamental and continuous task in any culture to devise ways of maintaining a boundary between ourselves and what, on the other side of that boundary, we call 'nature'. Douglas (1966) and Shotter (1975) describe some of the social, cultural and political consequences of drawing this essentially uncertain but nonetheless ecologically necessary distinction, in arbitrary but precise ways.

We may see the nature of our uncertainty simply by considering the nature of the standard questions we often set ourselves in psychology:

'why do we act as we do?' 'What is it that enables/makes/causes, etc., us to do what we do?' As stated the questions are ambiguous in that we might be asking: (1) 'What *in us* enables us to do it?'; or (2) 'What enables us *ourselves* to do it?' (1) is of course the classical form of the question and requires as an answer a description of some 'mechanism' within us, whereas (2) requires a description of some process of social exchange productive of increased self-directed, self-regulated, or self-determined activity, an account of something that goes on between people rather than within them.

Of the two approaches, however, the hermeneutical approach is basic, irreducibly basic (Gauld and Shotter, 1977), for a theory is a human phenomenon, a humanly constructed entity, and as such the terms in which it is couched present a task for hermeneutical analysis (see Bhaskar, 1979, and chapter 2); they cannot be given an interpretation free from frames of reference, practices and paradigms (Kuhn, 1962), traditions or cultures. Thus to explain, say, developmental practices, we must *already know* what it is to concern ourselves with developmental phenomena from a position within, presumably, a tradition concerned with their study; there is no presuppositionless knowledge to be had.

The Beginning and the End of Developmental Studies

I want to propose, then, that the aim in studies of mother–infant interaction be described as an attempt to account for the social practices by which human abilities (including our knowledge of them) are transformed from more primitive into more developed forms. But what should be the starting point for such studies? In accord with his concern only with the growth of knowledge not its origins, Popper (1972) – along with all those concerned with the study of everyday social practices – has argued for commonsense with all its vagueness and error as the starting point for all scientific investigations; for its inadequacies may be eradicated in the course of its growth.

Is such a methodological maxim any help to us here in studying the development of young infants? Surely before infants acquire any human knowledge, they must first be accounted merely as organisms and investigated as such? In that case, is not a starting point in common sense useless to us? Must we not begin from some theory of biological or organismic functioning? Well, perhaps not, for, said Stout (1938, pp. 407–8) – who considered in his 'genetic' approach many of the issues we are considering now –

What we are attempting is a descriptive analysis of the process through which knowledge of the material (and the social) world in all the essential aspects of its being passes from more primitive to more developed stages. What we are emphatically *not* attempting is to show how such knowledge is or might be generated from a prior experience in which it is not present. . . .

In other words, we must begin by taking the same commonsense view that mothers take of their infants at birth, that they begin life as in some sense persons – albeit as very primitive ones. For if we do not, and we take them to be organisms, then we face, as Stout pointed out, not simply the task of describing how their knowledge grows from primitive origins, but how something essentially organic is transformed at some point into something essentially personal. So, to be true to our starting point in commonsense, we must assume that babies are born *as* persons – or at least, as Macmurray (1961, p. 50) puts it, they live 'a common life as one term in a personal relation'.

Life as One Term in a Personal Relation

Now while mothers may treat their babies in a personal manner from birth (Macfarlane, 1974), it used not to be an assumption which found much favour among scientists studying child development. Many assumed that the child at first *is* 'asocial' (Schaffer, 1971, p. 13), 'animal matter' (M. P. M. Richards, 1974a, p. 51), developing only as an aspect of 'embryogenesis' (Piaget and Inhelder, 1969, p. vii) into a person later. Trevarthen (1974, 1975a) was one of the few to insist that infants must be treated both practically and theoretically as persons right from the start. And a part of what it is for infants to be in a personal relationship right from the start is for their mothers to treat their activity, not in organic terms as merely reaction to a stimulus, but in personal terms. That is, regarding the form of their activity as personal, she does two things: (1) one the one hand, she acts to elicit from them certain forms of no doubt innately organized activity, but activity which makes sense to her and which, without her intelligent adjustment of the eliciting circumstances would undoubtedly remain unexpressed (see the example from Newson and Newson, 1975, described below). In other words, a mother 'affords' or acts to motivate certain types of activity in her baby – Schutz (1953) would say, she provides a because-motive: her baby acts because of her 'invitation'. On the other hand, having motivated some characteristically human activity, she now acts to interpret it as having a meaning: 'Oh, look,' she says, after having got her infant to look at her by cooing and smiling at her, having placed her face in his line of regard, 'she's looking at me'. So she replies to 'her' (?) look with a 'Hello, hello, you cheeky thing'. The point here being that whatever mothers do to motivate their babies' activity, when they respond, mothers still interpret their response as something which their babies themselves do, not merely as something which they have succeeded in eliciting from them; it is thus treated as activity worthy of being an expression in a dialogue, an expression requiring a meaningful reply. Mothers thus supply their children with what Schutz (1953) would call an in-order-to-motive as well: for in this situation babies can learn what they can bring about by their own actions.

The process above, because it entails mothers acting contingently upon what their children do, may seem to some to be like 'reinforcement learning', *à la* Skinner. Nothing could be further from the truth: it is the way in which mothers 'reply' in terms of their interpretations which is crucial. Only by replying in socially proper terms to their children's responses are their children offered or afforded an opportunity to learn the proper social use to which their activities may be put. If, for instance, every time they made a pointing-like movement they were given a reward, a sweet, say, or anything (other than their mothers attending to their actions in socially relevant terms, i.e. looking towards the object they were looking at, or in some contexts, naming it, or giving it to them), then one may indeed increase the frequency of their pointing-like movements. But infants could never possibly learn from 'reinforcement' of this kind that such movements could be used, not for getting sweet rewards, but for the socially relevant purposes mentioned above.

As another example of the way in which the intelligent, interpretative adjustment of an adult to a child's own activity may function to elicit complex human action from him or her that they might not otherwise express, Newson and Newson (1975, p. 442) have described well the task of getting a supine four-week-old infant to follow visually a dangling ring:

> In this superficially simple task, the test demonstrator will carefully attend, not just to the general state of arousal of the infant, but to his precise focus and line of regard. Having 'hooked' the attention of the infant upon the ring, one then begins gingerly to move it across his field of vision in such a way that the infant's eyes continue to hold the object with successive fixations until eventually the head follows the eyes in that co-ordinated overall movement pattern which denotes successful tracking. If the test object is moved too suddenly, or is left static too long, the visual attention of the infant will flag and the attempt will have to begin all over again from scratch. In this

instance, what is in fact happening is a highly skilled monitoring by the adult and a consequent adjustment of the dangling object, moment by moment, depending on the feedback which is being obtained from the spontaneous actions of the infant.

And, as they go on to say, 'the resulting action sequence of the infant is therefore a combination of his own activity and an intelligent manipulation of that activity by the much more sophisticated adult partner'. It is in the sense, then, that children can be competent participants in such interactive exchanges as these (in a way that, presumably, other organisms could not), that they may properly be counted as one term in a genuine personal relationship.

Interpretations and Implications

But what is the character of this 'intelligent manipulation', upon what kind of understanding of the child is it based? As Smedslund (1969) points out, mental processes are logically related to one another by implication, not causation: an act is known for the kind of act that it is in terms of the future acts that it implies. Or, to put the matter in Smedslund's own words (1969, p. 8):

> Having a belief or wish in itself *implies, contradicts,* or *changes the likelihood of* many other beliefs and wishes. Believing that something is a stone implies a belief that it will sink if thrown into the water, and wanting to have one's cake contradicts (conflicts with) wanting to eat it . . . . A crucial difference between a cause-effect relationship (A causes B) and an implication (A implies B) is that the former involved logically independent phenomena, which must be shown empirically to succeed each other, whereas the latter involves logically dependent phenomena. Physical phenomena may be linked by a theory from which it follows that A leads to B. On the other hand, a mental phenomena A in itself implies B, without any theory.

Due to the intentional nature of all human action, people's acts are necessarily intrinsically related, logically, rather than extrinsically related – a characteristic reflected in the fact that linguistic categories, as Chomsky (1965, p. 55) insists, are structure-dependent: they are known for what they are only in terms of their relations to one another.

Now the force of the discussion above for studies in mother–infant interaction is this: if actions are to be known for what they are in terms of their implications, then we should expect to see mothers (without any theory) interpreting their children's acts for their implications. Also, of course, we may see them check, if they so desire, the validity of their interpretations by testing them for their further implications – e.g. 'my baby's reaching for that object implies she wants it, thus if I hand it to her (given that I know she can grasp things) she should grasp it, thus I'll hand it to her, and . . . she does grasp it': the mother's 'insider's knowledge of the 'logic' or 'grammar' of wanting, reaching and grasping being a help here in her practical interpretative reasoning.

The situation for the interactants in social processes is, then, one where their acts are motivated by being included or implicated within the structure of more overarching, ongoing acts. Being thus 'situated', acts have a meaning; they 'point to' or imply other acts, necessarily, without a theory, as a logical part of what it is to be an act. Thus it may seem, even in quite unreflective exchanges, as if the interactants are continually making 'inferences' about one another, although strictly they are not (see William James's, 1890, II, pp. 111–13, criticism of 'unconscious inference'; see also chapters 4, 9 and 11). They are merely acting within a shared field of implications. A person's acts imply, contradict or change the likelihood of the other person's possible replies to it, intrinsically, as a necessary part of what it is for social exchanges to occur at all. And this, clearly, is what Mead (1934, p. 77) means when he says, 'the mechanism of meaning is present in the social act before the emergence of consciousness or awareness of meaning occurs. The act or adjustive response of the second organism gives to the gesture of the first organism the meaning it has' – the adjustive response of the second organism is 'implicated', as he says earlier (p. 76), in the act of the first.

Thus we may find mothers responding (adjustively) to their children's acts quite unreflectively, in unproblematical, 'taken-for-granted' ways (Berger and Luckman, 1967; Schutz, 1967) which reflect the goals and techniques of the social traditions of which they are a part. And while we, as investigators of a mother's exchanges with her child, may 'see' an intention in the character of her (adjustive) responses to her child, she may be aware of no such intention; she may merely declare herself to be doing what seems only 'natural', the 'taken-for-granted', matter-of-fact 'way' of going on. The source of her intention must be sought, not in her emotional states or intrinsic nature, but in the history of the development of the social practices of which she is an exponent (Shotter, 1975; C. Taylor, 1971). We must understand the ideological context within which mother–child interaction takes place (Busfield, 1974); the ideas, beliefs and values in terms of which such interaction is conducted.

Early Social Practices

If long, interlaced sequences of exchange are to be established as activities people can themselves *do* rather than simply have happen to them, then people have to learn how to 'turn-take', i.e. how, on the one hand, to submit themselves to the influence of others, and, on the other, how to initiate appropriate action themselves. Involved is what one might call an 'ontological skill'; the ability to change one's own mode of being oneself, in this case, from being a recipient of an action to being an actor, from being a looker to being a doer, from being a listener to being a speaker, etc. Newson and Pawlby (1972) have studied the development of these 'turn-taking' games. Often, mothers seem to seize upon opportunities initially offered by their infants to establish a back-and-forth sequence of acts. For example, they describe the exchange between Tilly (at twenty-eight weeks) and her mother as below:

> (Following an exchange involving some play with a rattle)
> Tilly makes a vocalization (like a cough)
> Mother repeats vocalization
> Tilly repeats it
> Mother repeats it
> Tilly puts rattle to mouth
> Mother: 'Are you going to eat that one?'

Inserted into the episode with the rattle, then, is this short back-and-forth exchange in which Tilly took her turn and did, clearly, what her mother expected (required) her to do. Tilly manifests here, then, in some small degree, that she can be an agent in her own right, that she can *herself* do something appropriate to the social situation that she is in, that she can herself make what can be interpreted as a sensible response.

In an incident Shotter and Gregory (1976) describe, a mother is attempting to show her young child (Samantha, aged eleven months) how to place shaped pieces on a form-board. Having just physically helped her little girl to place one of the pieces, Samantha's mother says 'Oh, clever girl'. But Samantha had not paused in her activity and signalled by eye-contact and smiling that she knew she had done something socially significant; she just went straight away on to manipulating something else. So her mother leant forward, caught her eye, and repeated her 'marker' with emphasis: 'AREN'T YOU CLEVER?' Samantha then stopped and smiled.

Mothers are not just satisfied with their children doing the tasks that they require of them. They must also give indications in their actions that they did what they did as a result of trying to do it, that 'they' knew what was required of them, that their actions were based in some knowledge of the socially defined requirements of the situation. Thus children must come to show in their actions, not just awareness of their physical circumstances, but *self*-awareness: an awareness of the nature of their relations to others. Such a quality of their consciousness cannot, of course, be directly observed. In terms only of observational criteria, people do not differ from organisms in the structure of their activity. But indirectly, people demonstrate their self-knowledge by the way in which they respond to the consequences of their own actions. It is in terms of what it implies for future action that the knowledge informing people's actions is revealed; often, for instance, in the way they 'mark' their own acts as socially significant ones, or, perhaps, the surprise they manifest when the result is not as they had expected. Thus here, mothers do not just attempt to get their children to complete socially acceptable actions, they 'analyse' the concepts that they are developing practically, just as concepts should be analysed: by testing them for their implications – 'If she knows that what she's just done is significant then she should expect and accept acknowledgement from me . . . I will give it . . . she does accept it . . . thus she does know': again using her insider's knowledge, not just as a person, but as the child's mother, knowledgeable about her current level of competence, skill, knowledge, etc.

As a result of her help, as a result of the way in which a mother completes the realization of what might possibly be her child's intention, her child's actions may become incorporated into the circle of reciprocal exchange between them both. Thus children learn to act in ways which – in both expressing themselves and in manipulating the things about them – at least make sense to her, children themselves not understanding till much later the nature of what it is that they are actually doing, it being enough at first that they understand how to do it. And thus the process continues, with children being 'helped' by their mothers in this way to evaluate retrospectively the consequences of their actions, and their states of feeling. Now it is not so much in this process that they experience new states of feeling or perform new patterns of action that have never occurred to them before, ones which would otherwise be biologically unavailable to them; but that they learn meanings or socially significant uses for feelings that they may have, or movements that they might make, at any time. They come to learn the way other people fulfil the meaning in their movements, so that later they may fulfil their meaning themselves. Thus, in acquiring knowledge of how to order their activities in relation to others, children themselves learn how to act; they learn, gradually, how not to rely upon others to complete and give meaning to their behaviour, but to relate what they do and what they feel to their own knowledge of their own momentary 'position' in their society; they relate their own activity to themselves as now autonomous individuals, responsible themselves for 'their' own actions.

Conflict and Negotiation

If a child is to become an individual personality, a person amongst the many like him- or herself, but not so identical as to be indistinguishable from them, then he or she must not only grasp 'the-way-things-are-generally-thought-to-be' in the community (at that moment in history), but also 'the-way-things-seem-to-him-or-her' individually. Children may learn 'methodologies' (Garfinkel, 1967), ways of seeing, ways of feeling, thinking, acquiring knowledge and of communicating, and all the other kinds of social practices inherent in the conduct of everyday, communal life. But they must also learn how to express their own particular version of the communal world, as experienced from the momentary position they and no one else occupy in it. There is an intrinsic conflict, then, between an individual's interpretation of the world and the communal world of which he or she is only a part. And we might expect that, in mother–infant relationships, before children have acquired much knowledge of the way things are thought to be in their community, there will be a degree of conflict in their relationships with their mothers requiring resolution.

We suggested earlier that the interpretations mothers put upon their children's activities are important in determining the meanings the children learn for their actions. But now we must suggest that the process cannot be just a simple 'one-pass' affair; it must be a matter quite often of an initially wrong or inadequate interpretation being modified in the light of subsequent 'investigations', until a result acceptable to both parties is achieved. In other words, there is a social practice of the *negotiation* of interpretations involved here. But now, we must be careful about the sense in which we take the word 'negotiate'. For as C. Taylor (1971, p. 23), from whom much of the emphasis upon social practices here is taken, remarks,

> Our notion of negotiation is bound up . . . with the distinct identity and autonomy of the parties, with the willed nature of their relations; it is a very contractual notion. But other societies have no such conception.

In fact, it would seem, ways of negotiation must themselves be something put under investigation in the developing child. As Taylor points out, our ways of negotiating are not necessarily the only ways that there are: the traditional Japanese village, as he describes it, for instance, puts a high premium on unanimous decision; such a consensus would be considered shattered if two clearly articulated parties were to separate out, and one win out in opposition to the other. And besides these different practices, in our own society, ways of negotiating settlements are different in relation to different kinds of conflict. Thus to be an effective personality, the child must learn the proper practices of negotiation with others (as indeed must mothers with their babies), i.e. the rules of all the games in our daily micro-social power politics.

And the point here about negotiation is quite general: the meaning of an action (or utterance) is not just a matter of the intention it expresses, but also of how it is taken. The character of people's activities is something to be negotiated amongst those (here, mother, child *and* those who study them) who are concerned with the meanings being communicated and the commitments being undertaken. It is this more than anything else which will distinguish the nature of the investigations proposed here from those that have gone before in psychology: there will be no one, single, true account of the situations being studied, only an account true for certain 'practical intents and purposes' situated in a community. The same activity may be seen as having any one of a number of different interpretations according to the overarching projects or intentions it can be seen as tending to realize. So: not only will we mislead ourselves, methodologically, if we set out to characterize mother–infant exchanges in purely formal terms, we shall also mislead ourselves theoretically if we think we can obtain the one true account of what is happening. We must remember that subjective accounts (if forthcoming) of 'the-way-things-seem-to-each-of-us' are different from the objective accounts of 'the-way-things-are-thought-to-be' in the community. Whilst it is the mother's task to negotiate her children's development with them as best she can in terms of how 'things-seem-to-them', it is the scientist's task, not to render the actual experience of mothers explicit, but to give an account (*a*) of how 'things-are-thought-to-be' for the proper development of a child is our community, *and*, (*b*) of how 'things-must-be-if-personhood-is-to-be-achieved'. And for it to be possible, our social ecology must contain regions and moments which offer to our newborns opportunities to become the kind of persons competent to live in our society, as individuals, but nonetheless as one of us.

6

The Ecological Setting for Development: Implicate Orders, Joint Action and Intentionality

Being Ecological

In the development of the child, the individual and the social are, I believe, necessarily and inextricably interlinked. In discussing their mutual relations, I shall follow Gibson (1979) and adopt essentially an *ecological* approach. Gibson was, of course, mainly concerned with the study of visual perception. But in attempting to understand the relation between social and cognitive development in early childhood, it may be fruitful to extend his mode of analysis and to generalize his descriptive vocabulary to apply to other modes of perception.

The strength of a thoroughgoing ecological approach is, it seems, that it emphasizes the interfittedness of things and directs attention away from the child as a wholly isolated entity (and away from the hidden 'inner' processes presumed to be going on inside her somewhere). It directs us instead towards what is out there *in her world* at each moment in her development for her to grasp or to 'pick up' (as Gibson puts it); it directs us towards the totality in which she is embedded. While such an externalized concern need not in itself be an ecological one, it becomes so if we insist that the child and her world exist only in reciprocal relation to one another, that they are mutually constitutive and mutually defining. Then, what we might call the child's practical environment-for-action, her effective environment, or her *Umwelt* (Uexküll, 1957), becomes a very special environment existing just for her. It becomes 'her' world, a world into which she is dovetailed, feels at home in and knows how to operate because it is a world made (with the help of others) by her. The child then acts as she does in such a world, we might say, in accord with the ecological imperatives it provides; she acts in response to what her world, her *Umwelt* as she apprehends it, offers, demands or affords her. But the 'help' that she is afforded by others is such that, of course, she makes a world that they understand too, for she is not afforded the opportunities to make just any world. Although the world is hers in one sense, in another it is a world afforded her by her society – these issues, issues to do with the development opportunities made available in the different regions and moments of one's social ecology, are discussed in chapter 7. Here, I shall concentrate upon the problem of how such opportunities themselves might best be imagined and described.

As 'the first principle of *Umwelt* theory', Uexküll (1957, p. 10) states that:

> all animals, from the simplest to the most complex, are fitted into their unique worlds with equal completeness. A simple world corresponds to a simple animal, a well-articulated world to a complex one.

I shall rely upon this principle of reciprocal completeness a great deal in what follows. For I shall take it to mean that the child and his environment, what is 'inside' him and what is 'outside', interlock in such a way that the structure of one fits into the structure of the other. However, in the case of human *Umwelten*, we must modify Uexküll's principle by extending it in at least two ways: (1) Human *Umwelten* contain other human beings and thus of necessity, we shall argue, special systems of social 'affordances' (Gibson, 1979)[1] or 'affordings', which inform the human action within them, systems which include moral orders of often great complexity. They also contain many other humanly constructed artifacts of both an objective and an intersubjective kind which also 'live on' in everyday life, not just from one moment to the next, but from one generation to the next. These accumulate over time in such a way as to give everything in human *Umwelten* an implicit historical aspect – a network of implicit connections and ramifications in time, relating what might be in the future to what has been in the past. For human beings in a society with others, an environment-for-action is not a timeless world, but a space-time (or better) a time–space structure (see Gidden's, 1979, views discussed in chapter 11).

(2) Besides acting in their *Umwelten*, human beings can also act upon them and make a difference to them, thus creating new conditions for their own existence – not, of course, by creating new worlds afresh, but by remaking or remoulding those they already have to hand. The new effective environment so created is only maintained in existence though if

people 'agree' practically to establish and institute it, i.e. if they continue to act in terms of the 'world' posited in their 'joint action' (see below). Otherwise it fades from existence as soon as the action appropriate to it is complete.

To repeat: it is important to be clear that by the term *Umwelt* we mean the unique environment reciprocally defined by the person actively immersed in it, who as a part of it only exists as such in interaction with it; an environment which can be 'developed' as the person develops. From within her *Umwelt*, a person's world appears to be full of demands and requirements, opportunities and limitations, rejections and invitations, enablements and constraints. And her knowledge of what her environment affords will inform her action in it. So: ecologically, what is suggested is that the child, as a fragment of biological nature, relates herself creatively to her environment. And that the relation is actively made by the functioning of the natural formative processes constitutive of all human activity (see chapter 11 and Shotter, 1980a); by the operation, in fact, of a form-creating activity continuous with that at work in biological growth and evolution at large. So, although perceptually distinguishable from her environment as an individual, she is not as such physically isolatable from it; she exists (as an open system) only in mutual relation to it. Thus, in developing from a simple, undifferentiated being into a more complex, well-articulated individual, a child may also be thought of, ecologically, as at each moment remaking her world, her own effective environment. This means that her world is not for her as adults experience it. It is her own world and she acts accordingly in *its* terms – not just as she would like or wish, but sooner or later in ways only appropriate to what it affords. In fact, as I shall argue later, she experiences such opportunities as being 'out there', as external to herself and as a part of the world in which she finds herself placed and in terms of which she feels she must act – the 'must' being if not a moral must, at least a normative one, there being a usual, normal or 'natural' way in which to act in such a world of one's own.

Epistemologically, in such a view, it is not by observing single people, specific features, or isolated objects that the infant gets to know his *Umwelt*, building up his knowledge of it additively, piece by piece. On the contrary: he only gets to know about the people and things in it as they appear to him in terms of his current effective environment. But he can (under the appropriate conditions) remake that world in the course of his active involvement with the people and things he meets within it, continuing until he arrives at a world in which (for all practical purposes) he can co-ordinate his actions in with those of all the other people in his society. Such an achievement is possible for, as Gibson (1979, p. 43) notes in relation to spatial perspectives, although no two individuals can be in the same place at the same time, any individual can be in the same place, position or situation at different times. Thus the 'information' (in Gibson's sense) implicit in the structure of people's surroundings is available for all to pick up and, in principle at least, all may live in similar *Umwelten*. Though similar, each individual's *Umwelt* will remain nonetheless his own unique environment-for-action, with its own special combiniation of openings, barriers, offerings and obstructions. In action, the individual is completely enveloped in it. As such, it is at any moment known to him as a whole, with every part of it related in some way to every other part; he experiences no gaps in it – while sensing at the same time that it contains regions, people or things with awesome powers to call whatever he knows into question. Indeed, he only possesses his knowledge in virtue of it not being questioned or challenged by powerful others, or by the natural outcome of events as they unfold. Interpersonal assertions of power and the need to negotiate with significant others (to transform the character of what they afford) are inescapably involved in the experience of developing human beings; the legitimacy of one's knowledge always remains open to criticism, correction and amendment.

Ecologically, I am proposing, then, that cognitive development can be best understood, not as in the conventional psychological approach, in terms of processes developing independently within the child, but in terms of an evolving context for further action, a change in the effective environment, an expanding *Umwelt*. Thus I take it for granted (as indeed do all caretakers) that, although psychology may not yet possess an adequate account of principles of learning, the potential for the child to develop greater degrees of understanding is nonetheless there, and will function naturally, given that the individual is healthy and intact and appropriately embedded in some coherent cultural context. Ecologically, the task is to specify the nature of that embedding, the instructing or instructions people require to produce it. Thus our view is, we would say, a practical one: we are concerned simply with describing the actual methods or procedures of instruction, the 'developmental niches', available to children in their 'position' in their society.

By contrast, traditional cognitive psychology has set its sights upon discovering the nature of the 'inner computer', or 'program' people use (and children) use in performing their actions, and speculation currently centres upon the precise kind of 'data-processing operations' and 'inner representations' involved. I have criticized this view, at least by implication, in many places in this book, so little time will be spent discussing it here: the main objection against it is, I think, that it is very difficult to see how any 'inner object' could be anything more than, say, an *aide memoire*. For many such objects could, for instance, share the same 'relational structure' yet not represent the same things in the world, e.g. one inner representation could represent the workings of Kelvin's tide predictor (i.e. those of the actual object out in the world), and another inner representation, with the same structure, a person's knowledge of the world's tides, and nothing could represent which representation was which, or that just one might be used for both purposes. The point here is that a 'cognitive structure' is one thing, and the use a person could or does make of it, their intention regarding it, is quite another − and there is no way of representing that.[2] Furthermore, this approach raises the problem of how people express their knowledge of themselves in their actions, for is it the person, or his 'data-processing' operations which are responsible for his actions? Without at least potential control over every aspect of his own activity it is very difficult to see how a child could develop and modify his activity in response to what his circumstances may, or may not, allow 'him' to do. If 'he' is not present in his own actions, how he could learn *to be* the kind of person required of him by his society? The issue of mediation by 'inner representations' will not be pursued further here (but see chapter 11, and Shotter, 1982).

Ecologically, a quite different stance is taken: attention is not concentrated upon the supposed relation between people's 'outer' behaviour and their 'inner' workings, for it is not focused upon individuals at all, but upon the relations between people. And developmental psychology focuses upon the special case in which caregiver (parent) and child constitute *Umwelten* for one another appropriate to each other's development − the development of initially a caregiver into a competent caretaker, and of a child into an adult, into an autonomous new member of the caretaker's society. Central at certain moments in a person's *Umwelt* and establishing the appropriate environmental conditions for the natural functioning of that person's inner developmental processes − howsoever one may choose to characterize them in traditional cognitive terms − is a special kind of personal 'affordance' or affording constituted by another person. And it is our task to attempt to establish for developmental psychology what, in any given society, these environmental conditions are. This task is made easier than the cognitive psychologist's by the fact that the activities constituting them go on out in the open, between people, rather than inside their heads, hidden from being directly perceived by others.

Implicate Orders and Gibson's 'Ambient Optic Array'

Our interest is, then, in the nature of *Umwelten*, in both their formal structure and in the principles of their making and remaking − in, to use

Goodman's (1978) happy phrase, 'ways of worldmaking'. Below, in an attempt to set out an appropriate way of describing the structure of *Umwelten*, I shall explore and generalize (from the physical to the social) Gibson's notion of 'the ambient optic array'. Though not described as such by Gibson (1979), I shall note (*a*) that it has a holographic structure such that everything in it is represented[3] everywhere (at all times), and (*b*) that such an order is best described in Bohm's (1973b, 1980) terms as an *implicate* order. People's social surroundings, although not explicitly structured, are not, I suggest, utterly without order, and it is from 'information' (Gibson) implicit in the social activities in which they are involved, that people pick up what specifies their social *Umwelt*. Just as the child comes to appreciate the 'suckability' of a proferred teat or the 'graspability' of a cup handle, so he also apprehends in an equally direct manner, I suggest, the moral force underlying a serious maternal prohibition, and begins to distinguish between a deliberately harmful insult to his person and one which is merely a humorous form of play. He perceives these social barrier reefs and high seas, the harbours, havens and horizons directly in people's stony silences and fixed expressions, in their nods, winks, grimaces, gestures, stances and smiles – all of which activities occur, one must add, in relation to what he does.

Here then, in this section, I shall explore forms of order, implicate orders, appropriate to describing the formal structure of *Umwelten*, and in the next section I shall turn to the intentional processes involved in their construction. All human action is intentional in the sense that it is 'directed'; it 'points to' or 'contains something' other than itself; in short, it means, or is a means to something. Rather than in terms of 'pointing' or 'containing', this property of action is more fruitfully expressed, I believe, in 'specificatory' language (Gauld and Shotter, 1977): to act is to make something other than what it would have been if we had not acted, we give it a structure it did not already possess. So in acting we can be said to be determining or specifying something in terms of the differences we can make to it or in it. Thus any action in progress can, while serving to produce a degree of specification into its content, leave that content open to yet further specification – but only of an already specified kind, with what is past determining the style of what is yet to come (Rommetveit, 1976; Shotter, 1980a). It is thus that an action in its very occurrence, posits or implicitly specifies a world, a realm of other possible actions serving to specify, articulate or transform that realm yet further. I shall explore this difference-making or specificatory property of human action further, in the next section. Let us turn now to the more static aspects of mental phenomena.

Following Piaget (1950), as I outlined in chapter 5, Smedslund (1969) discusses the holistic, intentional qualities of mental phenomena, and claims that their contents are intrinsically related to one another, by implication, rather than extrinsically related. Having a belief or wish in itself implies, contradicts or changes the likelihood of many other beliefs and wishes, he points out: it could mean, for instance, that if a child cries and manifests discomfort, it implies something like 'Give me something different'; it definitely does not imply 'Give me more of the same' (see Lock, 1980, who has explored the implicational structure of many such situations). Implicit in the child reaching for something is that possibility that she wants it, is trying to get it, and will thus try even harder if barriers are put in her way. Acting on those implications, her mother responds to her accordingly. A child, in claiming to know that a cat is an animal must, by implication, be assumed to know what in general animals are, what are not animals, and thus whether the new entity confronting her is an animal or not (ignoring controversy about the law of the excluded middle here); thus her claim may be checked out in her subsequent behaviour. At every moment in their interactions with their children, mothers can be observed as acting upon the logical implications in their child's actions, treating even not well-articulated expressions as if their meanings were clear (see chapters 4 and 5). Children, too, clearly act upon what are for them the logical implications in their circumstances: it not being illogical in itself to treat the exit of an object from one's immediate perception as meaning that it has ceased to exist – consider a flame, a puff of smoke, a sound, a touch, etc. Clearly the logic of what implies what takes a while and a deal of experience to sort out. In 'failing' to reason as adults reason, children are not necessarily acting illogically; it is just that they are acting in an effective environment quite dissimilar to that of the adults who test them (this issue is discussed in chapter 7). Indeed, the very fact that the child is a human being implies that she is a being capable of behaving logically – a presupposition inherent, as Smedslund (1970, 1977) shows, in all our dealings with our children, whether as researchers or parents. Going even further, knowing how to recognize people as people implies that we already know (but only implicitly!) the whole nature of the circumstances in which human beings are constituted as persons – a claim for which Smedslund (1978) also provides evidence.

Relating these implicational phenomena to *Umwelt* theory, I can point out that in fact they follow directly from what I have called Uexküll's reciprocal completeness principle. For, to the extent that ecologically an organism's behaviour is fitted completely into its environment, the whole of its *Umwelt* can be said in some sense to be 'known' to it. Although obviously not all explicitly known, anything new is already implicitly known in kind, as the organism can only operate within the capacities it has available for information pick-up, and cannot operate outside of them. Thus for the developing child as for the mature adult, each difference made, each distinction drawn, serves to structure the whole of a person's knowledge of his *Umwelt*: if something is not this then, by implication, it must be either that, or that, or . . . . The very nature of a person's reciprocal relations to his *Umwelt* are such that whatever he does has implications, connections and ramifications (implicitly) with everything else within the wholness of his *Umwelt*. It serves to specify (*a*) what else he might do further; (*b*) what else he might have done but did not; (*c*) what his current place or position in his *Umwelt* is – his situation; (*d*) how, as a result of his action, his situation is changed and his *Umwelt* differentiated or transformed; and so on.

Gibson (1979) in his notion of 'ambient' as opposed to 'radiant light' captures very clearly the idea of an all-enveloping visual environment, in which at every point (place or standpoint) the whole of one's actual surroundings are implicitly represented. This is caused by light, in being scattered in every direction from the things and objects in that environment, reaching and making a contribution to the light at every point in one's surroundings. Thus, for Gibson, ambient light is structured in the sense that, at any given point of observation, there are differences between the light coming into that point from different directions (principally differences of intensity), invariant differences. One's environment can thus be specified visually, he claims, by 'picking up' the invariant differences available in 'the ambient optic array', differences which will change in an invariant manner as one moves from standpoint to standpoint. To the extent that they are 'there' whether anyone is present or not, as offerings of nature or 'affordances', they are there as possibilities or opportunities for anybody to pick up. Thus on Gibson's theory, the visual world at least is or can be the same for everyone. Social affordances are a different matter: they can only offer invariant differences for pick-up, clearly, if people act to make invariant differences in their own behaviour, that is, if people act in relation to one another in conventional ways – but more of this later. A final point of importance to mention here, which Gibson makes, is one which we will state but not expand upon: he points out that the invariances specifying, say, an object need not in themselves be obviously patterned, they can be 'formless invariants'. For instance, a single, global change in an optic array may specify *both* an unchanging object *and* the changing of some of its properties (as well as, perhaps, one's own movement in relation to it at the same time). The changed differences in the array overall, intermingled together, need have no discernible form as a whole; different specific forms are, nonetheless, implicated in the structure of that whole, and clearly may be extracted with the apropriate modes of pick up. I shall return to this most important point almost immediately below.

Strangly absent from Gibson's account of the ambient optic array is any mention of holograms, which may be said to represent in a many-to-many, or whole-to-whole way, the ambient optic array quite directly. Holograms are made by using coherent light usually supplied by lasers. No lens is used. A scene is encoded on a photographic plate by recording the interference patterns (differences) made by a (reference or comparison) beam falling on the plate interfering with light from that same beam, after it has been reflected from the scene – its original pattern of wave-fronts now being disturbed in a way corresponding to the structure of the scene. If, after having been exposed and fixed, the plate is illuminated with the same laser light again, it serves to reconstruct just the same complex pattern of wave-fronts, carrying in their differences just the same information as the light reflected from the original scene. A virtual three-dimensional display thus appears (Leith and Upatnieks, 1965).

The essential feature of a hologram, which makes it quite different from an ordinary photograph, is that instead of the point-to-point relation between scene and photograph, there is a whole-to-whole relationship. In the exposure of the holographic plate, each point in the scene reflects light on to the whole plate, while each point on the plate receives light from the whole scene. In other words, on the holographic plate, everything is represented everywhere. As such, the hologram is an example of the same form of order as Gibson ascribes to the ambient optic array, and we may take the hologram as a model or paradigm for it.

In so doing, a number of interesting features become evident immediately:

(1) Viewing a hologram is like looking at a visual scene through a window; as one moves about, new aspects of the scene come into view while others disappear. Furthermore, just as one may see as much of a scene through a smaller window (even a pinhole, if one moves close enough to it), so a hologram will still show the whole scene when cut in halves, quarters, etc. The whole scene remains represented implicitly in the differences still present in every one of its parts.

(2) Another feature apparent in holograms is that the structure visible on the surface of the holographic plate itself bears no formal resemblance to the original scene. Indeed, for scenes of any complexity, the pattern in the emulsion on the plate appears quite random, formless in fact (see Leith and Upatnieks, 1965). The forms it encodes are only revealed when it is 'interrogated' by an appropriate beam of coherent light. The hologram may even encode several different images superimposed upon the same

plate, each being recovered by using appropriately different 'interrogation' procedures – just as, in Gibsonian language, different pick-up procedures may reveal different invariances encoded in the same optic array.

(3) A final point here concerns the nature of the pick-up process, unelaborated by Gibson (1979) himself. In a hologram, the scene is encoded (as an interference pattern) in the differences between the outgoing, incident light of the reference beam, and the incoming, reflected light from the scene. This may give us a clue as to a fuller account of 'information pick-up' than the one offered by Gibson, simply in terms of 'extracting invariants', 'resonating', or 'being attuned'. Instead, I suggest, the pick of, say, visual information involves acts of looking, such that the relevant invariants are extracted from the relations (or differences) between the activity which we ourselves direct outwards upon the world, and that which results in us from its incoming consequences (see Bohm, 1965, discussed in chapter 4). Thus the pick-up of information can become, not only a matter of skill, but also a matter of choice and selection as to which of all the information available we actually attempt to pick up. While looking may be up to us, what we see when we do so is not; the information we pick up is clearly 'there', in the structure of our visual environment – Gibson is surely right in insisting on this.

Bohm (1973b, 1980) parallels the contrast between the ordinary photograph and the hologram, with the contrast between the accepted mechanistic order in physics and what he calls the new implicate order. In a mechanistic form of order, the world is regarded as constituted of entities which are outside of each other, in the sense that they exist independently and are locatable in different regions of space (and time), and interact in ways which do not bring about any changes in their essential natures. This, as Bohm terms it, is an explicate order, in which separately existing, localizable parts, by interacting, form a whole. It was the optical lens, he feels, which served in science to suggest – by its point-to-point imaging, by its use in recording things too big, too small, too fast or too slow to be seen by the naked eye – that everything can be observed in such a way. The hologram suggests differently. Holographically, in an implicate order, everything is in some sense enfolded or implicated in everything else; inseparable interconnectedness is the fundamental reality, and relatively independent, localized parts are merely particular and contingent forms within the whole. Essentially, forms and their influences are not locatable, but are spread out and present everywhere. To the extent that any 'elements' *are* apparent within the whole, their basic qualities and relations with one another will depend upon the whole in which they are embedded; if that changes they will change. In an implicate order, its 'parts' (mostly) exist inside (implicated in) one another, and at any one moment they owe not just their character but their very existence as 'parts' both to one another and to their relation to what were the 'parts' of the whole at some earlier point in time (see chapter 3 for a discussion of growing systems).

The study of implicate orders is as yet in its infancy (Bohm, 1980). Yet I hope I have said sufficient here to make clear some of the amazing properties of any environment ordered in such a way, containing (implicitly) properties not locatable but spread out everywhere within it. It remains now to explore not the nature of people's *Umwelten* as passively constituted for them by their physical surroundings, but as constituted for them actively, by the presence of other people within them.

Joint Action and Intentionality: Moral *Umwelten*

While there are many activities in which we as individuals know what we are doing and why, there are also many others in which we remain deeply ignorant as to what exactly it is that we are doing. Such is the case in joint action, in which people must interlace what they do in with the actions of others. We remain ignorant of quite what it is we do, not because the 'plans' or 'scripts', etc., supposedly in us somewhere inform-ing our conduct are too deeply buried to bring out easily into the light of day, but because its formative influences are not wholly there within us to be brought out. The actions of others determine our conduct just as much as anything within ourselves. In such circumstances, the overall outcome of the exchange is simply not up to us; in fact, it cannot be traced back to the intentions of any individuals. Thus rather than being experienced as a product of those actually producing it, it is experienced as an event which just happens – e.g. the child is treated as just happening to acquire language – and its occurrence is thus attributed to the operation of an external device (LAD), force, cause or agency, rather than to the efforts of the people actually involved in it producing it.

Although unintended and experienced as produced externally, other than by the joint action of its participants, the products of joint action still retain an intentional quality: they serve to specify (see previous section) the style of what further there might be to come. In other words, in joint action each person's act serve progressively to specify or articulate an *Umwelt* within which it takes place. Thus there can be, in Bergson's words (1920, p. 188), a gradual passage from the less realized to the more realized, from the intensive to the extensive, from the reciprocal implication of parts to their juxtaposition.

Such, I suggest, is the process by which an *Umwelt* – experienced as an external world containing a realm of as yet unexperienced possibilities within it – is 'developed'. The process is not one of realizing or actualizing in it a potential already in existence elsewhere – in some mysterious Platonic realm, for instance – but is one of gradually rendering explicit (collecting and localizing) what is already present implicitly (spread out everywhere) within it.

Let us turn now to apply our analyses to some concrete examples. Consider an episode involving Alan (roughly two years old) and his mother:

> Alan, playing with a toy train, looks up and sees his mother standing, looking at him. He continues playing for a short time, but now in an exaggerated, 'silly' way. He stops and walks over to her, then stretches his arms up to her in a characteristic gesture. She picks him up, holds him tight, and tickles him. He wriggles and laughs. She does it again. He wriggles again, but this time grimacing and grizzling. She puts him down and attempts to interest him in his train again, by 'working' it in such a way as to attract his attention to it. He ignores it. She redoubles her efforts, and this time he begins to show some interest in it. 'Train', she says. He stops and looks at her. 'Train', she says again. 'Rain', he says beginning again to play with it. 'That's right,' she says, 'train.'

Illustrated in this episode are a number of points. First there is the natural embedding of cognitive factors in the child's social experience. Then there is the way in which real feelings and emotions are inevitably aroused, affording further openings, barriers, etc., to the continuation of the interaction; the exchange is essentially mediated by affect (see chapter 4). Furthermore, in their more deliberate actions the participants offer one another opportunities for different forms of further action, often in the form of invitations to action which may, of course, be deliberately refused. Above all I want to draw attention to the interrelatedness of all these aspects within the unifying flow of a 'spontaneous dialogue' between mother and child, a dialogue of a quite unplanned kind.

I do so to argue against explaining the above episode solely in terms of a 'rule-following' model of human action. Both children and adults are not just rule-followers but rule-makers. Yet even before they have managed to establish anything like rules, their behaviour is still orderly, each act flows meaningfully into the next. Alan's mother, in acting in response to what he does – in putting him down when he grimaces, in redoubling her efforts when he fails to attend – responds particularly and precisely to him, directly in terms of her immediate perception of him in that situation. If she were working in terms of general rules she would still have to decide (on the basis of information picked up in the situation) *which* of all the rules available to her was the one to apply here, as well as precisely *how* it should be applied. And what applies to his mother also applies to Alan, his actions are also, I suggest, informed by his immediate perceptions: on perceiving himself observed by a powerful other, he acts in a 'silly' way in an attempt to have his behaviour discounted, his behaviour directly informed by his perception of his mother's power to call it into question. Rules are at issue only in a later stage of development, when matters of accountability and responsibility for deliberate action become more prominent.

Let us consider some further examples:

> Child: (sitting in her high chair, grizzling and whimpering, reaches in a grabbing fashion for her bottle, rocking back and forth)
>
> Mother: (gives it into her hand) Is this what you want? Suck your nice 'bockle' then.
>
> Child: (throws the bottle down and cries)
>
> Mother: (picks her up, but she 'won't' be comforted – she possibly 'wanted' to be picked up and nursed, but her initial behaviour was insufficient to specify that, and now her mother has made a 'mistake' by acting too late)

Here the (unintended) 'state' that the child is now 'in' has been progressively formed both by child and mother. Clearly, both would like it not to be as it is; at least we can take it that implied in what it is to be a child is the desire to be happy rather than miserable if circumstances will afford it. And thus the mother continues to experiment, both upon the basis of 'the state' the child appears to be 'in' *and* the implication that somewhere is to be discovered the circumstances that will afford her child an escape from it.

To take another example:

> Mother: (offers bottle)

Child: (takes the bottle but throws it down)

Mother: (smacks the child and offers the bottle again)

Child: (looks at mother and throws the bottle down again)

Mother: (a contained) Grrr . . . .

The 'mistake' initially made by the mother (if indeed it was a mistake) has been converted into a 'wrong' that the child is now 'in'. And both mother and child are going to have to take notice of the precise character of that 'wrong' if they are to deal with it appropriately. Already specified to a degree, the situation only affords further action within it of an already specified kind. Of course, with a child, the mother may 'break' the pattern of action above in which they have entrapped themselves, by distracting her child with an utterly 'silly' act:

Mother: (clowning about by popping her tongue in and out, and rolling her eyes) Look . . . look. The big blue meany is coming to get you. Ohoo . . . o.

Child: (laughs)

She still appreciates her act as a silly one, i.e. as an act which is not a fitting continuation in the circumstances they had constructed between them.

Above I have illustrated activity in which people act spontaneously, without being conscious while acting of having any particular reasons for their conduct. If asked to account for their actions they would probably experience difficulty. Not because they are unconscious of their reasons and lack the vocabulary and skill to articulate them, but because they do not possess *the* reason for their conduct wholly within themselves. The influences determining it are spread out between them (non-locatable in any real spatial sense), implicit in the individual *Umwelten* they constitute for one another. Rather than by reference to their ideas or their knowledge, to anything in their heads, their actions are explained by reference to the contents of their *Umwelten*, in terms of the qualities and interrelations of the entities they contain. And these are the terms in which the people themselves would account for their actions if pressed to justify them:

Researcher: (to mother) Why did you smack him?

Mother: Because he was in the wrong to throw his bottle down like that . . . wasn't he?

It is possible, however, to give a much fuller account of why she laid her hand violently upon the flesh of her child – *the* reason for *her* reason, in fact.

She did it, we might say, because (*a*) she believed, given her child's initial 'state', that if she offered him the bottle he would take it (that he is a human child of a certain age implies amenability to such offers); (*b*) she believes it to be a part of civilized conduct (upon which the continued existence of the social order depends) that helpful offers should not be rudely spurned, and if declined, declined politely, i.e. in a way which calls nobody's personhood into question: (*c*) she believes the spurned offer did offend her personhood, by suggesting her incapable of properly appreciating another person's state (an ability implied in what it is to be a person); (*d*) she believes herself a victim of an injustice, the social order has been transgressed, and, she believes, punishment of the transgressor will restore it; (*e*) she believes a smack to be just such a punishment, one which humiliates her child sufficiently to indicate that she will not tolerate such treatment; and so on. Clearly, the implicational structure of the mother's whole *Lebenswelt* – not just the *Umwelt* in which she acted, but her social ecology as it appears to her in thought and reflection – is such that everything in it is connected to everything else. Others are immersed with her in that same implicate order. Thus it is enough for her to justify her smack by referring to the child's 'wrong', for it serves to indicate to others in her *Lebenswelt* what the effective environment for her action was: her action was indeed informed by her perception. And we accept, within limits, that persons have a right to act as they see fit. These 'workings' of daily life are what the child must learn as he develops into the *Umwelten* constituted jointed by himself and his caretakers. And they *are* what he will learn, naturally, as long as the appropriate conditions for their acquisition are established.

A notable feature of social *Umwelten* is that not only do they provide norms – in the sense of only affording at any moment further action of an already specified kind – but also an (implicit) moral framework, such that certain 'regions' of it offer risks to self or personhood, i.e. there are 'places' or 'positions' in which people may 'lose', if not themselves, then at least certain aspects of their personal status, certain crucial rights, duties, privileges and obligations.

The necessarily moral character of human *Umwelten* is discussed in chapter 8, so we will not repeat that discussion here. There it is suggested that their moral nature can be understood, or unpacked, in terms of moral 'affordances' or affordings – in terms of the rights and duties, etc. – which mothers afford or attribute to their children in the course of their interactions with them. As long as the appropriate conditions are established, children will, we have assumed, grasp (or pick up) naturally that which is afforded them by their caretakers, and come to act in ways informed by what they pick up, i.e. by the rights accorded them and by the duties demanded of them (this view is further discussed in chapter 9). At least, this is how, I suggest, those actually entrusted with bringing up children proceed practically; and, initially at least, it is the appropriate conditions for such natural developmental processes which we as researchers wish to understand. Other ways of learning, other sequences of development may in general be possible; some are demonstrated by laboratory experimentation. In our ecological approach, however, we wish to understand what in particular and how in particular, children in a particular society learn to be members of it, the conditions under which they grasp what is there in their surroundings to be grasped, as well as the conditions under which they may fail to grasp it. And further: whether their surroundings are deficient, and the opportunities they need to develop themselves are simply not there to be grasped (or picked up).

Conclusions: Hermeneutical Explanation as a First Step

As phychologists observing mothers and children, we know that in some of the episodes we observe developmental exchanges are taking place. In a global, not very well-articulated way, we appreciate the processes at work: we 'see' the child learning an interactional or communicative competence, grasping meanings, expressing intentions, accounting for 'him-' or 'herself', etc. We want to know the details of the process, the significance of each interactional episode, what it means, what it permits or affords or indicates for the future. As mentioned in chapter 5, the task of transforming a superficial, global and perhaps misunderstood grasp of things into an accurate, well-articulated account of its actual meaning is essentially a hermeneutical one (C. Taylor, 1971; Gauld and Shotter, 1977; Shotter, 1978). And the search for entirely general laws or rules, for 'objective' presuppositionless knowledge is irrelevant to such a task. Primarily, warrantable understandings from within a frame of reference, a tradition or a culture are what are required. Once discovered, of course, and the frame of reference articulated, then the nature of the frame itself, its necessary and contingent features, the formal and substantive universals it embodies, may be investigated (see chapter 8). And finally, the question may be raised as to what must be the fundamental nature of physical reality for such phenomena to be possible. Hermeneutical explanation – the interpretation of what is actually happening or being done – may not be the final step in scientific explanation in psychology, but it is I believe a necessary first step. Returning to one of the examples, the 'wrong' which that mother saw her child as being in, constitutes, I maintain, an initial, irreplaceable and irreducible datum which any further investigation cannot ignore.

From a practical point of view (whether proceeding to a deeper scientific analysis or not), the products of a hermeneutical study can be very useful. Having their source in the practices of daily social life, in the spontaneous activities going on between mothers and children in which children develop naturally, they may be turned around to reflect back into those activities. They can be applied both to extend them and to make their operation amenable to rational deliberation (see chapter 5). Thus, unlike the 'block diagrams' and 'rule-schema' resulting in the traditional cognitive approach, our more ecological results may be 'put into practice' immediately: as that is from where they were derived. Furthermore, our own methodology, to the extent that it also involves the progressive rationalization of a social practice (child development), achieved in the course of an active involvement with those under study, may be self-developing in the same way, reflecting back into both the developmental practices of daily life as well as the practices involved in their study.

All societies must incorporate in the operational procedures of their daily life, devices, 'mechanisms', social practices to do with 'manufacturing' from their newborns the basic elements capable of maintaining their social order, i.e. persons. To the extent that a society remains in existence, these procedures must exist somewhere (non-locatable) in its ecology, spread out in its constituent interrelations. Thus, irrespective of what goes on in people's heads, it seems both an important and a feasible endeavour to discover what those procedures are. Thus: ask not what goes on 'inside' people, but what people go on inside of – though if everything is represented everywhere (implicitly) in an implicate order, it hardly matters, for everything inside is represented in what is outside anyway.

7

Models of Childhood in Developmental Research

This chapter attempts to identify the direction in which developmental research into models of childhood has been moving during the last ten years, and to provide some pointers for the future. Regarding such pointers, let me say straightaway what the tenor of my conclusions will be: the trouble with developmental psychology is its *child-centredness*. Gradually, it seems to me, we are learning to be less parochial, to be less concerned to account for the world and ourselves *as we at present experience them*, and to be more concerned to account for *why* we currently experience them as we do – for why at this moment in history we experience ourselves in such an individualistic manner, as if we all exist from birth as separate isolated individuals, containing 'minds' or 'mentalities' wholly within ourselves, set over against a material world itself devoid of any mental processes. Psychology so far has studied, not so much behaviour itself, as how we currently talk about, think about and account for it in our normal everyday experience; we have, as Goodman (1972) puts it, mistaken features of the discourse for features of the subject of the discourse. However, we are beginning, I think, to repudiate this 'Cartesian starting point' – localized in the 'I' of the individual, which assumes all developmental problems to be solely to do with the acquisition of knowledge – and to replace it by a starting point (or situation) located within a much more diffuse and flowing process – a process with not only social, cultural and historical aspects to it, but with biological and ecological ones too; a large-scale developmental process which is productive of individual, localized subjectivites, but which itself is, as Popper (1972) puts it, 'without a knowing subject'.

As well as in developmental research, such a trend is currently manifesting itself in many other quarters: in the philosophy of science

(Kuhn, Popper, Lakatos, Althuser); in structuralist and semiotic 're-readings' of Marx and Freud (Althuser, Foucault, Levi-Strauss and Lacan); in the renewed interest in American Pragmatism (James, Dewey, Mead and Peirce); in the now growing interest in Vygotsky – occasioned no doubt by the new *Mind in Society* (1978) book; and in Gibsonian 'ecological' writings (Gibson, 1979) – as well as in sociobiological works (e.g. Wilson, 1975; Dawkins, 1978). All, in one way or another (though not in a way immune to criticism), repudiate the starting point for research in the social sciences or humanities in the experience of the autonomous and self-sufficient individual (thus dismaying, of course, liberal–democratic opinion). All emphasize one way or another the embedding of individuals in a larger, ongoing, unending, evolutionary or developmental process, in a special 'discourse' which, to an extent, predetermines not only their present nature, but also the character of their future opportunities for development, either genetically, historically or both. A trend which calls, not only for new kinds of theory, but for new methods of research also.

Ecology Mediates Between Biology and Social Life

The task that Martin Richards specified in 1974, albeit vaguely, of 'build-[ing] a holistic view of the developing organism which can include both biological structure *and* the [social] world in which it lives' (my emphasis and additions) is thus, I think, being faced. With the help of the concept of an ecology – where an ecology is that set of relations within an organic totality necessary to the survival of its individual parts as the individuals they are – with that concept to mediate the relation between our concept of our biology and of our social life, there is now a real possibility of constructing a unified view, and of moving beyond research concerned merely to argue the percentage contributions of heredity and environment.

Accounting Practices and Their Models or Paradigms

That is the general drift of what I want to say. When I turn to a discussion of some of the models actually used in British developmental research, I hope it will be possible to see how they exemplify the themes and issues I have outlined above. However, I want to make a couple of preliminary remarks about the nature of my brief.

Reconstructing Theorist's 'Models' From the Way Theorists Talk
Firstly, I want to say in defence against the inevitable inadequacies of my account here, that the task of discussing the 'models' in British developmen-

tal research is not an easy one. Workers do not begin with well-articulated models of childhood, at least those engaged in experimental or applied work do not. They begin, and rightly so, with a problem or a question; in fact, they begin by being socialized into a research tradition or 'paradigm' (Kuhn, 1962) which provides what Popper (1963) calls a 'problem-situation' – and they do not have to articulate the character of that situation fully, nor make fully explicit the character of the model of childhood implicit in it in order to conduct their research. It may remain implicit. Teasing it out is like doing archæology or psychoanalysis: a complete and explicit version of the set of largely unconscious and unquestioned assumptions constituting the research tradition, has to be reconstructed piece by piece from a collection of diffusely gathered fragments. The process is essentially a hermeneutical one (Palmer, 1969). In such a process, one must of course pay attention to what is in the foreground: namely, the experiments done, the findings made and the theories proposed. But of equal importance also is the scientists' background talk: (*a*) the talk to do with constructing the research situation as problematic, and (*b*) the talk to do with how they make sense of their findings and construct them as proposed problem-solutions. It is this talk which in fact reveals the 'model of childhood' implicit in their approach; the implicit model against which they can 'measure' their explicit theoretical proposals for their intelligibility, and their findings for their match with their expectations.

For example (although I must emphasize how invidious and discriminatory it is to name an individual for a fault for which, as will become clear, we are all of us responsible), Bower (1974) in *Development in Infancy* – and I shall return to Bower in a more systematic context in a moment – proposes an 'epigenetic or 'chreodic' theory of development, in which the developmental process is seen as a 'trajectory' determined by environmental events through a 'landscape' of possible, genetically determined, innate outcomes. This is his *theory* of development, But what is his 'model' of the child? We must pick that up, I think, from how he talks in presenting his experiments and the results they provide.

What we find if we pay attention to his talk in this kind of way is that in discussing the rationale of his experiments and in making sense of his findings he continually talks of even very young children as 'believing', 'thinking', 'realizing' and 'knowing', and of events as taking place in 'in the mind of the infant', and so on – and that he only uses his epigenetic theory to explain the observed character of all this early thinking and believing, etc. If we add to this a consideration of what he explicitly does not mention: namely, (*a*) the nature of humankind's historical achievements, and the fact that discriminations which took thousands of years to clarify – such as the distinction between impersonal, causally related events and those of a personal, intentional kind – are now apparently grasped by young children, partially at least, in a matter of months if not weeks; (*b*) the way in which adults, with knowledge of the nature of such distinctions, construct the 'invitations' and 'barriers' to action in the child's behavioural environment (what its surroundings 'afford' it, as Gibsonians would say), and continuously and intelligently adjust their behaviour to what they perceive their children's developmental require-ments to be; and (*c*) the problem of the articulation of the child's reflexive knowledge of *him-* or *herself*, how the child becomes a certain kind of person, knowing him- or herself to be capable of doing certain things, and not just being observed as doing them by others. If we take all this into account, both what he says *and* what he does not say, then I think Bower's actual model of the child (if not of childhood) becomes plain.

Developmental Self-Sufficiency   It is in fact the familiar image implicit in the Cartesian starting point, the image of individuals who exist in the world as independent beings, developmentally self-sufficient in the sense of containing already – on receipt of the appropriate 'trigger events' from the environment – all that is required to develop themselves; where their development consists in simply acquiring the knowledge already possessed by those around them. It is, in fact, as Norbert Elias remarks in his 1978 book *The Civilizing Process* (upon which I shall draw below), a model of the child as already in one sense an adult; the child is seen as a being already in possession of a degree of self-conscious knowledge as to what his or her own capacities *are*, as well as a degree of self-conscious control over them, such that the child can already do seeing, thinking, remember-ing, realizing, etc. But is that an assumption we are warranted in making about very young children? I think not.

The Concept of Childhood

My second comment concerns the nature of the brief implicit in the title of this chapter: I am discussing, not models of the developmental process, nor models of the child, but models of childhood. The very title indicates, I think, the kind of shift in concern in developmental research, away from processes within individuals towards the more diffuse concern with larger situations, which I have already outlined. For 'development' as such is essentially an organic or biological concept: it is to do with a process of growth by the 'unfolding', 'realization' or 'expression' of a tendency already prefigured in some way in an entity's current nature; it indicates a certain kind of irreversible progression from a simple, less well-articulated being into a complex, better-articulated individual; and so on. 'Childhood', on the other hand, is not only a social and cultural concept, but if Ariès (1973), Elias (1978) and Shorter (1977) are correct, it is a historical one too: socially, it is the state or stage in life one must pass through before becoming an adult, in which one has the status of a child, and as such is justifiably regarded and treated in a way quite different from an adult. In other words, childhood is not something to be found within children, but within the larger society within which they exist; it denotes the niche, so to speak, which a society constructs for the development of its newborns into autonomous members. And the characterization of what childhood actually *is* requires the description of what that niche is, psychologically. But historically, Ariès claims, the self-conscious grasp of the fact that such a stage in life exists, and the use of that fact in planning and structuring (and sanctioning) aspects of family life (as well as in depicting the character of childhood in art and science) is an achievement of the modern world – a part of that same historical process which has led to the particularly individualistic image we have of ourselves today.

In medieval society, there is little evidence of people being able self-consciously to treat and depict children in ways any different from adults, except that children were seen as smaller and imperfect. Only from the sixteenth century onwards does the idea of childhood as a special stage in life appear: first children are seen as distinct from adults, but only as sweet and simple, as a source of amusement and relaxation for adults. But in the late sixteenth and seventeenth centuries, texts begin to appear which suggest that the levity of childhood is a mistake, and that by the use of correct 'methods' during childhood, children can be made into persons of 'probity and honour'. And then by the eighteenth century, the child begins to take a central place in family life, along with the feeling that what happens there is of crucial importance in determining what the child is to become – thus, in order to correct the behaviour of the child, an attempt is made to understand child development, and the texts of the late sixteenth and seventeenth centuries are full of comments on child psychology.

Now to say that in medieval society the concept of childhood did not exist is not to say that people before the late sixteenth century simply treated children as adults in every respect; clearly, they could not have done so. They must have spontaneously and unreflectively adjusted their behaviour to some extent to meet what they unselfconsciously perceived to be the needs of their dependent, developing children. Otherwise, their offspring would have become 'wild', feral children, and this clearly did not happen – the chain in the reproduction of culture remained unbroken. But it does mean that they were not self-consciously aware of the differential character of their own behaviour regarding children, nor of the special consequences of their so acting; thus they did not plan and devise special programmes of activity aimed at promoting their children's development. As Ariès points out, the archaic, medieval attitude to infants was that until they could take part in adult life, they did not count (and could disappear from life without any great concern being shown); they simply appeared as a part of the taken-for-granted background to a life with a single stage to it, adult life. Not that the form of adult life current then would be thought of today as being properly adult. As both Ariès and Elias suggest, it would now strike us as rather puerile, as somewhat 'childish' in fact: society now places many demands and prohibitions on adult behaviour not present in medieval society, and requires a greater degree of discriminating self-control (implying less spontaneous, unreflective activity) in meeting them. Indeed, there is a sense in which we can say, Ariès and Elias argue (contrary to Levi-Strauss, 1966), that our society is psychologically 'older' or 'more grown up' than medieval society, and that for us now, childhood is more clearly separated from adulthood, with taboo 'boundaries' (M. Douglas, 1966). Thus 'growing up' in our society now requires the traversing of a greater psychic distance in the process than in medieval times. This also means, by the same token, that we as adults, as investigators of the world of childhood, must accept that its nature may be very strange and alien to us indeed, and not necessarily at all like the world of adulthood present to us now in our own experience.

The Civilizing Process   This raises the question of the approach we should adopt in our attempts to conceptualize its nature; for we face the problem of conceptualizing not just a social world of a familiar kind (which is difficult enough), but a niche within it with a nature quite alien to us. How might the niche of childhood be best described? (1) As a *status*, it could be unpacked as a complex of special rights and duties, of expectations and sanctions, on analogy with a legal status. (2) But we must go further and characterize it in a more psychological fashion: it could be described as 'place' or 'position' within a field of Gibsonian 'affordances'[1] which offer a 'landscape', so to speak, of other people who provide the child with 'developmental opportunities' – a special developmental land-scape or ecology, which adjusts itself both to its own requirements and to the child's, and offers at each moment a number of alternative develop-mental paths to traverse (see chapter 6). Here the child would develop in an environment which is itself intelligent, and which applies that intelligence to the child's development. (3) Or then again: we can go even further to take into account the historical course of what Elias calls 'the civilizing process'; that is, the way in which a society – by its members reproducing and transforming it in the course of its history – reproduces in them a certain psychological make-up (which is also transformed in the course of them making their history). And such a psychological 'make-up' in fact 'grows' more complex as the 'division of labour', etc., within the society within which it has its being grows more complex. This is the view which I shall support, and which is, I shall now argue, implicit in current developments in British developmental research. So let me turn now specifically to that research.

The Research Traditions

Currently, developmental research is both a respectable and an exciting topic. The well-worn joke, that infant research is one of the few spheres of activity in this country at the moment in which any growth is to be found, is true. In the UK, at the moment, we have a fair number of our own distinct traditions: I have characterized them as (1) the psychoanalytic (object-relations school); (2) the perceptual-inferential; (3) the biological-ethological; (4) the social-developmental; (5) the cognitive developmental (Schaffer, 1971); and (6) the liberal-democratic policy research traditions (concerned, of course, simply to look into current developmental issues of the day). The influence of two great developmentalists – Darwin and Freud – is apparent in all of them. There is not sufficient space here to discuss them all, but I hope that from what I say about those that I do discuss (1, 2, 3, 4), what I would say about those I leave unmentioned (5 and 6) will be apparent.

The Object-Relations School

All writers agree that Bowlby's (1940, 1944) early work, relating the character of juvenile delinquents to experiences in their early family life, must count as one of the beginnings of British developmental research. Trained in psychoanalysis, he emphasized the importance, following Melanie Klein (1932), of the early mother–child relationship, especially the way in which the child coped with the contrast between the mother's presence and absence. (In fact, the theme of conflict between presence and absence, between what may in general be called polar contraries – the mutually constitutive polarities of a discrimination which cannot exist at all as isolated entities – runs through the whole of Freudian theory, and has now, of course, become one of the main themes in structuralist writing also.) Bowlby followed up the depressive effect produced in children by separation from their mothers first noticed by Klein, and went as far as to claim on the basis of his research that such 'separation . . . during the first five years of life stands foremost amongst the causes of delinquent character development' (Bowlby, 1940) – thus setting the stage for a whole tradition of 'maternal deprivation' research. Now it is not my task to evaluate that research claim, but it is my task to try to outline the model of childhood implicit in it.

Bowlby was a member (although subsequently he made excursions into ethology) of the so-called 'object-relations' school in psychoanalysis, which – in emphasizing primarily a subject's need to relate to objects rather than the reduction of instinctual drives – might be thought of as more oriented to social rather than biological concerns. For my brief outline of object-relations theory, I shall turn to the version of it offered by Winnicott (1974). The first thing to say about it is that the child is conceived of, not as an agency surrounded by other agencies, but as a subject surrounded by objects, which because they are objects do not themselves act to instruct the child, nor do they act to shape the child's opportunities to express him- or herself. Winnicott conceives of children, as indeed do all Freudians, as not at first differentiating themselves from their surroundings; thus in such circumstances it would be illegitimate to talk of children as if they themselves interacted with their mothers, as they are not functionally separate from them. Indeed, Winnicott maintains that it is by an almost 100 per cent adaptation to her infant's requirements that the mother affords her infant the opportunity for the illusion that her breast is a part of the infant. Thus psychologically, whatever onlookers may observe, there is no actual interchange between individuals as such (that, says Winnicott, is an illusion of the psychologist). Psychologically, the infant takes from a breast which is a part of the infant and the mother gives to an infant which is a part of herself. However, the 'good-enough' mother, as Winnicott terms her, is one who not only adapts her activity to what she perceives her infant's needs to be, but who also gradually adapts her adaptation to her infant's growing abilities, namely to her infant's abilities to account for failures and to tolerate frustrations. Having given her infant the opportunity to create the illusion of a wholly satisfactory subjective world, she must now begin the process of disillusionment, thus to afford her infant the opportunity to discover a world, to an extent, recalcitrant to his or her desires.

The beginning of this most important 'illusion–disillusionment' process is marked by, as Winnicott calls them, 'transitional phenomena' – the patterns of behaviour displayed by babies in their use of their first 'not-me' possession (here Winnicott refers to Linus's blanket and Christopher Robin's Winnie-the-Pooh). He calls such objects 'transitional' as they seem to have a half-way character between objects in a wholly inner[2] reality and those presented from without. They occupy a third, intermediate realm of experience to which, he says, 'inner reality and external life both contribute' (1974, p. 3), and through which the child relates to objects as entities outside and separate from his or her *self*[3] (see Shotter, 1982, and chapter 11, for an account of mediatory processes with 'duality of structure'). As with all Freudian developmental processes, it is assumed that this 'illusion–disillusionment' process is unending, that no human being is ever free from the strain of relating inner desires to outer contingencies, but that the strain can be controlled by reference to this intermediate area of experience, which serves to organize the otherwise conflicting relations between inner and outer reality.

This is, I think, a most tremendously important idea, and those familiar with Lacan will recognize that it parallels his claim that 'the unconscious is the discourse of the Other' – where the Other is not a second-person other, but a third-person 'symbolic order' which, to quote him, 'organizes the relations between the subject and the real world' (Lacan, 1977). It means that the concept of childhood implicit in object-relations theory is a concept of a whole process in transition, within which a fragment of the process, not at first recognizable as an individual within that process, comes gradually to localize within itself the resources necessary for at least an independent status within the process – if not for an actually independent existence outside of it. The situation is well described in the words of the Kantian philosopher John Macmurray (1961), when he says of the infant,

> he cannot, even theoretically, live an isolated existence . . . he is not an independent individual. He lives a common life as one term in a personal relationship. Only in the process of development does he learn to achieve a relative independence, and that only by appropriating the techniques of a rational social tradition.

Macmurray was influential upon some members of the object-relations school, so I take it that they would not see that statement as incompatible with their views. The statement requires careful reading though: 'he is not an independent individual . . . . Only in the process of development does he learn . . . .' Does the child him- or herself learn, or is the child instructed by others? Whether Macmurray is clear upon this issue or not, Winnicott is: in discussing the 'mirror-role' of the child's mother and family in the child's development, he says:

> This to which I have referred in terms of the mother's role of *giving back* to the baby *the baby's own self* continues to have importance in terms of the child and the family. Naturally, as the child develops and the maturational processes become sophisticated, and identifications multiply, the child becomes less and less dependent on getting back

the self from the mother's and father's face and from the faces of others who are in parental or sibling relationships. (1974, p. 138)

What Winnicott fails to mention here is the degree to which a child's behavioural 'environment', or social ecology, affords him or her this or that kind of activity, thus to experience in the faces of those around him or her the kind of person the child is being given the opportunity to be. He simply takes it that the child can act freely, as the child's 'self' determines.

Thus for Winnicott the developmental task is clear: it is to provide babies with the environmental opportunities they require to develop their 'selves', whatever they may be. In their development, babies 'make use of objects', 'feel omnipotence', 'give up hope', 'make forecasts', etc. (to quote some of the phrases he uses). In other words, Winnicott treats even very young babies as if in some sense they are already adults, but are simply lacking, not so much knowledge, as the appropriate relations, the 'object-relations' required *to be* appropriately motivated. In fact, Winnicott sees babies as possessing a 'self' right from birth, and it is the mother's task to attune herself to it in order to allow it its proper growth. He is thus the first of our theorists to assume the 'developmental self-sufficiency' of the young child – even though in chapter 7 of his *Playing and Reality*, 'The location of cultural experience', he criticizes Freud for his failure to locate the developmental process within a cultural setting: 'Freud did not have a place in his topography of the mind for the experience of things cultural' (p. 112).

Poetics in the Political Economy of Developmental Opportunities Before turning elsewhere, I want to elaborate upon the implications of just one word in Macmurray's statement: we only ever achieve, he claims, a *relative* independence. The 'strain' of relating our desires to what the objects in our surroundings will afford us is always present – there is always in reality, one might say, an intrinsic scarcity of desired affordances, for in being oriented to seek developmental opportunities from others, we are developmentally unavailable to them. I want to draw out two points from this fact: (1) The first is that it is only in the 'symbolic realm', only in play that one can act without the challenge of direct empirical reference; as soon as one moves out of the area of play, there are inevitably conflicting tendencies; one moves into the Freudian nightmare world of flowing processes without stable boundaries (a fact which, as Russell Jacoby (1975) points out, we continually repress): illusion, fantasy and magic, displacement, projection, introjection (the determination of the me/not-me, inside/outside, real/not-real, good/bad boundaries); of depression, guilt, anger, obsession; of blame, forgiveness, redemption, and so on.

All are, as Freud continually emphasized, a normal part of the everyday world. It is a modern illusion to treat the real world as purely a matter of clear boundaries and systematic logic; that attitude is only possible in play and scientific theory. The real world, to use a short-hand expression, must be treated poetically; if, that is, one is concerned with accuracy of description, rather than with power of action. And that is why, at the moment, there is a burgeoning interest in tropes, in figures of speech, in 'metaphors for living', as Lakoff and Johnson (1980) call their new book on the subject.

(2) The second point I want to make is that, given the inevitable scarcity of people prepared to afford to others all the developmental opportunities they perceive as being needed by them, we all must continually suffer disappointments and frustrations. A 'political economy of developmental opportunities' exists within which the scarcity of the appropriate affordances is apportioned – with some people clearly gaining more of their fair share than others. This political economy is with us throughout our lives; one can see it at work, as Judy Dunn and Carol Kendrick (1982) have documented, in the continual squabblings of siblings, and as E. P. Thompson (1982) has outlined, between nation states concerned with their identities. In fantasy at least if not in reality, others (even our children) are always a threat to us, either in requiring, or by refusing to provide, a scarce psychological resource, without which we cannot grow.

The Perceptual-Inferential School

Let me turn now to the second school on my list, which I termed 'perceptual'. I have already mentioned Tom Bower, and the other worker I have in mind under this heading is Peter Bryant. The essential point uniting them, I think, is that, contra Piaget, they do not believe logical inference to be beyond the capacities of very young children. For them, development is a process in which children rely less and less upon the immediate perceptual context, and come to rely increasingly, they say, upon 'internal' categories in organizing their activities. We are all familiar with Bower's (1971) experiments studying the reactions of six-week-old babies to disappearing objects, and with Bryant's and Trebasso's (1971) experiments with four-, five- and six-year-olds on transitive inferences, so I will not give an account of them here. But let me state what Peter Bryant sees as their main point: that the errors and failures of children in solving problems, in the ways adults conceive of as appropriate, stem not from their lack of basic mental capacities, but from a difficulty in putting these capacities to use – a subtle, but I think a very important point. What he is suggesting is that in their development, infants themselves gain both an awareness of what their capacities *are* – what looking is, what remembering is, what it is to relate things remembered to things seen, i.e. what recognizing is, and so on – and, also, they learn how to apply and control these capacities. The capacities themselves, however, reveal themselves in the basic perceptual activities of the child; they are there from the start.

I shall return to the issue of children's own responsibility for their actions in a moment; but let me now extend the earlier complaint that I made against Bower to Peter Bryant. Following Helmholtz's 'unconscious inference' theory for depth perception, he also calls what the young child does perceptually, 'inference'. However, William James (1890, vol. II, p. 279) criticized Helmholtz's theory on the ground that if we already knew that a particular relation signified 'depth', then we could infer that upon its reappearance it signifies 'depth' once again. But that unless we had been provided beforehand with the knowledge of what the relation signifies, inference as such cannot establish its signification. Here also, I think, is the weakness in Bryant's position; and here also is his model of the child revealed.

It is in fact the same as Bower's: the child is treated as being in some sense already an adult, as developmentally self-sufficient, containing all that is required for him or her to develop themselves, if placed in the appropriate environment. What is missing from the individualistic picture presented by Bower and Bryant is the socio-historical process within which significations are established – in *their* view, these must be taken to be innate (as indeed Helmholtz, good Kantian that he was, took them to be); i.e. they are inherited genetically rather than culturally.

This leads on to something else which is also missing from their approach: a concern with the growth of infants as social beings, able at some point themselves to be responsible for their actions, and to 'answer for' them when required to do so by other members of their society, living in a social world fundamentally concerned with the legitimacy and accountability of actions. Clearly, under the appropriate experimental conditions, one can show that even very young babies can react in a characteristically differential manner to a great range of circumstances. Bower (and also, it seems to me, must Bryant) takes this as indicating that children 'already know' very early on (perhaps innately, in advance of experience) how to do all kinds of things. But do such observations indicate this, do they indicate that the baby him- or herself knows it in the proper social sense of being able, if required, to account for his or her action to others? In chapter 4, I tried to show both how self-conscious, responsible actions and their significations could be established together. And that what it was for children to be responsible was for them to know as they acted what the significations of their actions would be, and to be able to check them for their legitimacy and their tendency to arouse sanctions, etc.

The Biological-Ethological School

These same difficulties – to do with responsibility and legitimacy – arise also, I think, with the next position I want to discuss: what might be called variously the biological, ethological or sociobiological view. In concentrating upon what might be carried over from one generation to the next genetically, scant attention is paid to what resides in the socio-historical context, and how it is continually reproduced (and trans-formed) by people in their myriad daily activities. That context, as Vygotsky (1978) makes clear, is full of mental instrumentalities and technologies, devices for organizing and making use of one's basic capacities, e.g. 'memory aiding devices' (Hunter, 1979), which at one time or another human invention has placed in the cultural treasure house. For instance, Trevarthen (1974, 1975a and b, 1980), in discussing what he calls 'primary inter-subjectivity' points out that babies react in a distinctly different way towards people than towards objects; he takes this as indicating that babies perceive them differently. And he talks of babies as being innately organized to make such a discrimination, and of the origins of language as being embedded in 'an innate context of non-verbal communication'. This I am sure is so. But what is missing from this claim is attention to what those perceived by the baby *do* in response to what the baby does in perceiving them. While the possibility for mutal influence *must* exist innately, its signification need not. We are all aware of how various 'moral experts' have pronounced from time to time upon the significance of infant behaviour, and how, as Newson and Newson (1974) have documented, people have responded to their children's activities in distinctly different ways at different points in history (and in different cultures – cf. Margaret Mead). The non-verbal context, al-though no doubt partially specified innately, is further specified this way and that by determinants accumulated in the social history of the culture, in the unreflective discourse of everyday life. It is in this 'practical discourse' that people – by their stance, their nods and grimaces and smiles, etc., by the practical architecture and geography of their living spaces, as well as in their more lengthy and reasoned expressions – indicate the character of their social relations to one another. It is within this total discourse, I suggest, that members of a society 'construct' their newborns as different kinds of person according to the 'positions' they offer them in that discourse, in the linguistically and historically consti-tuted developmental environments they provide for them.

These comments are reinforced if one compares Trevarthen's recent work (1982) – on what he calls 'the primary motives for co-operative understanding' – with, say, C. W. Mills' (1940) 'Situated actions and vocabularies of motive'. Mills begins by pointing out that it is not the function of language to 'express' something already existing within individuals, but that it serves a 'social function', i.e. that of 'co-ordinating diverse action'. And that it can only do this if it works to indicate future action, to indicate intentions, i.e. what people are trying to do in the future by what they are actually doing now. In other words, intrinsic to a language, Mills maintains, is a 'vocabulary of motives', of goals at which one may legitimately and justifiably aim in one's society, goals which reflect its socio-historical development – for instance, it may at one stage have been in general puritanical, while now it may be hedonistic. Developmentally, of course, motives are imputed by others before being avowed by oneself. Mothers control their children by saying: 'Don't do that, its greedy.' In so doing, they not only afford their children the opportunity to learn what to do and what not to do, but they are also introduced to and instructed in a standard mode of justification, a linguistic device which they can themselves use to legitimate and prompt future action, as well as to dissuade and proscribe it.

Trevarthen argues, I think correctly, that the motives for 'co-operative understanding' must clearly be presupposed as existing in all human social activity – they are, as he claims, what makes the human form of life unique. But can we specify their innate nature in detail in a way uncontaminated by our own ideological preoccupations, uncontaminated by the further specifications introduced into them in our own particular form of social life? To attempt to do so is to act as if these motives can first be pursued by the young child on its own, and that in the course of so doing, society's 'vocabulary of motives' becomes superadded to them, so to speak, from the outside. Yet this is, I feel, how Trevarthen does attempt to specify them.

Thus, it seems to me, he presents a picture of childhood as being essentially a process of 'organic development' within a 'socio-historical' context, and it is during childhood that the child as an organism incorporates what its culture has to offer. In other words, unlike Bryant and Bower, Trevarthen does not implicitly treat the child as already psychologically an adult; but he does nonetheless accredit it with a great degree of self-sufficiency for its own development. The infant contains within itself as an individual the motives for its own initial development – where the alternative view is to see such motives not as located initially within the child at all, but as diffusely spread out within a whole bio-historical-socio process at large, an ecology, within which the child can be seen as embedded, as a small component region or moment (see chapter 11).

Anti-Piagetian Research: Bryant, Smedslund, Donaldson, and Walkerdine

Now the developmental psychologist who most clearly takes this view – that what ultimately we treat as being located within individuals we must first see as being implicit within the whole historical course of social life at large – is Vygotsky (1962, 1978). And the next and final position I want to discuss seems to me to reflect a number of his views. I want to give it the rather cumbersome title of 'the developmental social psychology of everyday social life', and to represent it by two pieces of writing: Margaret Donaldson's *Children's Minds* (1978) and Valerie Walkerdine's *From Context to Text: a Psychosemiotic Approach* (1982). Both emphasize the 'primitive matrix' or the 'discourse' of daily life within which the child develops – within which, to quote Margaret Donaldson (p. 76), 'all our thinking is contained'. Rather than from within the child, they see the child's development as originating within the flux of daily life in which the child is embedded. This research is also, like Bower's and Bryant's, an explicit or implicit critical reaction to the Piagetian tradition preceding it.

In this respect, concerning the difficulties faced by young children in experimental conditions, Peter Bryant (1974, p. 52) had already remarked that 'they may be so bemused by the oddness of the situation that they fail to exercise their normal ability to put experiences together in an effective logical manner.' The operative word here, of course, is the word 'normal'. In fact, under normal conditions in everyday life, no matter how young the children are, the presupposition that they are behaving logically is implicit (Vygotsky-like) in all of our dealings with them. Smedslund (1977), another lapsed Piagetian, has outlined why this is so: he points out that if we are to test whether children behave logically or not, we must first instruct them in a problem. If we are then to check whether they have understood the meaning of the instructions, we must do so by observing whether (in what they go on to do) they have grasped what is implied by, contradicted by or irrelevant to their meaning; in other words, in order to check out their understanding, we must take it for granted that the children are acting logically. Understanding and logicality presuppose one another. But even at a very primitive level, with very young children, the normal presupposition in everyday life is logicality: as mothers demonstrate when they check out their babies' 'understanding' by acting towards them on the assumption that certain consequences are implied in their babies' current activity, and that these consequences will follow, and the baby act logically, as long as the mother arranges the circumstances appropriately – normally, for instance, reaching will lead to grasping if a mother presents an object to her baby appropriately (see chapter 5). Only in unusual situations, as Smedslund points out, is understanding presupposed in order to check out logicality. But it is this unusual stance, however, which is the stance taken in Piagetian and in many other experimental situations – but as subsequent experimental work has shown, such an untested reliance upon a child's understanding is unwarranted.

Children's Minds   This is the theme around which Margaret Donaldson has built her approach: that when children properly understand what they are supposed to do, they show none of the difficulties Piaget claims children to be prone to at various stages in their development. Further, they understand directly what to do in situations involving people's motives and intentions (see chapter 4, for a discussion of the 'direct perception' of human expressions). For instance, in Hughes's (one of her workers) replay of Piaget's 'three mountains' experiment – which, Piaget claimed, demonstrated the egocentricity of the young child's world view – a new situation is presented to the child which now contained people trying to do things, namely, to chase and to hide from one another (where Piaget's mountains had been peopleless and thus motiveless). In understanding the situation now, in terms of particular people's practical intentions and motives, even very young children can grasp the contents of 'other minds', i.e. how those in the different positions in the display would see *their* situation – thus at three and a half years, half the age Piaget claims at which children cease to be egocentric, 90 per cent of children were able to say who could see whom and who was hidden from whom. The 'old primitive matrix', as Donaldson calls it, of everyday life activities, with which children are to an extent already familiar, clearly served here to help to organize and structure children's activities for them, spontaneously – children, rather than acting 'out of' their own resources, act 'into' a motivationally structured situation (see chapter 11 for a discussion of action being structured by being directed 'into' a context).

   Now central to life within such a matrix, as Donaldson sees it, is a direct and immediate understanding by all the participants in it of one another's intentions; and it is this assumption, she claims – the assumption that children must from the start possess some ability to grasp meanings, rather than, say, Chomsky's (1966) suggestion that human beings possess a specific language acquisition device (LAD) – which makes the approach she takes a new approach. Languages are inherent in the ecological relations between human beings, not in their biology. 'The newer account differs from this,' she says (p. 38), in the most fundamental way. The primary thing is now held to be the grasping of meaning – the ability to 'make sense' of things, and above all to make sense of what people do, which of course includes what people say. On this view, it is the child's ability to *interpret* situations which makes it possible for him, through active processes of hypothesis-testing and inference, to arrive at a knowledge of language. (my emphasis)

But again with echoes of Helmholtz and Bryant, she goes on immediately to say: 'Now there is an important condition which must be satisfied if this account is to hold: the child must be in a general way capable of *inference*' (my emphasis). This is, to my mind at least, confusing hermeneutical, perceptual and ontological issues with cognitive, epistemological and information-processing ones (see chapter 9). Only children who already know in what their world consists can make inferences on the basis of 'information'; they cannot gain their knowledge of how to be in the world, in the ways required of them by their society, in that manner.

I have now said enough, I think, to draw out what I think Margaret Donaldson's model of childhood is – and I must emphasize that I think that it *is* a model of childhood, for it takes into account the special character of the social matrix within which the child's development takes place. But notice, it is not the child him- or herself who is embedded in that matrix, but the child's thought. Ontologically, the child remains distinct from its context; only epistemologically is the knowledge the child acquires spread diffusely throughout the system. Reasoning (or inferring) goes on inside 'the mind' of the child, while the matrix of pre-existing socio-historical knowledge remains on the outside. What is missed in such a view is that in the course of its development a child must not only gain knowledge, he or she must also acquire certain 'ontological skills' – as Donaldson herself recognizes (pp. 93–4) when she discusses briefly Vygotsky's views on the nature of children's abilities to control and use their own capacities, and to become responsible themselves for what they do. Children have to learn how to be listeners, how to be speakers, to be watchers, thinkers, rememberers, imaginers; how to be storytellers, requesters, insulters, etc. They have to learn how to be certain kinds of person, and this necessitates them learning how *to do* certain things within themselves, some 'ontological skills', not just 'facts' about such activities: they have to learn to articulate their own relation to themselves in a socially appropriate manner. But, in this ontological respect, the child is treated in Donaldson's position still as developmentally self-sufficient.

The great virtue of Donaldson's position as I see it is its emphasis upon the character of the 'primitive matrix' within which development takes place. It is of course a research task of mammoth proportions properly to articulate the nature of that matrix; it is a biological, ecological, sociological, anthropological and historical task. But it is a task, I think, which is in fact already under way in many quarters of social theory, social phenomenology, hermeneutics, semiotics, ethnomethodology and social psychology. It is the task of attempting to render explicit what already exists, but is implicit in the current character of our corporate social life. And in particular here, my task is to render explicit what is implicit in the special social practices known as doing developmental psychology. In doing so, I am not so much taking up a particular position within that discourse (although clearly, I am) as attempting to reflect upon the actual structure, so far, of the discourse itself.

Psychosemiotics   And this is, in fact, precisely the character of Valerie Walkerdine's (1982) psychosemiotic approach to developmental problems. She is sympathetic to Margaret Donaldson's views, but criticizes both her and others for attributing to the child, as I have been putting it, too great a degree of developmental self-sufficiency. She sees such theorists as inevitably erecting unwarranted distinctions and boundaries right at the start of their research, by their talk of what is inside the child and of what is outside in the world. For the actual setting of such boundaries is something which is at issue in the course of development. Thus it is not that such terms can have no psychological use; on the contrary. But their use, clearly, only exists within a discourse, and what is 'inside' in one discourse, in one manner of speaking, may be 'outside' in another. We must not mistake features of the discourse for features of the subject of the discourse (Goodman, 1972); and, as I said earlier, in our own current discourse about ourselves, we are at the end of a long tradition of western thought in which we talk (with no empirical justification) of every human being as possessing right from the start, an inner subjectivity of one kind or another. And this misleads us in our research into always beginning our study with individuals, and into thinking of society as only a group or collective of interrelated individuals.

What Walkerdine does in her research — and I have no space to describe it in detail here — is to study children's ways of talking, their discursive practices, to discover both what they actually do and can be brought to do, and how they achieve their aims by the use of certain discursive devices — such as metaphors and other figures of speech. Now the essential point about studying 'discourse' as such — instead of what might be said to go on (or not) in 'the mind' of the child — is that in constituting the nature of one's relation to others in discourse with them, one also constitutes the nature of one's relation to oneself. Rather than oneself determining one's part in the discourse, it is primarily one's part in the discourse which determines one's relation to oneself – in other words, our systems of social accountability 'speak' us more than we speak them. For instance, speakers may develop different forms of self-consciousness: speakers who direct their attention inwards while speaking, towards the speaker–ego relation, who are concerned to maintain their self-consistency, their ego-integrity, etc., are clearly conscious of themselves in a way quite different from those speakers who direct their attention outwards, towards the speaker–community relation, who are concerned with its current state of harmony, etc. (Washabaugh, 1980). Hence, Walkerdine begins by assuming neither children's 'selves'[3] nor their knowledge to be 'within' them, but by seeing both the nature of their putative 'selves', *and* their knowledge, as being diffusely present in the socio-historical practices in which they are embedded. Within such an approach it becomes possible to tackle both the epistemological problem *and* its ontological counterpart simultaneously: (*a*) the problem of how children learn to do this or that kind or mental activity, and (*b*) to be this or that kind or person.

This is not an easy position to describe, and even though I think that it indicates a direction in which future research must go (see chapter 10), I have been able to do it scant justice. It requires a set of background assumptions about the nature of physical reality quite new to us (see chapter 11). The model of childhood it contains is best summed up by Elias (1978, p. xiii):

> the specific process of psychological 'growing up' in Western societies, which frequently occupies the minds of psychologists and pedagogues today, is nothing other than the individual civilizing process to which each young person, as a result of the social civilizing process over many centuries, is automatically subject from earliest childhood. The psychogenesis of the adult makeup in civilized society cannot, therefore, be understood if considered independently of the sociogenesis of our 'civilization'. By a kind of basic 'sociogenetic law' the individual, in his short history, passes once more through *some* of the processes that his society has traversed in its long history.

To lessen the apparent extent of this task, remember that, in the process, society has differentiated; that there is now a great 'division of labour', and that not only are knowledge and skill socially distributed, but so are different modes of being also, i.e. kinds of 'selves' or identities.

To sum up then: what I have been tracing – in outlining these models of childhood in British developmental research in the last decade – is a progress *away from* (see Kuhn, 1962, p. 171) a peculiarly 'closed', individualistic image of young human beings. While clearly dependent biologically upon others, young infants are presented in this view as independent of others psychologically. They are seen as able seemingly to gain knowledge of the 'external' world in a completely autonomous way. To grow to adulthood, infants do not apparently have to live in a special relationship to adults. The only question raised by such an image is whether the infant's knowledge is gained empirically, by the structure of the 'external' world impressing itself upon 'the mind' of the infant; or whether it is a rational matter, with the external world exerting only a selective function upon a body of knowledge the child already possesses innately. Progressively, this image of the child has been criticized, and the Cartesian starting point it implies repudiated. But it is exceedingly recalcitrant: opening up the infant to contextual influences in one region of its being often leaves it still closed and developmentally self-sufficient in others. However, this critical process continues and, rather than in individuals, we are beginning to learn how to locate the starting point for our researches diffusely within the self-reproducing flow of the social ecology of ordinary everyday activities. Within such a view, development is seen as a part of a flowing process, within which something – which is at first spread out in an implicit, vague and non-locatable form within that flowing process – is progressively given a refined, explicit and locatable expression. This is a view expressed by Vygotsky (1978, p. 57), but still in an individualistic terminology, in his remark that all intrapersonal processes are first interpersonal ones. In this view, childhood is simply the initial part of the trajectory of that social flow as it reproduces itself – with each individual's psychogenesis recapitulating at least an aspect of its sociogenesis. That, given the models I have discussed, is one direction at least in which I think British developmental research has been moving during the last decade – towards a more explicit understanding of its own implicit origins.

Part Three

Social Accountability

8

Vico, Joint Action, Moral Worlds and Personhood

Human choice, by its nature uncertain, is made certain and determined by the common sense of men with respect to human needs and utilities . . . . Common sense is judgement without reflection, shared by an entire class, an entire people, an entire nation, or the entire human race.

(Giambattista Vico (1975): *Scienza Nuova*, 1744, paras 141 and 142)

Part of what it is to be recognized as a competent member of a society by others who are already competent members of it is to be able to sense or know directly – without the need to stop and reflect, nor to have to gather any evidence relevant to the matter – what should appropriately be said or done in most of the mundane circumstances one confronts in that society. Such an ability seems to involve our possession of what we call 'common sense' – common in the sense of it being vulgar, i.e. being widely distributed in everyone. And under normal circumstances, as different matters arise and make demands upon us in daily life, we say that 'We know by common sense what to do.'

A Universal Commonplace Competence?

It is the nature and structure of that vast system of implicit but organized common sense knowledge, and the way in which it, amongst other things, informs our social life with others – in terms of what might be called the 'indigenous' psychology it contains – that I want to discuss below. First, I want to show that under normal conditions (and the notion of normality is central), we are able to understand other people's doings and sayings directly and immediately, in a skilful manner, because we can participate with them in such activities. This gives us access to a kind of knowledge unavailable to us as mere observers of happenings in which we are uninvolved. Also, prior to all such acquired knowledge and belief, we possess the same corporeal form as other people. And possession of such a form, if nothing else, provides us with immediate access to the intentional nature of human action: with such an access we find that human action, in its very nature of always 'pointing to', or of 'containing' or 'specifying' something beyond or other than itself, posits a context of possibilities within which it occurs; in other words, it posits a world. It also, in its requirement that an agent be 'there', so to speak, continually to control and direct its conduct, 'points to' or posits in its every aspect an author, the person him- or herself who is involved in its outcome.

However, people know that although they may have some powers to act in the realization of their intents, they are not omnipotent, and much human action (and thought) remains incomplete, and thus vague, 'pointing' towards ends or objects it never fully attains or specifies; vagueness and intentionality are, in fact, two sides of the same coin, for only in a really uncertain world is true human action necessary – in an already completely determined world, all activity in it could only be of a preplanned or statistical kind, and human action and agency, as such, would be unnecessary, redundant.

People know, then, something of what it is to be a person. In possessing such special kinds of 'insider's' knowledge, of both a substantive and a formal kind, about the content of activity in their society and its formal structure, it would be surprising indeed if we were not able to use it to understand others of our kind in a way quite different from the way that we understand those things of which we know nothing 'from the inside'.

I shall, in fact, attempt to make out a case for the existence of universals of common sense, not only for substantive universals (such as the concept of personhood, as well as other notions relating to one's membership of a society, involving knowledge of, for instance, birth, sex and death, care of the young, weak and aged, treatment of those transgressing the social order, and so on), but also for even deeper, more formal universals (such as the universals already mentioned to do with the vague and abstract properties of action and intentionality of which one is also aware as a human being).

I shall not, however, follow Chomsky (1965) in claiming that such universals have the character of 'innate ideas' present to children at their birth in advance of experience; instead I shall follow Vico, and claim that such universals arise naturalistically, out of the intrinsic properties of human societies and the nature of human agency within them; there is, as

Vico might say, an immanent providence at work in human affairs providing for the peculiarly human forms of order which arise. For Vico, common sense played a very special part in the 'workings' of human societies, and the maintenance of their social order.

Vico

Giambattista Vico was born in Naples in 1668, and died there in 1744, having hardly ever left his native city (see Berlin, 1969, 1976, upon which I have relied heavily for my account here). He first published the work for which he is now known, his *Scienza Nuova* – the new science in question being the science of history – in 1725. His main concern was to show that human phenomena are accessible to human understanding in a way that natural phenomena are not. Although beginning as a Cartesian, he became convinced that the notion of timeless truths, founded in 'innate ideas' common to everyone, was a chimera. The validity of all true knowledge, even that of mathematics and logic, could only be shown, he argued, by understanding how in precise historical detail it came about, and why it came to be accorded its place in human affairs. He became convinced that, whatever the splendours of the exact sciences, there was a sense in which we could know more about our own and other people's experiences – in which we acted as participants, indeed as authors, and not merely as observers – than we could ever know about non-human nature, which we could only observe from the 'outside'. Full knowledge can only be knowledge 'through causes', *per caussas*: according to this principle we can only be said to know a thing fully if, and only if, we know *why* it is as it is, or how it came to be, or was made to be what it is, and not merely *that* it is what it is, and has the attributes it has.

This is Vico's *verum ipsum factum* principle, the claim that we can logically only guarantee the truth of that which we ourselves make (about which more later). To apply this old medieval maxim to such provinces as mathematics, mythology, symbolism and language is, Berlin claims, evidence enough of philosophical insight, a revolutionary step on which the cultural anthropology and the philosophical implications of the new linguistics theories of our own time have cast a new and extraordinary light. But Vico did more than this, much more, and Sir Isaiah sums up his achievement under seven theses (Berlin, 1976, pp. xvi–xix) which, before I go on to look at a number of them in more detail, I will list below:

1 That is there is no fixed, essential human nature, but that people in their efforts to understand themselves and their world, and to transform it to their needs, transform themselves.

2   That those who make or create something can understand it, as mere
    observers of it cannot. Thus people cannot fully understand nature.
    Only God, because he has made it, can understand it fully.
3   That people's knowledge of the external world – which they can
    observe, describe, classify, reflect upon, and of which they can record
    the regularities in space and time – differs in principle from their
    knowledge of the world that they themselves create, which, as such,
    obeys rules which they themselves have imposed upon it.
4   That there is a pervasive pattern which characterizes all the activities of
    any given society: a common style reflected in the thought, the arts, the
    social institutions, the language and the ways of life and action of an
    entire society.
5   That people's creations – laws, institutions, religions, rituals, works of
    art, language, songs, rules of conduct and the like – are not artificial
    products created to please, or to exalt, or teach wisdom, nor weapons
    deliberately invented to manipulate or dominate people, or promote
    social stability or security, but are natural forms of self-expression, of
    communication with other human beings or with God.
6   From this it follows that people's doings and makings must be
    understood, interpreted and evaluated, not in terms of timeless
    principles and standards valid for all people everywhere, but by a
    correct grasp of the purpose and thus the peculiar use to which such
    doings and makings are put, a use which belongs uniquely to its own
    time and place at a stage in a society's cultural growth.
7   That, therefore, in addition to the traditional categories of
    knowledge – *a priori* (deductive) and *a posteriori* (empirical), that
    vouchsafed by revelation and that provided by sense-perception – there
    must now be added a new variety, that of reconstructive imagination.
    Understanding involves 'entering into' (*entrare*), working one's way
    into a means of expression not one's own; working back from the
    purpose and use of expressions to the larger mode of reality motivating
    them and in which they play their part, then back again from the whole
    to a more detailed rendering of the parts in terms of which it is
    actualized – this is, of course, the now familiar two-way trajectory of
    what Dilthey called the 'hermeneutical circle'.

All these notions will be indispensable in the task of elucidating some of
the universals present in our common sense, indigenous psychology – the
indigenous psychology of contemporary western humankind. In particular there are two topics I propose to explore further in Viconian terms: one
is the nature of the knowledge one has when, as a person, as a member of a
society, one knows not just *that*, or *how*, but *what* something's meaning or

use or purpose is, and seeks to understand *why* it is as it is. The other is the nature of the 'constructive' process, the unintended but nonetheless human process involved in the making of moral worlds, the systems of judgement, evaluation and, above all, accountability, in terms of which people, if they are to be proper members of their society, *must* operate.

Vico and Divine Providence

Vico was convinced, as we are now, that individual people are at once both cause and consequence of a social order: it is, he said,

> a truth beyond all question: that the world of civil society has certainly been made by men, and that its principles are therefore to be found within the modifications of our human mind. (1975, para. 331)

Yet clearly such worlds (of civil society) were not deliberately made or planned – it is a misleading 'conceit of nations' or 'conceit of scholars', says Vico, to suggest self-conscious thought went into the matter. The 'making' of social institutions simply cannot be explained by reference to anything like motives, plans or purposes, in terms relevant merely to individuals explaining their actions in an intelligible fashion to one another. For: (*a*) 'this (social) world without doubt has issued from a mind often diverse, at times quite contrary, and always superior to the particular ends that men had proposed to themselves' (para. 1108); and in any case (*b*) such terms (as motive, plan, etc.) are only properly attributed to individuals acting already as members of a social institutions, who explain themselves by reference to events and entities and use of a 'vocabulary of motives' (cf. Mills, 1940) within the social reality appropriate to that institution. Too often we attribute to those who must 'make' institutions for themselves abilities only possessed by those who are already members of them.

What is at work in the 'making' of social institutions is, suggests Vico, something special, something which *sui generis* works 'without human discernment or counsel, and often against the designs of men': he calls it 'divine providence'. But by that he does not mean the working of any supernatural agency or agencies external to intelligent human activities, coming in from the outside to impose an order upon them (indeed, he would also exclude natural agencies if they were external to human action itself, e.g. Chomsky's Cartesian 'innate universals'). Nor does he mean by divine providence the workings of chance, or fate, or any blind cause and effect processes. For, he says:

> That which did all this was mind, for men did it with intelligence; it was not fate, for they did it by choice; not chance, for the results of

their always so acting are perpetually the same (i.e. they produce a
social world with a moral order). (para. 1108)

Thus what he means by a divine providence at work is that, although the
'making' of a moral order is not an 'accountable' or 'visibly-rational-and-
reportable' activity within the social reality of a particular society – for
such activities are a precondition of people being able to give reports and
accounts to one another – nonetheless, there is, in fact, a natural provision
for it in the very nature of social action itself. It is this, Vico maintains,
which all social philosophers before him have missed.

Thus, just as Newton explains how both apples fall and planets stay in
their orbits (but not why) by reference to the 'occult quantity' gravity, so
Vico introduces the special notion of a divine providence: although
literally, he does not know what he is talking about, he feels certain that a
special principle, something *sui generis*, is required. Although he is unable
to say *why* it operates as it does, he is able to say in some respects *how* it
works; he is able to describe further properties of the process:

(1) In para. 1108, to back up his point that providence often works in
ways both contrary to and often superior to men's own particular ends, he
cites a catalogue of examples beginning, 'Men mean to gratify their bestial
lust and abandon their offspring, and they inaugurate the chastity of
marriage ... (and so on).' The point of all such examples being to
illustrate, as I shall go on to show in more detail below, the discrepancy
between people's 'reasons for' and the 'institution producing consequences of' their actions; for frequently what people intend and what results
from their actions can be two quite different things. This is because often,
in performing their actions, people must interlace what they do in with
other people's actions, and *their* actions are just as much a formative
influence determining what people do as anything within themselves.

(2) In fact, suggests Vico, providence has often made such 'narrow ends'
into 'means to serve wider ends, [which] it has employed to preserve the
human race upon this earth' (para. 1108). In acting in their social roles, in
acting as persons, people cannot but help to reproduce their social order in
their actions, and as such contribute to its maintenance in existence.
Ecological necessities are at work here, as I shall suggest later: human
beings act so as to retain their status as the persons they are, thus acting to
reproduce in their actions a social order which gives them their statuses.

(3) But providence is *divine* providence; it is hidden *in* the consciousness
of men: 'the philosophers have been altogether ignorant of it,' he says,

as the Stoics and Epicureans were, the latter asserting that human
affairs are agitated by a blind concourse of atoms, the former that

they are drawn by a deaf [inexorable] chain of cause and effect. . . . But they ought to have studied it in the economy of civil institutions, in keeping with the full meaning of applying to providence the term 'divinity' [i.e. the power of divining], from *divinari*, to divine, which is to understand what is hidden *from* men – the future – or what is hidden *in* them – their consciousness. (para. 342)

What unfolds or is made explicit in social activity is, in some sense, already present implicitly hidden in human consciousness. There are relations between divination, interpretation, psychoanalysis and hermeneutics to be explored here. The hermeneutics concerned in the actual unfolding of social processes may be called a practical hermeneutics.

Vico sees social change as occurring under the press of individuals' self-interest. Normally, a man 'unable to attain all the utilities he wishes, he is constrained by [his society's] institutions to seek those which are his due; and this is called just' (para. 341). But, for Vico, people in striving to satisfy their needs cannot help but continuously change the conditions of their own existence, and they thus transform themselves, generating new needs, new categories of thought and action (and thus experience) and new characteristics. Although still persons, still intentional beings with an understanding from the inside as to what it is to *be* a person – unlike stars and stones – although still able to reproduce their social order in their actions, their actual nature (in terms of their personality characteristics, modes of thought and action, their vocabulary of motives) may be utterly new. Vico *denied*, in the face of the highest authorities of his time, as well as the central (still continuing) western tradition, the existence of an unchanging human nature whose properties and goals are fixed and knowable. A viconian social psychology would not be concerned with discovering theoretical principles, but with the practical task of moving on to new forms of human being; with people actually discovering within themselves how to exericse new powers of mind – and how to avoid being bewitched by linguistic and theoretical constructs of their own making.

Vico's Concept of Social Institutions: the 'Making' of 'Moral Worlds'

Vico also explored the actual nature of human creations in the social sphere and the ways in which individual people are at once both cause and consequence of a social order. The problem he faces here is that although we do, in some sense, make our own cultures and thus ourselves, it is not something that in any sense people do deliberately, in control of the processes of production; as products they are not the result of any identifiable human purpose; they are not a making for which persons as such can be held accountable: knowledge *per caussas* is thus unobtainable. Yet Vico writes:

> It is true that men themselves made this world of nations (and we took this as the first incontestable principle of our Science . . .) but this world has without doubt issued from a mind often diverse, at times quity contrary and always superior to the particular ends men had proposed to themselves; which narrow ends, made means to serve wider ends, it has always employed to preserve the human race upon this earth. Men mean to gratify their bestial lust and abandon their offspring and they inaugurate the chastity of marriage from which the families arise. The fathers mean to exercise without restraint their paternal power over their clients and they subject them to the civil powers from which the cities arise. The reigning orders of nobles mean to abuse their lordly power over the plebians and they are obliged to submit to the laws which establish popular liberty. . . . That which did all this was mind, for men did it with intelligence; it was not fate, for they did it with choice; not chance, for the results of their so acting are perpetually the same. (para. 1108)

Many things are striking about this passage, especially, perhaps, the way in which Vico distinguishes between people's reasons for, and the institutional consequences of, their actions; this feature, of what I have called 'joint action', will occupy us greatly in our concern with dilemmas of responsibility attribution. But for the moment let us consider another point: although arising as apparently unintended consequences of human action, Vico denies that human institutions arise by chance, for, he says, 'men did it with intelligence', and 'the results of their so acting are perpetually the same'.

Pompa (1975), in discussing the intelligence or reason at work in such a social process, pairs this passage with another, similar, in which the same sequence of institutional development is proposed, going from a purely bestial state, through family life, to both a civil and a national life, except that now institutional life is approached from the opposite direction, i.e. not from what leads to its production, but from the constraints it exerts once produced. Having established the fact that man (!) in his bestial state desires only his own welfare, Vico goes on,

> having taken wife and begotten children, he desires his own welfare along with that of his family; having entered upon civil life he desires his own welfare along with that of his city; when its rule is extended over several peoples he desires his own welfare along with that of his

nation; when the nations are united by wars, treaties of peace, alliances and commerce, he desires his own welfare along with that of the entire human race. In all these circumstances he desires principally his own welfare. Therefore it is only by divine providence that he can be held within these institutions to practise justice as a member of the family, of the city, and finally of mankind. Unable to attain all the utilities he wishes, he is constrained to seek those which are his due; and this is called just. That which regulates all human justice is therefore divine justice which is administered by divine providence to preserve human society. (para. 341)

People may never cease to act for what they take to be their own particular ends. But as a consequence of existing only as members of a society, what they take their interests to be depends upon their position in that society; the various institutional roles they occupy influence the goals they pursue. This is the way in which 'narrow ends [are] made means to serve wider ends'. While people never cease, Vico suggests, to desire principally their own welfare (because that is a part of their 'corrupted nature', he says), they are restricted of necessity by others in what they can do, and thus each, 'unable to attain all the utilities he wishes . . . is constrained to seek those which are his due' – his 'due' in the position, the role he occupies. Thus, concludes Pompa,

> the 'mind' referred to in the earlier passage as the possessor of these wider ends is not some transcendent, non-human mind but the intelligence of human agents under the determining influence of human institutions. (1975, p. 26)

Institutions determine the direction of people's activity in determining people's sense, their common sense grasp, of what is due to them, of what it is legitimate or socially appropriate in the circumstances to do, of what, perhaps, is the most they can justifiably 'get away with'. Inherent in institutional life is what one might call a 'structure of normality' in terms of which one must judge and evaluate, and be able to account for, one's actions. It is the normative or evaluative aspect of human action which, more than any other aspect, distinguishes it from mere behaviour. People unable to account for their actions in this way cannot be accounted by others as fully competent members of their society – they are yet to qualify as persons.

Here, then, Pompa urges, Vico is arguing that a 'providence' is at work in human affairs – not a transcendental providence coming from the outside (even though Vico calls it divine) – but an immanent providence in the sense that human social nature is such that it makes natural provision, in the institutionally structured activities of individuals, for the working of wider social processes – processes which, because they are genuinely social, the product of joint action between people, individuals cannot account for, and of which they thus remain largely ignorant. (The peculiar properties of joint action are the topic of the next section.) While people do not act for the sake of the 'structure of normality' inherent in their common sense (see above, Berlin's point 5), while people do not deliberately set out to invent it, they nonetheless act in its light and evaluate their actions by reference to it – hence its normative quality. People make judgements (without reflection) in a way common to all those who share in the same system of institutional activity. So although the making of a social structure is not to be explained by a motive or purpose proper to an individual as such, neither is it to be explained by reference to some superhuman agency; it is, we shall say, a product of joint action, a human product of human intelligence – not fate, nor chance, 'that which did all this was mind, for men did it with intelligence'. The making of a 'moral world' is something naturally provided for in the structure (the intentional structure) of joint action; providence – 'divine providence' – is such that a social order arises naturally in a human society.

Vico's Concept of Knowledge Per Caussas: Verum and Certum

Vico uncovered a new sense of knowing, Sir Isaiah Berlin maintains, which is basic to all humane studies:

> the sense in which I know what it is to be poor, to fight for a cause, to belong to a nation, to join or abandon a church or a party, to feel nostalgia, terror, the omnipresence of a god, to understand a gesture, a work of art, a joke, a man's character, that one is transformed or lying to onself. (Berlin, 1969, p. 375)

This is a species of knowing, Sir Isaiah claims, on its own – knowledge indigenous to a way of life, to membership of a social institution. If a man claims to know what it is like to lose his religious faith (to use Sir Isaiah's example), to know the way in which his world and his self is transformed as a result, then his claim may or may not be valid (he may be lying or deluding himself, or misidentifying his experience), but the sense in which he claims to know it is quite different from that in which he may claim to know, for example, that this tree is taller than that, that the temperature today reached 70 degrees F, or that the King in chess can move only one square at a time. In other words, such indigenous knowledge is not a form of 'knowing that' such and such is the case, and neither is it a form of 'knowing how' to do something like riding a bicycle (see Ryle, 1963). It is a form of knowing founded on memory and imagination; the kind of knowing which participants in an activity may claim to possess when they know *what* things are and *why* they are as they are.

In elucidating the nature of this knowledge, we can follow Vico. He begins by distinguishing between *certum* and *verum*, between certainty and truth; between (*a*) acquaintance with and beliefs about particular matters of fact, and (*b*) knowledge of universal truths. *Verum* for Vico is truth based upon *a priori* principles, the kind of truth that is reached, for example, in mathematical reasoning, where starting from certain axioms, one comes to irrefutable conclusions. But *verum* is obtained only at the cost of empirical content, for people can only, according to Vico, logically guarantee the truth of that which they themselves make (his *verum ipsum factum* principle mentioned above). If *verum* is made by us, how can it reflect or describe in a demonstrable, irrefutable way the world outside itself?

The answer, according to Vico, is that no matter what Cartesians may claim for physics, it cannot. Once one attempts to make one's own constructions (in this case, of thought) conform with things outside themselves and independent of them – with reality, say – then one can no longer guarantee them as *verum*, for the matter is no longer wholly within one's own control – reality must have its say too. Thus at best, Vico claims, one can only speak of *certum*, not logical truths but truths of ordinary understanding and perception, the *certainties* in terms of which we live our daily lives.

However, as it is, one exists in a specific historical context, occupying a particular place within a particular society; and no one can escape the particular categories, social and psychological, mental and emotional, which obtain at that particular historical moment, for that particular place. This is the world, as Sir Isaiah points out, of the *sensus communis* of a society, the 'judgement without reflection, shared by an entire class, an entire people, an entire nation, or the whole of the human race', a 'sense' which is, furthermore, continually being evolved (in the sense of what is implicit and potential within it being made explicit). One's 'certainties' are thus specific to one's way of life.

However, the character of our knowledge of both our, and the world's 'whatness', is such that, literally, one does not know how to doubt it – one is unable to formulate an intelligible doubt about it, because to do so would be to use in its expression those self-same categories about which one wished to express a doubt.

The nature of the 'bind' we are in here can be appreciated by exploring the relations between *certum* and *verum*; they can be illustrated as in figure 1.

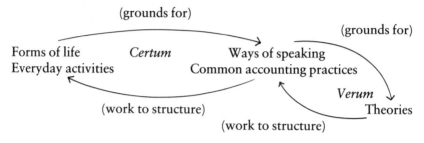

FIGURE 1   *The relations between* certum *and* verum

As the figure shows: the *verum* implies the *certum*, while the *certum* in its turn is structured by the *verum*. Or to put the matter another way: the *certum* must exist as the grounds of the *verum*, while the *certum* supposes that it is certain about something, namely the categories of the *verum*. For example: we feel that the law of falling bodies $s = 1/2gt^2$ is *true (verum)* as we are certain (*certum*) that if distance (s) and time (t) *are* as we must assume them to be – in the form of life within which the law has its being, in which distance is measured by rulers and time by clocks – then they are indeed and in fact related as the law describes. The *verum* both has its grounds in and works to *structure* the *certum*, to such an extent that our experiences appear to us as indubitably structured for us in the categories of the *verum* (where in their partial and selective nature such categories inevitably produce, of course, distortions – see Shotter and Burton (1983)) – whilst the *certum* are grounded in everyday activities structured by our common-sense ways of speaking.

Certum arise out of the totality of social practices in which we continually reproduce our being, which 'have us', so to speak, and through which we make ourselves what we are. Our form or forms of life provide us with a practical or implicit understanding (an intuitive, unformulated understanding) which is prior to any explicit, systematically expressible understanding that we might achieve. Many other writers have expressed such a view similar to Vico's: 'What has to be accepted,' says Wittgenstein (1953, p. 226), for instance, 'the given is – so one could say – *forms of life.*' Or as Heidegger (1967, p. 191) says, 'The ready-to-hand is always understood in terms of a totality of involvement . . . . In every case . . . interpretation is grounded in *something we have in advance* – in a fore-having.'

But forms of life, however, do not have *a* structure to them, at least not a single structure; although they are structurable (Goodman, 1972). Their character is vague, really vague, in the sense that they can be known only in terms of the activities possible within them; [1] i.e. in terms of their possible further specification in practice; or more strictly, in terms of their already specified, further specifiability. Events in them can have what some writers have called 'duality of structure' in the sense that they can be seen as both means (known in terms of their use) and *meanings* (requiring interpretation). 'What is most difficult here is to put this indefiniteness, correctly and unfalsified, into words' (Wittgenstein, 1953, p. 227). This 'no-thing-ness' character can only be described metaphorically (see chapter 10); Bohm's (1980) 'implicate order' (see chapter 6) is just such a metaphor – an order amenable to multiple explications, while remaining itself indeterminate.

Because people know what it is to be a person, what it is to have knowledge, to be a member of a society, to act unselfconsciously as well as according to a plan, etc., more than 'knowing how' and 'learning that', they also 'know why'; they can know the kinds of reasons *why* people act as they do. For they can set themselves also to 'make' or to 'create' outcomes which for all practical purposes are equivalent to those produced by other people. In so doing, they can 'enter into' a mentality other than their own; they can, given the practical details of other people's settings, appreciate their reasons for their actions, *why* they acted as they did. It is possible, though sometimes very difficult, to do this – but Vico describes something of what is involved in doing it, and in so doing describes some of the special methodology appropriate to a practical hermeneutics.

The knowledge we have of ourselves, of our ideas and volitions, our experience, both past and present, individual and social is not simply given to us as brute fact; yet we know such things, and in a way quite different from the way we know about things 'outside' ourselves. But quite in what way is unclear, for people are nothing if not ambiguous creatures, not in every respect their own creators. While they can come to do much for themselves, deliberately, with reflection, there is much also they do spontaneously, without reflection, not requiring their personal control. Not fully under their own control, they are unable, on Vico's *verum factum* principle, even to understand their own mental activity wholly. However, to the extent that it is potentially under one's own control (Vygotsky, 1962; Shotter, 1973a, 1974b), it is potentially understandable in a way other things are not. It is, Sir Isaiah points out, understandable but with difficulty, for it involves appealing not just to what we know because of what we are, but to what we could know in virtue of what we could become. We have to make the effort, at least in thought, to go through what is involved – the thoughts, feelings, fears, hopes, ambitions and imaginative experiences, constitutive of a mode of being currently not our own. An enterprise which involves us in continually asking ourselves about the motives, intentions, purposes or volitions that people must of necessity have had, in order to have done what we know they did.

To grasp motives and intentions, to understand, however imperfectly, *why* men act and live as they do, is, Sir Isaiah points out, to have in Vico's terminology, knowledge *per caussas*, the knowledge possessed by a creator when he understands his own creations and constructions, what he did to get them, to bring them into existence. As such, knowledge *per caussas*, however incomplete, is for Vico superior to, 'more godlike than', mere 'knowing that' – the awareness 'from without' which provides the data of the natural sciences, or of the ordinary knowledge of the external world. Equally, it is superior to 'knowing how' – the mere acquisition of a skill or method – for it leads to a grasp of the whole outlook within which an act, an activity, a skill or a method plays its part.

Joint Action and the Making of Moral Worlds

There is, then, something special in the nature of human action such that people, although unaware of doing so, construct social worlds of meaning between themselves in the course of social interaction, and in so doing determine the form of their own consciousness, their own categories of thought, perception, feeling, action and expression as well as their own modes of being in the world within which such categories are applied. Of late, action rather than behaviour has gained a certain prominence in psychological theorizing (Harré and Secord, 1972; Shotter, 1975). Initially such theorizing was concerned with marking out a sphere of activity in which autonomous action was possible, a sphere in which it could be said that, rather than being caused to behave by they-know-not-what forces acting externally to them, people themselves are the originators or authors of their own actions, and they can be said to have reasons for their actions. Thus, instead of explaining a particular event by showing how, in the circumstances of its occurrence, it is an instance of a general law, a person's particular action is explained by discovering what in particular the person was trying to do in executing it. In this sphere of autonomous action, as Hollis (1977, p. 21) says, 'rational action is its own explanation': that is, people are 'there' as agents 'in' their actions, and are executing them in terms of certain grounds and other rational considerations. And their actions are explained when, roughly speaking, those grounds are as plain to outsiders as they are to those performing the actions. The rational considerations in terms of which people act explain their actions.

However, not all human action is accountable or justifiable; not all of it is performed by autonomous persons. There are many everyday activities in which, it seems, we remain deeply ignorant as to what it is that we are doing (*à la* Vico); not because the 'ideas', 'plans', 'scripts', 'theories', 'constructs', etc., supposedly in us somewhere are too deeply buried to bring out into the light of day, but because the formative influences shaping our conduct are not wholly there in-our-individual-heads to be brought out. In our everyday practical affairs we are in a social setting, and, as Vico remarks, our actions are influenced by the actions of others. Besides acting autonomously (or, at least, being treated by others as autonomous agents, an important qualification as we shall see), people also act jointly doing things collectively which they lack the 'power' (Harré, 1970a) to do singly. While many people (not only academics) may sit down and do things entirely on their own, counting themselves as the producers of the products so produced, being wholly themselves account-able for them, they also engage in such activities as conversations, academic lectures, greetings, insults, promises and all the other many intangible and invisible but nonetheless very real things which only exist 'in' social relationships between people – for instance, the wrong in which Jill seems to be 'in' in Laing's (1971, p. 21) 'knot':

Jill: You put me in the wrong.
Jack: I am not putting you in the wrong.
Jill: You put me in the wrong for thinking you put me in the wrong.

The result here is that Jill feels herself 'wrong', wrong in her being, ontologically. But the wrong she is in is, however, only partly specified, and further activity, which must take account of its nature so far, will be necessary if Jack and Jill are to clarify what is happening between them.

I want to explore, then, an aspect of people's 'social powers' in these types of activity: they have the power, I think, to create and sustain in the course of joint action a 'moral world' between them, a seemingly 'external' and 'objective' world in terms of which, when required as autonomous agents to do so, they can give reasons for their actions, and have them understood and accepted by those, and only by those, who inhabit with them that same 'moral world' or 'world of meaning'. And this is a quite different way of giving one's reasons for one's actions, of giving them a rational explanation, than in terms of rule-, plan- or script-following, or in terms of following anything of a pre-established kind; it involves, as we shall see, grasping the so-called 'intentional structure' of the 'moral world' from which the action draws its sense.

The Intentional Properties of Unintended Consequences

In discussing the nature of the 'construction' process involved in the 'making' of 'moral worlds', I want to explore two interrelated themes. The first comes straight from Vico. It is simply that in the world of practical human affairs, people must often interlace their actions with those of others. Hence, what they as individuals desire and what actually results are often two quite different things. The outcome of joint action is thus essentially independent of any particular individual's wishes or intentions. As it cannot be traced back to the intentions of any particular individual, rather than something done by persons who cannot account for it, it seems to have the quality of something caused 'externally', and thus it seems appropriate to attribute it to some 'outside' force or agency acting upon people and structuring their actions – not something for which people are responsible at all.

The second theme I want to explore relates to intentionality. The fact is that no matter how it is produced, human action always has an intentional quality to it: it is not only directed in some way, but it is also intrinsically interconnected with the world in which it has its being. In some fundamental way it always seems 'to point to', 'to contain', 'to mean', 'to be a means to', 'to be directed upon an object', or, in short, 'to be related to something other than or beyond itself' – even if that thing or state, like a unicorn or utopia, does not and cannot exist. In other words, it is a fact that we can act upon the basis of beliefs, trying thus to do things, even if our beliefs prove false or deluded, and our efforts fail, attempting to 'fit', either ourselves to our circumstances, or our circumstances to ourselves (Searle, 1979a).

It was Brentano who was essentially responsible for introducing this conception of intentionality into modern philosophy and psychology in an attempt to clarify the distinction between physical and mental phenomena: 'Every mental phenomenon contains something as an object within itself, although they do not all do so in the same way,' said Brentano. 'In presentation something is presented, in judgement something is affirmed or denied, in love loved, in hate hated, in desire desired, and so on' (1874/ 1973, vol. 1, p. 88). In its very occurrence, then, human action, human being 'in' action, implies or indicates something beyond itself. It posits a realm of other possible actions, a 'world of meaning or reference' which seems to make its appearance even as an action occurs, and can thus function as the context in which the sense of the action can be understood. Simply to glance at someone is to posit a world in which recognition of like by like is possible, in which 'recognition' is a possible activity.

Another way of grasping the meaning of intentionality (Gauld and Shotter, 1977; Shotter, 1980a) is to talk of the specificatory function of action: the way in which an agent is able, in the execution of an action, to specify, to indicate or to point to a particular region of the world beyond or outside the action itself. Thus an action in progress can, while having so far produced a certain degree of specification into its content, leave that content open to yet further specification – but only specification of an already specified kind (Shotter, 1980a).

The 'worlds' produced or 'specified' in joint action are thus experienced as places open both to further action and to further interpretation or specification. Merleau-Ponty describes our experience of them very well, when he says,

> Our future is not made up exclusively of guesswork and daydreams, Ahead of what I can see and perceive, there is, it is true, nothing more actually visible, but my world is carried forward by lines of intentionality which trace out in advance at least the style of what is to come. . . . Husserl uses the terms protentions and retentions for the intentionalities which anchor me to an environment. They do not run from a central *I*, but from my perceptual field itself, which draws along in its wake its own horizon of retentions, and bites into the future with its protentions. . . . Time is not a line but a network of intentionalities. (1962, pp. 416–17)

Action is thus quite distinct from behaviour, from mere physical movement structured by reference to a plan or programme. People's actions are not movements in an external world of physical time and geometrical space, but are a natural aspect of the intentionality inherent in the 'social world' in which they take place and which they help to create.

Taking the two features of joint action mentioned above – the fact that such action produces results which are then experienced as 'objective' in the sense of being 'external' to the minds of those producing them; and that, unintended though such results may be, they nonetheless retain an intentional quality and thus in their occurrence posit a 'world' beyond themselves – taking these two features together suggests something of what is involved when people, without being able to account for how they do it, create and sustain seemingly 'objective realities' between them.

Accountability and Personhood

What is it then to treat people personally? Clearly, in meeting people personally, as we frequently do in daily life, we do not, in attempting to understand them, have to stop and reflect, and cudgel our brains as to the meaning of their actions, nor do we have to look beyond their actions for some further evidence as to what they might mean – at least, not normally. We simply look to them as the authors of their own actions, and, miraculously, we seem to grasp the nature of their thoughts and feelings, the meanings, intentions and purposes in terms of which they act; at least, on most occasions we do. Human action would thus appear to be unique. Not because, from an external observer's point of view, it is unlike any other behaviour (from such a standpoint it seems in fact very similar to many other forms of behaviour, especially that of computers), but because we approach it, seemingly, in a quite different way to the way we approach other behaviour: we are able to apply, and sustain, a quite different set of interpretative assumptions, or attribution procedures (Heider, 1958), from those we apply in other cases. I shall now discuss some of these common sense rules for the attribution of agency and personhood, self and responsibility (derived from Gauld and Shotter, 1977, pp. 42–45).

Attributive Assumptions: Self and Accountability

While we attribute the pattern of a projectile's trajectory to the operation of impersonal, general laws or principles of a causal kind, we still, notwithstanding the efforts of battalions of behaviourists, attribute people's motions in everyday life, their trajectories, to them. Why?

There seem to be a number of good reasons for such attributions: first, as Winch points out, when it comes to rule-following behaviour, 'the notion of following a rule is logically inseparable from the notion of making a mistake' (1958, p. 32). Thus we do not congratulate the moon for managing to stay in its orbit last night, but we do congratulate young Johnny for having managed not to fall off his new skateboard this afternoon. The mistakes and errors to which human actions are prone do not issue from their being governed by 'looser' or 'more statistical' laws than those that govern motions in the natural world. On the contrary, what rules there are in social life – as Chomsky has shown in language, or as any examination of wrangles in courts of law would show – are extremely precise and may on occasion prescribe very fine distinctions indeed. Mistakes and errors occur because (we assume) skill, effort and care are required in applying and implementing them, and we know we can still succeed at doing what we have just failed to do by applying greater care. People can correct their mistakes – a most important point for the maintenance of a social order.

However, even more than skill at applying criteria is involved if we are to assume people themselves to be attributed as the true authors of their own actions. For they may still, so to speak, be 'going through the motions' or merely 'acting the part' (like Sartre's waiter). As Gauld and Shotter (1977, p. 44) point out,

> accepting a criterion as *the* criterion . . . by which the success or
> otherwise of an action is to be measured involved not just applying it to

one's directed movement, but as it were *committing oneself* to fulfilling it, guiding one's self-expression in accordance with its requirements.

One is oneself involved in one's acting in such a way that success or failure of one's action is one's own success or failure.

Such a commitment of oneself in one's actions is reflected in the fact that, normally in everyday social life, people who have qualified to be treated as autonomous are accorded the right of having most of what they say taken seriously, taken as 'meaning what they say they mean' – it being normal in everyday life only to question and request explanations or justifications of people's conduct when it is abnormal or suspicious in some way (see e.g. Mills, 1940; Peters, 1958; Scott and Lyman, 1968). All psychological knowledge, Abelson (1977) claims, is erected upon such a foundation, the right to express first-person, present-tense, self-descriptions (felicitously named 'avowals' by Gilbert Ryle), such as 'I am talking', 'I love you', 'I intend to walk', 'I want coffee', 'I believe in God', 'I feel cold', etc. Such assertions Abelson labels 'non-observational self-ascriptions', taking it to be the case that (*a*) as a part of what it is to be a competent member of a moral world, people already know how to express themselves, and do not need observational evidence as to what they think, feel or intend (see both Vico's views on this, and Gauld and Shotter, 1977, ch. 10) – indeed they are the sources of such evidence – and (*b*) in a moral world, no one but the persons in question have the status, the authority, under normal conditions, to decide what their experience means to them. Thus to be autonomous, not reliant like a child upon others to complete and give the appropriate meaning to one's acts, is to be accorded the right of expressing oneself, of telling others one's thoughts, feelings and intentions, and the right to be accorded their author, to be taken as responsible for them.

Thus being an autonomous person, in relation to others in one's society, is not to be a creature of impulse, able to ignore the limitations and constraints of social codes, customs, rules and so on. Such a one might act as they pleased, but they would soon find themselves in a social void, robbed of their everyday purchase on human affairs. Being autonomous means being the author of one's own actions. But one only qualifies for that right if it is possible for others to treat one as responsible, that is, as able to 'answer for' one's actions with reasons for acting as one did. One is able to do that if indeed, as one acts, one monitors one's actions in terms of certain considerations common to all other people in one's society. Thus, in our ordinary, everyday, common sense view of people as autonomous, we assume people know how to make their actions conform to something in their common sense, and furthermore, we also assume that they are able, potentially at least, to report upon, or to account for, how they made them so conform. In a moral world, self-expression and accountability are inextricably interlinked.

Social Order and Personhood

Although people may represent themselves to themselves and one another in many different ways in different cultures – as having a mosaic, context-dependent 'self'; a fixed and predetermined 'self'; a context-free, potentially infinite 'self'; an outer public and an inner private 'self'; an impersonal slot-filler 'self'; in short, as existing within many different modes of relation with things taken to be other than oneself – we can still feel reasonably safe in saying that, nonetheless, a concept of personhood exists in recognizable form in all human groups; it is, Geertz (1973) maintains, a cultural universal, a substantive universal of a people's commonsense. Why?

If the comments about joint action made earlier are true, and most outcomes of action in a social world are outcomes of joint action, then rather than individuals, why not take particular interpersonal relations as the units productive of action in a society: the speaker/listener as a unit, the teacher/pupil, mother/child, master/slave, boss/worker, husband/wife, etc.? If individuals never have an isolated existence in actuality, but are merely 'terms' in one or another 'personal relationship' (to use Macmurray's, 1961, expression), then what is to be gained by ignoring that reality – especially when, as at the moment, important scientific gains may be made by taking such an interactive view? The answer, I think lies in the fact that a society, if it is to remain a society, must amongst other things be able to maintain a social order. For that to be possible, the elementary units in that order must be able to detect whether that order has been transgressed or not, and if so, be able to act in some way towards its restitution. In other words, the basic elements of a social order must not only know what they are doing, they must also be able to account for their action, as well as knowing how to correct mistakes, redeem themselves, acquit themselves, make reparation, and so on.

Such could not be the case, as is already clear, for interpersonal units acting jointly. It would simply be utterly unclear as to who should do what in relation to the repair and maintenance of a social order – and that order will not of its own nature endure (Vico). As it is, the concept of persons, as having localized within themselves rights and duties, abilities and constraints, although it may be misleading for many purposes (e.g. scientific purposes), seems necessary to a social order maintaining itself in existence. The concept of personhood is implied in that of a 'moral world'.

Furthermore, though I have not the space to show it here, the converse is also true: the idea of a moral order is implied in the concept of personhood; for only within a relatively stable social order is the development of a conferred social competence, and thus autonomous and responsible personhood, possible.

Apparently, then, the moral demands placed upon people by the necessary membership of a (developing) social order, and the psychological reality of their existence as social beings engaged in joint action, can conflict. How, morally, things *must* be treated, and what, psychologically or scientifically, they are, can be widely discrepant. And as the social order develops (through the stages of Vico's 'ideal, eternal history'), the discrepancy can increase. For as the primitive unity of a moral world is differentiated (with the division of labour) into more and more sharply demarcated categories of existence, so the grasp upon what unites it is lost: the reality of joint action recedes from view, and its operation (which is never accountable) becomes unintelligible. A 'second barbarism of reflection', as Vico (para. 1106) calls it, ensues. At such a stage, in which everything is done deliberately and nothing unaccountably, 'without reflection', the basis for genuine communication in joint action disappears, and anxiety-ridden individuals live in their own private, self-centred worlds, unable to communicate with their fellows. It is often suggested that we are moving towards just such a stage of development in our society now. Only by returning to that primitive unity (on, one hopes, a higher level of awareness), and grasping what it means to treat social worlds as intentional entities, might it be possible to understand how the categories of existence which seem sharply demarcated to us now are in fact deeply interrelated.

Concluding Remarks

Psychologists have been far too impressed for far too long by physics and physicists, by the science of what we call our 'external world' – that part of the world which, for each of us, embodies that which is other than ourselves. A science of the human or social world, containing regions within which people themselves are embodied, still remains to be constructed. Besides being long misled concerning questions as to the nature of methods and theories appropriate to psychological investigations, psychologists have also allowed themselves to feel their jurisdiction limited to what goes on only within people's skins. Beyond that boundary physics and physical principles are thought to rule, people being held to live in physical time and geometrical space. It is just that inhibition which I wish to question here, in discussing the nature of social and moral 'worlds', and the views of human nature necessarily implicit in being an inhabitant of such world. In so doing, I have tried to show that, although the 'workings' of such worlds are just as invisible to us as the world of modern physics, in their intentional nature they are no less full of charm and strangeness. Their special peculiarity resides in the apparent paradox that, while people quite clearly do construct their own ways of life for themselves, their own 'worlds', they nonetheless experience them as 'given', as realities existing somewhere in that world, But what with quantum mechanics, Heisenberg's uncertainty principle, relativity, etc., even views of the physical world are changing profoundly. The idea of the world as a place characterized by number, metric, causality and objective existence, is being replaced by new ideas based on notions of order (Bohm, 1969). This is because, as Bohm makes clear, even in physics, people participate in an essential way in the order studied; the world is known to them in terms of their doings in it (Bhaskar, 1979). But what *are* they? Here the problems of the physicist and the social scientist overlap.

Individuals who become competent members of a society, inheriting from their predecessors the culture of that society, clearly know a great deal 'from the inside' of what it is like to be a person in that society. Claiming at least a degree of social competence, my analysis is to an extent informed by it; I write here in the light of it.

It is informed also, though, by Vico's remarkable theories: for him, our common sense (or common sensing) does more, much more, than merely help individuals, through the provision of a shared framework, to communicate and to co-ordinate their actions in communal projects. It helps to form social institutions with the very special property of transforming actions done in the naked, self-interest of individuals, into actions conducive to the creation, maintenance and progressive development of a social order. The 'moral world' so produced contains within it, implicitly, a view of what people in it *ought* to be like. Such a view is, if Vico is right, specific to a particular point in its historical development. But such a view also contains, we can say, substantive common sense universals, to do with the particular things which must exist in all cultures, basic elements without which such cultures would be impossible – e.g. the idea of personhood, of sexual relations, authority, rights, duties, etc.

While much remains to be done to elucidate just what, precisely, our embodied being might contribute to the 'common sense' informing our actions, it is clear that, if nothing else, as human beings we are informed as to what it is to act, as to what the nature of human action is. And furthermore, 'in' acting we have access to the nature of intentionality, to the fact that action is always connected in some way with something beyond itself, no matter how vague that something – and one's relationship to it – is. Possessing such a 'sense' of intentionality, it provides us, implicitly, with a view of our world as open to our actions, of other people as recipients of our communications. Such a deep and abstract aspect of common sense may be called a '*formal universal*', a pervasive aspect of all social worlds everywhere. Possessing it, we have the basic prerequisite to enter into 'worlds' other than our own, and to transcend the limited modes of existence allowed us by the 'world' of our own moral community. What we *ought* to be, and what we are or may become, however, can be very different things.

9

Telling and Reporting: Prospective and Retrospective Uses of Self-Ascriptions

Here I want to explore what is involved in people explaining and justifying both themselves and their actions to one another, in an ordinary, everyday fashion – how they are able as individual personalities to take responsibility for things they do as their actions, for judgements they make, as their judgements. Can we give an account of people's reasons for acting which preserves their individuality and autonomy, which does not see their actions as necessarily flowing from something else – from 'rules', or 'scripts, say – 'outside' of and other than themselves? To preserve their autonomy, people must be able to account, not only for their actions, but also for themselves, i.e. who and what they are. In general, the process of accounting is one in which people can make their actions seem propitious or appropriate by further elucidating, to the extent they remain unclear, the 'situation', the meanings, purposes, beliefs or reasonings, etc., informing them. But we may do this in one of two ways: either by stepping out of the flow of social action, so to speak, to give an 'account' (noun), or from within the flow, accounting (verb) for what we have just done by further action which clarifies it in some way. While much research at the moment focuses upon the collection of 'accounts' and the problem of their interpretation, it is this second form of accounting, practical accounting, which interests me here – in which the intrinsic intentionality of human action is such that people can, in the course of their actions, progressively specify regions of the world beyond themselves.

People's Use of Actions in Expressing Their States and Statuses

Morally, it simply is not open to us to do just what we want when we please. What we have a right to do in one situation, we have no right to do in another; conditions we have no obligations to satisfy here, we must attempt to satisfy there; privileges accorded to us now, we may or may not be accorded tomorrow; and so on. Our moral world is an ever changing sea of opportunities and limitations, enablements and constraints, invitations and rejections, with its character transformed by each action which takes place within it.

I want to discuss what might be called the 'political economy of developmental' opportunities which people make available to one another in their interpersonal relations in such a world. The currency at stake is made up of the rights and duties, privileges and obligations which, on the one hand, people claim or demand for themselves, and which, on the other, are placed upon them or acceded to by others. The having of such rights and duties, etc., is not something people can just do on their own.

Clearly, while essentially concerned still to retain one's membership of one's society, people act whenever they can to increase their rights in relation to other members of their society and to reduce their obligations to them; there being point to such an aim, of course, only if one does remain a member, one's currency otherwise becomes valueless. Thus at every moment, where one is, how one is placed in terms of what one has a right to do and what one is being required to do, is important knowledge in determining one's momentary action. Those who do not properly grasp where they are, so to speak, do not know how to act in ways appropriate to their situation. But how do we, in such a sea of change, keep a grasp upon our position within it?

Strangely, it is unusual to spend most of our time in bewilderment and confusion. Normally, we know what we are doing and why, we know how we stand, and we grasp what those around us are at also; at least we do so to an extent sufficient to conduct most of our mundane activities with some degree of success. The many difficulties and dilemmas possible in theory in social life – as Wittgenstein (1953) noted in the case of language – hardly ever arise in the normal conduct of daily life. Actual human institutions seem to be structured so that in practice such problems are either minimized (see chapter 8 for a discussion of how in a social order 'dilemmas of responsibility attribution' are minimized), or they are carefully avoided, or they are dealt with in some other way – perhaps by being treated as special, and removed from the realm of 'real life' and conducted within circumscribed regions, such as in 'theatres', or on 'playing fields' or 'campuses' (Huizinga, 1949). Or perhaps again, what raises a difficulty in theory turns out in practice to be a foundation tenet of actual social life, something simply taken for granted.

For instance: the fact that people in daily life are unable to provide distinctive empirical evidence in support of what they tell (or avow) of themselves to others, although it raises many problems in theory – in the causes/reasons debate, say (Buss, 1978; Harvey and Tucker, 1979) – raises few problems in practice. In daily life, the fact is that we assign people a right to make such unsupported self-ascriptions, to make as Abelson (1977) calls them 'non-observational self-ascriptions'. The normal functioning of social life is founded upon such a convention; it could not operate as it does without it. For being accorded the right of having most of what they say or do taken seriously and responded to without question is a part of what it is for human beings to be treated as first persons, for them to be accorded their status as full and competent members of their society. It is only normal to request explanations of people's conduct when it is enigmatic or suspicious in some way (Peters, 1958; Scott and Lyman, 1968), when what the agent has in mind is not immediately perceptible, or if perceptible, not easily acceptable to others; or when, perhaps, their behaviour seems not wholly to be under their own control, not an action of theirs (R. Taylor, 1966). In conferring upon one another such a right, people give one another the opportunity to use self-ascriptions in asserting their states and statuses in relation to one another; and while people may simply assert things of themselves and have them accepted or rejected by others, they may also be invited by others to make such assertions and they may accept or ignore them as they see fit. The tension in every moral transaction follows from the existence of such options, each party to it is able to act in ways that other parties may neither desire nor expect.

In using a self-ascription in a status-assertion, I may, for example, say to a woman 'I love you.' In so saying, I may, but I usually do not, mean that I have carried out an extensive observational analysis, *à la* Bem, of my inner states and outer behaviour – my heart rate, breathing, sexual arousal, time spent looking at her and attempting to be near her, etc. – and have made my statement as a report which sums up the results. There are, as I will discuss below, occasions upon which such reporting is appropriate, but is questionable in a way in which a status-assertion is not. The fact is that here my declaration is not a reporting but a telling; it is a moral statement which once uttered (whatever its causes) commits me to going on in the future with the woman to whom it is uttered in a way different from my relations to her in the past. Now, my status in relation to her is changed; that was my reason for my utterance. I am now, however, vulnerable to her rejection of me; my status is not yet as I desire. Hence the circumspection which is always associated with such declarations. If she accepts me, then the new rights she accords me over her person are tempered with new obligations, Thus when next I am off to a football match with the boys, and have not consulted her beforehand, she will say to me reproachfully,

'But I thought you said you loved me?' And I will feel guilty and embarrassed. Realizing the commitments involved, we do not make such declarations lightly.

Above I am using my self-ascriptive utterance in a prospective manner, in an attempt to project the whole of myself in a certain way towards the future. And I sense the risk to myself in my project falling to the ground and coming to naught. However, in suggesting that the statement 'I love you' is usually used in such a way (by men?) does not rule out the possibility of it also being used retrospectively, as a report upon one's state of being, as Bem's (1967) 'self-perception theory' would suggest. People do on occasions find themselves puzzled as to why in the presence of a certain person their hearts go 'pit-a-pat', and they feel compelled to gaze at him/her with rapt attention. Then they may report that such events are happening 'because, I suppose, I must love you'. But then they could go on to say, 'But I'm not ready for it yet, let's just go on as we are for a bit longer,' thus clarifying that their statement *was* meant as a reporting and not as a telling. Further, as a report, their statement could be quite wrong: to be fascinated or attracted by a person is not necessarily to be in love with them; rather than your liking them, your inner goings-on may be due, if you are already locked in an unavoidable attachment to them, to your hatred of them, or to some other sentiment that you might have regarding them. In formulating such a report upon the events leading up to and constituting one's current state, one's self is split: an aspect reports while an aspect is reported upon. The uncertainties and risks in relation to myself in such retrospective uses of self-ascriptions, in which only a part of myself is actively involved, are clearly ones of quite a different kind to those in prospective uses, in which I risk the whole of myself. To be wrong in one's report is not to be wrong in one's being.

The Ethogenic Perspective

I shall return to make a few more comments about the different logical grammars of telling and reporting in a moment. Here, however, is a convenient point at which to break off in order to say something about the ethogenic perspective, and my relation to it. The practical-descriptive approach I propose may be considered as essentially belonging to the ethogenic school (Harré and Secord, 1972), for it is concerned with how ordinary, everyday social life is actually made to work by the human beings who conduct or perform it. Ethogenists are interested in the devices, techniques, procedures, methods, ways, stratagems, ploys, etc., which people actually *use* in 'bringing off' their aims in social life, not just anyhow, but in a 'rationally accountable' or 'socially responsible' manner. This is my interest also.

But, following Harré and Secord, it might seem that ethogenists should study only what already exists in social life. They state their position as if, on the one hand, there was a pre-established set of devices available in social life, and on the other, users of them, who, if they possess any competency at all, have such devices at their disposal. But, if that is their view, it would be tantamount to the old idea, scotched by Wittgenstein and his followers (e.g. Winch, 1958), of people as first being given a language, with words having meanings, and so on, which exists independently of its use in social life, and of it then being put to use by people in their social conduct. Such may indeed be the case with large tracts of social life, in which later generations inherit preformed 'conventional', 'ritual' or 'rule-governed' structures from their predecessors); and Harré's and Secord's 'dramaturgical standpoint' is well suited to their study. But one cannot appeal to such pre-established structures in accounting for the ultimate meaningfulness of behaviour. People are not just rule-users and rule-inheritors, they are also rule-makers; and as the rules governing social life must be made in the course of its actual conduct, and are only intelligible in relation to the context out of which they arise, rules as such cannot be the source of order in social life. There must be a non-rule-governed way in which people can be meaningful to one another, due to the intrinsic intentionality of all human action. Rules may be necessary if one is to perform in a socially skilful or competent manner, or to discourse upon or account for one's social conduct, without being necessary to meaningful conduct *per se*. For to perform incompetently is often still to perform in a socially meaningful way, as the parents of every child can attest.

There is thus another side to the ethogenic coin than the concern just with routinely available, preformed devices: there is the concern also with how such devices may be brought into existence in a society in the first place, with how they might be transmitted to new members of it, or with how once in existence they may be developed and changed – a concern with broadly 'developmental' issues (Gauld and Shotter, 1977) rather than with 'dramaturgical' ones. Here, rather than social competency being taken for granted, its very existence is rendered problematic. This does not, however, prevent our concern from still being an ethogenic one, for now we may be concerned with, among other things, the actual devices available in a society for transforming incompetency into competency. Unfortunately, we must add, ways of transforming competency into incompetency will interest us also (see Goffman, 1968, and Garfinkel, 1956, for discussions of 'status degradation ceremonies'). Such is the danger in 'attribution theory' in current social psychological research, as I shall argue in a moment, if it is taken too seriously as an account of how people actually do things in everyday life: in ignoring or distorting the actual processes necessary to people making and maintaining the social order in which they live, it may help to render them incompetent in its making and maintenance. Such concerns clearly relate to our interest in the previous section, in status-assertions and status-assignments.

I shall return to matters of status below; here I want to carry my 'developmental' concern with the use of non-preformed devices further. Clearly, such apparently routinely available devices as promises, loyalties, agreements, commands, accusations, excuses, endearments, insults, tellings, reportings, etc. are not things which endure in and of themselves as objectively existing entities in the world. Being quite invisible and intangible, and only existing 'intersubjectively' within certain patterns of interpersonal relation, they are constructed and reconstructed as and when required, to meet the changing exigencies of daily life. Existing only dynamically, they may exist explicitly at one moment and only implicitly the next. As such, they could just as easily fade from existence as remain in it. And one can easily imagine societies, or particular face-to-face relationships, in which, for instance, the social 'skills' of promising, uttering endearments or being loyal had been all but forgotten (as in Ik society – Turnbull, 1973), or alternately, elevated into high ritual skills (as in traditional Japan) – just as 'deference' is supposed to be disappearing from English society. The categories in terms of which people account for their relations to one another, and self-consciously think of themselves as having to one another, may change in many ways, from one moment in history to the next (Gergen, 1973).

However, as such categories wax and wane, one's personal actions do not necessarily gain or lose their immediate moral force. The effect of one person's action upon another, with regard to status assignments, status demands, and their satisfaction, does not depend upon that action as first being seen as falling into one or another category of action, and only then its precise moral content appreciated and acted upon. It may do; but especially in face-to-face exchanges people's actions derive their force very largely from the context in which they are used. Thus the raised eyebrow, for instance, is not usually first interpreted as either an insult, a question or an expression of surprise, and then reacted to. It is reacted to directly by the recipient stopping speaking, hesitating, attempting to explain, offering apologies, etc. In other words, people usually react to their immediate circumstances, rather than at one remove, to their categorization of them. As Harré (1981) points out, attribution and kindred processes are not necessarily modes of propositional reasoning; they are, I shall argue, only most unusually so, and are in fact usually 'done' as a mode of perceiving, as a practical hermeneutical process. Clearly, people may affect one another directly and immediately in a wholly non-propositional manner, understanding in detail how to use their actions to achieve particular effects in people much as carpenters and other artisans understand how to wield their tools in shaping the materials they work on (recall here Aristotle's distinction between 'theoretical, practical and productive sciences' discussed in chapter 2). In becoming socialized into a society, people clearly first learn its practices before they learn the theory (or the moral rhetoric) of them; they first learn how to act before learning how to account for or to justify their actions (see chapter 5). It is only later, when they already have some expertise in actual social manipulations, that as children they learn to discourse upon their conduct – and we all know of children who, even at six or seven years old, are able to argue: 'I didn't mean it. I wasn't being rude. That's not rude . . . anyway, she was rude first.' Moral practices initially precede the rhetoric of them, although later, of course, they come to include it.

Though my concerns below, then, will largely be with 'developmental' issues, and with the ways in which, in everyday life, we cope with the puzzles and difficulties they raise, my consideration of them will still be disciplined by the same considerations disciplining all ethogenic investigations: any accounts offered must attempt to render explicit, in one way or another according to one's purposes, what is already there implicitly in the actual nature of daily social life. Or, to put the matter another way, the explicit uses and functions proposed for people's actions must not distort or render inoperable the implicit uses or functions of those actions in making actual daily life work.

The dangers of such distortions are not unreal; the ethogenic concern with actual social practices in making and maintaining the social order is of crucial importance; it can serve to highlight particular concerns in and constraints upon people's actions not always present in laboratory experimentation. For instance, I have already argued that a part of what it is to attribute or ascribe moral autonomy to a person is to ascribe to them the right to make 'non-observational self-ascriptions', such as 'I don't believe you,' 'I've changed my mind,' 'I love you,' or 'I want coffee,' and to have them taken seriously even though there are no observational criteria to warrant them. The necessity to ascribe such a right or status to people does not arise out of anything empirically discoverable about people and their behaviour from a third-person point of view; indeed, empirically, even in daily life, people probably fail to take one another seriously on large numbers of occasions. The necessity that they do not always do so is one of a logical kind:, without the ascription of such rights to one another, the maintenance of a social order by those who are members of it – for who or what else is there to maintain it? – would be impossible (see chapter 8). Subjects in experimental studies are not always ascribed such a right; for the purposes of science, the normal moral order is often suspended.

It is for these reasons, and others still to be discussed, that although my 'developmental' approach may seem to be at odds in some ways with Harré's and Secord's 'dramaturgical standpoint' I still consider it to be essentially an ethogenic one, complementary to their standpoint, and far removed from that of attribution theorists.

An Hermeneutical Model for the 'Development' of Social Relationships

Classically, psychologists have tended to think of people's behaviour as something caused, as something which appeared as a final result of, or in 'response' to, a sequence of antecedent events; it was not something which people could, as social agents, in and of themselves just 'do'. Ethogenists do not want to reject this causal story in its entirety, for while they do want to assume that people themselves can be responsible for at least some of the things they can be observed as doing, they do not want to assume they can be responsible for them all. In general though, rather than being interested in the causes of people's actions, ethogenists are interested in the uses to which they may be put, as 'invitations' or 'opportunities' for future action, or as expressions serving to order or determine the nature of future social events. For people may use their actions either instrumentally, as means to an end, or expressively (Harré, 1979), in claiming a special status and thus a distinct kind of treatment by others.

While one may be puzzled as to what events, exactly, led up to the occurrence of a particular present event, another quite different kind of puzzlement is concerned with what, irrespective of the event's cause, the event means, what it is the means to, what it indicates, points to, specifies, etc. What is the person doing in doing it? Ethogenists would claim that a goodly number of the puzzles one faces in coping with everyday social behaviour are puzzles of the second kind rather than the first. And the aspect of accounting which interests me here is how, when the indications in people's actions are insufficiently clear as to the uses they intend them to serve, those indications are 'explained' or made clear. I am interested in what I shall call 'practical accounting', to compare it with 'rule or category related explanation'. An example will help to make clear what I mean here; consider the following episode:

They were walking very close now. Her hand brushed more than accidentally it seemed against his. He grasped it. She turned towards him, startled, eyebrows raised, a questioning look. He smiled and squeezed her hand more tightly in his. She turned away, head slightly bowed. He loosened his grip and silently her hand slipped away.

Here, the man 'explains' his gripping of her hand, I would claim, by his smile: he makes clear by it that he does not intend to drag her off by force, or to exert greater physical control over her, but just to initiate greater physical intimacy while still respecting her personhood – in response, perhaps, to her 'invitation'. And in so claiming, I am offering, of course, a rule- or category-related explanation, an account, the accuracy of which may only be properly established in negotiation with those to whom it is applied. Hence the initial uncertainty as to its precise nature. To continue with my account, I claim that she in turn 'explains' by her look and by the inactivity of her hand that either her 'invitation' was in fact accidental, not actually an invitation, or 'on second thoughts' she is withdrawing it. As a result of this exchange, he realizes that while she is still prepared to undertake an indefinite range of projects with him – her continued presence there indicates that, she is probably not at this stage prepared to investigate further with him the possibility of a more physical relationship between them. His status in relation to her in at least this sphere of activity is now, at least to a degree, somewhat more clear; and it will be a while before he takes her hand again. But as their relationship progresses, in the course of them explaining themselves (not their actions) to one another, what was a vague, global and unformulated mode of relationship is progressively shaped, specified or formulated at a practical level by them in their actual conduct of it. But how do actions like 'smiles' and 'failing to grip another's hand' serve to make more clear the intent in an earlier action; what is involved, practically, in them 'explaining' themselves to one another in this rather mindless fashion? For clearly, nothing like categorical perception and propositional reasoning was involved in the above episode.

Let me illustrate the workings of a practical hermeneutics, of practical accounting further with the following episode, selected almost at random, from Erica Jong's (1978, pp. 35–6) *How to Save Your Own Life*:

The door opens and Bennett appears. I continue to stare at my mail. Though we haven't seen each other in three days. I somehow have no desire to get up and face him. I force myself.

'Hi, darling', I say, embracing him. . . . He pecks me on the mouth and moves away unable to give himself to the greeting. He has missed me, but he hasn't yet seen his mail. It must be gotten out of the way like a bowel movement before screwing.

His rigidity angers me. Embracing him is like embracing a tailor's dummy.

'Aren't you really going to kiss me?' I ask.

He returns dutifully and kisses me very wetly (as he has ever since I ran off with a man whose kisses were wetter than his). He presses his pelvis against mine with consummate technique. I feel he is using craft. . . .

What is going on here?

Normally, implicit in the reunion of lovers (married or otherwise) is the anticipation that they will express a degree of enthusiasm for one another; this is evidenced in their concentration upon one another to the exclusion of outside concerns; it is a part of what it is to be lovers. In the above episode, Bennett enters and Isadora continues to stare at her mail. In a lover's world, this action is inappropriate; and it works to begin the specification of quite a different realm of next possible actions. Isadora draws back from its implications. But (as events depicted later show) too late: Bennett has already perceived her lack of enthusiasm, and attributed it to her hostility towards him. Already, the situation between them is specified as them not, in fact, being true lovers. In such circumstances her attempt to repair the situation with her forced 'Hi, darling' and her embrace jars; it fails to fit the circumstances. Yet they are still civilized, liberal, fair-minded people, aware of the patterns of privileges and obligations such people afford one another. So Bennett reciprocates her embrace. Not to have done so would indicate on his part a definite intention to destroy their relationship (and clearly he does not want to be the one responsible for any major change in its nature). Yet he reciprocates within the already specified context of them as no longer being true lovers (either that, or his stiffness is general, and he is always like it irrespective of his situation): whichever, it angers her. It means that he is withholding from her the right to affect him spontaneously; he has constituted his mode of being such that instead of being open and responsive to her every expression, charitably concerned to interpret them all as directed towards the enhancement of both their personalities, he becomes attentive to her in a much more circumspect way. Both he and Isadora recognize that, in general, criteria of appropriateness are socially constructed, and that between them they make the context within which what they do gets adjudged as being good or bad, as appropriate, or as legitimate or not. She, so far, has succeeded in constructing those terms. But in this case he tries (while veiling his motive) to get the lion's share of the making; he wants to control the terms in which they both must judge the appropriateness of their actions. Hence his dutiful wet kiss: it has the proper 'outward' form of a passionate embrace (but it is informed, Isadora feels, by self-controlled craft rather than self-abandoned desire); so she must initially at least treat it as sincere.

And so it continues: as a result of such exchanges, people make themselves, in relation to one another, what they are – or are allowed to be. The specification of Bennett's and Isadora's statuses now in relation to one another – the rights they are willing to accord one another and the duties they expect – as a result of the above exchange, are modified. And as their relationship progesses, in the course of them articulating themselves more clearly in relation to one another, what was a vague, global and unformulated initial mode of relationship is gradually and progressively shaped, specified, formulated or determined by them in the course of their actual conduct of it.

But how can a 'failure-to-look-up-immediately', a 'stiffness-in-an-embrace' serve to specify the intent in an action? What is involved, practically, in people meaning things to each other in this rather direct and immediate way? Clearly nothing like categorical perception or reasoning from general propositions can be involved: Bennett's and Isadora's own particular and unique person lives are being lived out here; each moment is unique; it is not a pre-programmed, routine career followed by all more or less identically.

A Hermeneutical Model of Social Perception

The primary process involved in such 'explanations' is not, I want to claim, anything like the inferential, 'information processing' procedures proposed by attribution theorists (e.g. Kelley, 1967; Jones and Nisbett, 1972) – nor for that matter does it illustrate the kind of 'mindlessness' studied by Langer (1978), in her experiments upon people performing highly practised skills, as if following a 'script' – but by a very different kind of process. For, to repeat, one is puzzled not by one's ignorance of what led up to a person's action, but by what their action actually *is*, by what it is that the person is actually trying to do in performing it – by their 'not-lookings', by their 'stiffenings', their 'smiling', their 'turning away', or their 'eyebrow-raising', and such like.

In modelling the process involved I shall draw, not from the natural sciences, but from 'hermeneutics', the discipline to do with the interpretation of (originally biblical) texts (Palmer, 1969; Ricoeur, 1970; C. Taylor, 1971; Gadamer, 1975; Gauld and Shotter, 1977). There, one's understanding of the precise part played or function served by a particular expression or piece of text is clarified by constructing (or reconstructing) the larger whole, its context, the wider scheme of things the author had in mind in expressing himself so; the construction being shaped and limited by having to accommodate the item of text in its every aspect. Thus the process does not begin with a pre-established order of things to which puzzling facts must be assimilated, with them being explained as particular instances of the general rules or laws constituting the order, with their uniqueness thus lost. It begins with the puzzling facts in their full individuality – known globally to be of a certain kind (text, facial expressions, or whatever), of course – and then proceeds by degrees in a back-and-forth process from part to whole, and from whole to part again, to articulate an order adapted to the undistorted accommodation of the initial facts. Or, to put the matter another way, in the process, an initially global, superficial and undifferentiated grasp of an action's meaning is transformed into a well-articulated grasp of its actual meaning. Rather than an inference from a pre-established order, the process involves the creation of a wholly new order of things within a globally determined whole. The action is understood by its being 'framed', one could say.

Interestingly (or ironically, for attribution theorists intent upon discussing all such processes as 'inference') one of the best sources to turn to for just such a discussion of the perceptual process is Heider (1958). Not only does he distinguish quite clearly between perception and inference, but he also describes perception as a 'constructive process' in which a 'whole' or 'unified structure' is produced within which events may be 'embedded', and which results in our 'direct experience of them as being the events they appear to be'. He distinguishes between perception and inference as follows:

> Perceiving is experienced as a direct contact with the environment; it is a means whereby objective facts enter the life space. . . . Then there is inference through which we arrive at conclusions on the basis of the existing contents of the life space. (Heider, 1958, pp. 15–16)

Then he goes on to describe (p. 34) the direct grasping of meanings in perception as follows:

> One might say psychological processes such as motives, intentions, sentiments, etc. are the core processes which manifest themselves in overt behaviour and expression in many ways. The manifestations are then directly grasped by p, the observer, in terms of these core

processes; they would otherwise remain undecipherable. By looking
through the mediation, p perceives the distant object, the psychological entities that bring consistency and meaning to the behaviour; p's
reaction is then to this meaning, not to the overt behaviour directly,
and this reaction is then carried back by the mediation to o, etc.

Motives, intentions, sentiments are not inner things represented in outer
behaviour, but are in the mediatory activity (joint action) going on between
individuals, and are directly perceived by those directly involved in it as
first-person actors and second-person recipients in that activity – only
third-person observers have to make inferences. As such, one might say,
motives, etc. exist less 'in' us than in the institutions between us.

And in these institutions, it is the rights, duties, privileges and obligations
of the different 'persons' (first, second, etc.) which seem to me to be of crucial
importance. The meaning of the episode between the man and the woman,
which I referred to in the previous section – written, of course, with an
'insider's' knowledge of it – was quite transparent to them both; for they
were making it transparent as they went along. And had the woman failed to
make her intent clear in her look and limp hand (or should it be, 'had the man
failed to grasp her intent'?), then she could have done something further,
perhaps said, 'Please . . . not yet', or whatever expressed her intention best.
For they are constructing in miniature, in a hermeneutical back and forth
between whole and part, a social order, a common world between them 'of
which neither is the sole creator' (Merleau-Ponty). What happened – where
they stood and where they now stand – although known to them, is
somewhat opaque to outsiders. They (outsiders) might infer, assimilating
the observed events to pre-established schemes, that indeed an offer of
physical intimacy was ventured and sadly rejected, but what that rejected
offer meant in the context of the man's and woman's whole relationship –
that it was the 100th such occasion in a 100-day ritual walk in the woods,
and thus the last, decisive rejection – would most certainly escape them.
Predicting at least the continuation of the relationship, they would be
surprised to observe that at the end of their walk, according to their pact, the
man and woman parted, never to meet again. But the ability of outsiders to
infer as much as they do comes, I suggest, from their ability to assimilate
what they observe to pre-established schemes constructed during their
direct involvements in exchanges as first and second persons.

Tellings and Reportings, Avowals and Appraisals

Returning now to consider the uses to which self-ascriptions may be put,
we can see now how on a hermeneutical model, but not an inferential one,

it is possible for people progressively to reveal to one another, in their interactions, what they have in mind. The procedure involved is, in fact, a 'developmental' one, involving processes of a differentiation and specification within a pre-existing but initially only globally articulated totality. In this context, it is the 'specificatory' nature of thought and action which is important (Gauld and Shotter, 1977, p. 127). Rommetveit (1976) has described just such a specificatory process also. He suggests that whatever is made known in verbal communications may be 'conceived of as expansions and/or modifications of a pre-established shared *Lebenswelt*', where a *Lebenswelt* constitutes, 'the initially shared, unquestioned, or free information onto which your very first question is nested or bound' (p. 206). And in discussing the progressive development of a shared social reality – using the example of a question-and-answer game – he goes on to point out that an 'answer at every successive stage is nested onto what at that particular stage has already been established as a shared social reality (or unquestioned, *free information*)' (p. 207). An interpretation of what a person might be doing in their behaviour can be arrived at, Rommetveit would suggest, by a systematic analysis of the way bound information is nested into already known free information.

I am now in a position to clarify further the distinction between telling and reporting, between explanation by revelation and explanation by description or classification, between the saying of such things as 'I want coffee' and statements like 'The coffee-spilling incident did indeed rather turn me against him' (the type of reports, presumably, figuring in Nisbett's and Bellow's (1977) experimentation, upon which I shall be commenting below). Ryle (1963) calls the two kinds of uses 'avowals' and 'appraisals' respectively, and I have already discussed their different prospective and retrospective uses. And it is important to emphasize that the distinction between them inheres *in the uses* to which people put their actions or statements, and not in the form of the statements themselves.

While the prototypical form of avowal may be first-person, present-tense, self-descriptive statements such as 'I am thinking,' many such statements may also serve equally well as reports, or combine both an appraisal with an avowal function, e.g. in saying 'The whisky's burning my mouth,' one might be saying 'I feel the whisky burning my mouth . . . help,' or 'I feel something (avowal); it is most likely the whisky which is burning my mouth (appraisal).' Furthermore, many other statements or actions not cast in anything like that form may, nonetheless, serve the same function: witness in this respect what the man and woman 'tell' one another in their actions.

It is in their 'logical grammars' (Ryle, 1963 that telling and reporting may be distinguished (Heaton, 1976)); that is, it is in what they imply for one's future action, being in receipt of one or the other of them, that is important. While statements or actions used as reports or appraisals may be checked out for their truth or falsity by reference to observational data, to establish whether the state of affairs depicted in the statement exists in reality, tellings or avowals are treated in quite another way. For someone to demand that I make available to them the particular observational data upon which I based my avowal 'I want coffee' would be distinctly odd, for in fact, as I mentioned before, there are none (Gauld and Shotter, 1977, p. 45). Such a someone may insist, and go so far as to say 'Look here, I've checked out your brain states and the rest of your physiology, and as far as I can see, you're just not in a coffee-wanting state at all.' To such a one I could still say, 'Nonetheless, I still want a cup of coffee . . . to 'punctuate' my day . . . to get a lift from the caffeine in it . . . to compare it with the last cup of coffee I had here . . . to be sociable as everyone else has one . . . to have something to throw in your face for being so boringly insistent . . . ', and so on.

While I may justify my wanting coffee by any one of a potentially infinite set of reasons appropriate to the context in which they are offered, it makes no sense to ask me to prove my wanting 'true', in terms of it having the proper antecedents. Thus in other words, avowals do not have to be warranted like reports, by reference to facts, to any antecedently or currently existing states of mind, body, or anything else, as they simply are not used like reports. They are used by people to reveal to others what they currently have in mind – what their needs, interests and desires are, etc. – in an attempt to order future action; executed now, they function to change the shared social reality within which the next action must occur. And rather than them being evaluated for their truth or falsity, as depicting already existing states of affairs, avowals may be evaluated for, say, the degree of sincerity with which they are uttered: i.e. whether the use claimed for them by the one performing them is indeed the use they actually intend them to have, for people may have altogether different, more hidden intentions than those they reveal in their performances. For instance, I cannot claim to be sincere in wanting coffee if immediately it is offered me I either ignore the offer, or I accept it but put the cup down again instantly, and ignore its existence from that moment on – unless, that is, I wanted the coffee to perform some kind of bizarre insult upon those involved in providing it for me. Thus, while reportings may be evaluated as to whether they are true depictions, and that is their use to depict and describe, avowals require evaluating much more broadly as to whether their apparent use is their true or sincere usage – something which is only revealed as the actions following from them progressively unfold.

In Criticism of Attribution Theory: The Rights and Duties
of Persons

At the heart of attribution theory is the assumption that 'the person-perceiver's fundamental task is to interpret or infer the causal antecedents of action' (Jones and Davis, 1965, p. 200). Given my views expressed above, it is clear that to the extent that such an assumption is considered to be fundamental, I think that it is wrong. In everyday social life the person-perceiver's fundamental task is hardly ever that of inferring the causal antecedents of action, but that of attempting to grasp what in their actions people have in mind – a task of quite a different kind: a hermeneutical task conducted from a second-person standpoint, rather than an inferential task from a third-person standpoint. On most occasions, person-perceivers are successful in their task; only occasionally do we fail to grasp quite what it is that people are up to in their actions. And it is most unusual for people's actions to be so bizarre that one can perceive no sense in them at all; only then does one resort to a causal analysis, as to what might have produced such a disturbance in normality, in the attempt to restore it (Peters, 1958; R. Taylor, 1966). Thus normally, I am claiming, people quite literally 'explain' what their actions are, in the course of their performances, each action in an exchange serving to clarify the actions preceding it.

The need for people to know what their own and one another's actions are, arises, I would claim, out of the fact that the world of everyday life is a 'moral world', which works in terms of people's rights and duties as members of a society. Within it people have a right to question the legitimacy of one another's actions, and to ask whether they are appropriately grounded in, or are a proper part of, the society's shared social reality; just as by the same token everyone also has a duty to ensure the legitimacy of their actions.

As in many other experimental studies in psychology, the normal moral order implicit in daily life is either suspended or considerably modified in studies by attribution theorists. Nonetheless, it is clearly enjoying a great vogue at the moment in claiming to meet the demand for a psychology more appropriate to daily life. As one exponent (Ross, 1977) of it has claimed:

> The current ascendancy of attribution theory in social psychology culminates a long struggle to upgrade that discipline's conception of man. No longer the stimulus-response (S–R) automaton of radical behaviourism, promoted beyond the rank of information processor

and cognitive consistency seeker, psychological man has at last been
awarded a status equal to that of the scientist who investigates him.

It is the claim that the struggle is over that I wish to contest, that its
culmination in people being awarded the status of scientists is an
achievement to be applauded. While such a status carries with it certain
rights – the right to question whether things are what they seem, etc. – it
also entails certain duties – to act only in relation to logical and explicitly
formulated theories, for instance. Both such rights and duties are quite
different from those in ordinary daily life, in which ordinarily, things are
what they seem to be, and people only account for things in unquestioned,
taken-for-granted terms. To award ordinary people the status of scientists,
from, perhaps, an egalitarian desire to attribute to everyone the ability to
conduct the supposedly most highly valued activity in our time, is, I think,
misplaced; it is a status which is clearly inimical in many respects to the
normal living of everyday life; a quite different moral order is involved.
Attribution theorists fail to take such 'moral' issues into account. In, for
instance, failing to distinguish between tellings and reportings, between
the prospective and the retrospective functions of self-descriptions, and in
treating them all as reportings, they have failed (while claiming exactly the
opposite) to accord the same social status to their subjects as
themselves – i.e. the right to make first-person avowals.
    An actual social order does not just allow for the existence of socially
autonomous individuals, with the right to make such avowals, such
'nonobservational self-ascriptions'; it demands it. If a social order is to
endure, then of necessity – for human beings are not born with, as far as
we can tell, any particular species-specific way of life – it must be possible
for the elements within it, who conduct it, to identify transgressions of it,
and for the transgressors to help make restitution. The elements of the
order, unlike atoms, have no intrinsic valencies; they must maintain their
social order by their own efforts. Without such individually responsible
and accountable elements, without in fact persons, a social order would
fall apart.
    As I argued in the last chapter, other (transpersonal) unities would not
do. In the moral world of everyday life, 'unities' cannot normally be
accorded any moral unity or autonomy, for in practice, the joint action to
which they would give rise is unaccountable (to be accorded the legal
status of a person, social institutions have to be 'properly constituted',
with clear lines of accountability, responsibility, etc.). Joint acts are
produced by people interlacing their actions in with those of others, thus
what they each intend and what is actually produced between them may be
widely discrepant. In such genuinely social activity, people may remain

deeply ignorant as to what it is, really, they are doing (or why), not because the 'scripts', etc., supposedly in them somewhere are too vague, or too well practised (Langer, 1978), or too deeply buried in them to bring out into the light of day, but because the formative influences shaping their conduct are not entirely there in them to be brought out. Some important influences exist in the situations between people. Other people's actions are often just as much a formative influence in determining what people do as anything from solely within themselves. Joint action thus raises difficulties for the maintenance of a moral order and requires special treatment: its occurrence is either minimized or prevented, or groups of people functioning as unities in society at large must, by law, organize themselves such that they *are* accountable, and the group then counts legally as a person.

Crucial to the conduct of daily life, then, are the rights and duties, privileges and obligations of human beings as persons. The concept of persons able to take responsibility for their actions is necessary to the existence of a self-maintaining social order, just as a rational, social order is necessary to people conferring such autonomy upon one another – the right to make unsupported self-ascriptions and the duty to be accountable for them. It is precisely to these factors that attribution theorists, and many other social psychologists concerned with 'theory relevant' research, pay little attention: the factors necessary to the reproduction of social orders.

The 'Findings' of Attribution Theorists: Telling More Than We Can Report

Nowhere are the unfortunate consequences of this failure made more apparent than in implications drawn from work by Nisbett and Wilson (1977) and Nisbett and Bellows (1977). They report studies in which people, after having done something within the context of an experimental manipulation, are asked to report upon what seemed to have 'caused' what they did. The same general result was obtained time and again: people seemed unable to give any accurate reports on factors which quite clearly influenced their behaviour.

As they report it, such a result seems surprising, especially so, for as Nisbett and Wilson (p. 232) are at pains to point out, it is 'obvious to anyone who has ever questioned a subject about the reasons for his behaviour or evaluations, that people readily answer such questions'. But, given their results, it would seem that we should put very little trust in what people say; the very title of their paper – 'Telling more that we can know' – suggests that the idea that people themselves are the best authority upon what they themselves think, feel, need, etc. is suspect. As

Nisbett and Bellows (1977, p. 624) conclude, 'it should be clear that the present findings raise serious methodological questions concerning the validity of subject reports as a tool of social science investigation.'

But how should we react to these 'findings'? Firstly, when the confusing and misleading language in which they are reported is clarified – the confusion between telling and reporting, reasons and causes, knowing and believing, and suchlike – the results are, in one sense, I think, trivial. They merely report once again the already well-known fact that while we do many things in social life, intelligently and intelligibly, in quite skilful ways, it is quite normal not to be able to report upon how we do them. Practice, in many spheres of social life, normally precedes the theory of it (see chapter 5). To assume otherwise is to believe in what Ryle calls the 'intellectualist legend', the crucial objection to which is this: if execution of an intelligent act requires the execution of some prior intelligent theorizing to provide the plan for the action, then either such theorizing itself is unplanned, in which case it cannot be intelligent, or it is conducted by reference to a plan fixed in advance, which again is not intelligent. We are not ordinarily able to report on our own inner workings.

Nisbett and his associates only succeed in surprising us by their results by misleading us into thinking that they are talking about tellings as well as reportings, and by making us feel that we have no right to be telling people all over the place about ourselves, as we cannot be trusted to be accurate. If that really were the case, why should we trust them when they say what their results were?[1] The fact is, contrary to what Nisbett and Bellows fear about the validity of subject 'reports' as a tool for social scientific research, there is nothing else for the social scientist to use except his subjects' avowals – what they tell us they see, feel, want, believe, dream, etc. – for these are the 'tools' they use in their 'makings'.

Furthermore, by suggesting that we should sell our right to mean what we say, and to have what we say taken seriously, for a mess of causal theorizing, Nisbett and his associates obscure the true character of the phenomenon under study; namely, its intrinsically social nature. Their whole approach leads them to suggest that it is the individual who is unaware of the 'causal' processes which, going on inside him or her somewhere, influences his or her behaviour; as if with special 'awareness training' or suchlike, he or she could become aware of them. Another interpretation of Nisbett and his colleagues' results might be that people's unawareness stems from the fact that the experimental setting is a genuine social situation in which subjects must interlace their actions in with aspects of the situation not under their control, aspects of it due to other people, the experimenters in fact. In such circumstances, the outcome is a product of joint action, and as such cannot be linked by individuals to any specific intentions of theirs, hence the inability of individuals properly to account for it. The individuals involved in joint action are unaware of how its outcome is produced because, to repeat, it is not a process going on wholly within them; it is something shared between them and others.

A paradigm example here is the movement of the wineglass on the Ouija board. Clearly it does not move unless people's fingers are on it. But so strong is the conviction that its movements cannot be traced back to any intentions of the people there present – while its movements nonetheless display intelligence – that they are attributed often to an external 'spirit', acting through the medium of the people involved. The 'workings' of such social processes as these, by their very nature, are not subjectively experienced by the individuals involved in them, for the workings are spread out in the processes going on between them – hence their 'invisibility', and the possibility of people finding themselves entrapped within mental 'prisons' of their own devising.

While I can be held responsible for what I avow of myself – for what I write here, for instance, in saying, 'I think attribution theorists are wrong' – it is unreasonable to expect me to be able to account for things to which I have only partially contributed; nor should I (or any other individual) be accorded the moral right to do so. The meanings, the usages served by the outcomes of joint action are matters for negotiation (Harré and Secord, 1972).

Concepts and People's Control of Their Own Behaviour

Attribution theorists have, however, turned up some interesting and important results, few more so, I think, than those demonstrating the apparent 'cognitive' control of emotional and other physiological and motivational factors: examples here are the 'misattribution studies' of Valins and Ray (1967) and Storms and Nisbett (1970), in which people are misled into attributing their fear, or their insomnia, to other than their seemingly original sources, thus changing the degree of their severity – one is reminded here of Levi-Strauss's (1963)[2] story of how, in a similar 'reattribution' procedure, a shaman helps a woman through a difficult childbirth. Given such remarkable results, what precisely am I complaining about when I say (*a*) that attribution theorists obscure the real nature of social processes; and (*b*) that they fall foul of the 'intellectualist legend'? How can such misguided people produce such effective results? Because, as it is the purpose of this whole book to argue, there are other than empirical methods for producing effective results in the social world; there are 'practical' methods too, methods for changing people in their being.

Something which makes a social world quite different from a physical world of matter in blind but lawful motion.

People can be changed in their being, as the persons they are, by telling them things; as a result their 'world', so to speak, changes. Only if a person's world remains unchanged is a report about events within it of any use. Hence the prospective nature of tellings and the retrospective nature of reports. Let me extend this point by asking which of the two functions, prospective telling or retrospective reporting, attribution theory itself serves. When looked at in this way it becomes clear, I think that the studies by attribution theorists – and indeed many other studies in experimental social psychology – founder in a deep misunderstanding of the difference between the empirical and non-empirical aspects of 'experimentation' in the social sciences (see chapters 1 and 2). The task of elucidating the language and the important concepts in terms of which we actually conduct our daily social life is not one in which experimentation need play a primary part, for it is not primarily a task of an empirical kind; it is a conceptual or non-empirical one. As Heider (1958, p. 4) remarks:

we shall not attain a conceptual framework by collecting more experimental results. . . . It is our belief that in the field of interpersonal relations, we have a great deal of empirical knowledge already, and that we can arrive at systematic understanding and crucial experiments more rapidly by attempting to clarify theory.

Such non-empirical research is required in social psychology, and this is the purpose of the practical-descriptive approach I am proposing. But at the moment both non-empirical and empirical research are confounded.

10

Social Accountability and Images of Selfhood

The main drift of what I want to argue here is this: that in our attempts to understand ourselves, we have been somewhat blind to the fact that in our everyday lives we are all embedded within a social order which morally we must continually reproduce (and perhaps to an extent transform) in all of the mundane activities we perform from our 'place', 'position' or status within it. We have instead concentrated far too much attention upon the isolated individual. As a result, we have failed to study the sense-making procedures made available to us by the social order (or orders) into which we have been socialized; procedures which have their provenance in the history of our culture. Such procedures are, I want to argue, constitutive of people's social being in a very deep way. For among other things, they enable the members of a social order, not only to account for themselves to themselves and to one another, when required to do so, but also very generally, to act routinely in an accountable manner – their actions informed in the course of their performance by such procedures. Besides enabling accountable action, such procedures also work to constrain members in what they can say and do. They put limits upon their behaviour, for people must talk and act only in ways which are intelligible and legitimate within their society, and which are appropriate to their momentary position (or status) as the persons they are within it.

Essentially what I shall be arguing, then, is that our understanding and our experience of our reality is constituted for us very largely by the ways in which we must talk in our attempts (to put it almost tautologically) to account for it. Where our experience and understanding of ourselves is a part of that reality; and we must talk about it and ourselves in certain limited ways, to meet the demands placed upon us by our status as responsible members of our society. However, if our ways of talking are limited in any way, then our understanding and experience of ourselves and our reality will, by the same token, be limited also. It is in particular the issue of 'entrapment' (Stolzenberg, 1978; see also the Epilogue to this book), or 'trained incapacity' (as Veblen called it) that concerns me here; the fact that our current ways of sense-making prevent us from experiencing and understanding certain aspects of ourselves. Indeed, as an aspect of the blindness induced by our current individualistic modes of accountability – which, as I have said, has led us to ignore what is made available to us by our social context for our use within it – we have also failed to attribute sufficient significance to the second-person standpoint in life, the standpoint from which the meanings of first-person actors are perceived and understood as such. Rather, we have concentrated almost wholly upon the viewpoint of the third-person, external observer; the position from which an actor's behaviour is seen only as a sequence of movements.

To an extent, to compensate for this neglect, what I have to say here will be a disquisition upon 'you', upon what it is to be the recipient of the actions of a first person and to create within oneself meanings on the basis of 'instructions' received from another person – from someone who is recognizably distinct, mentally, from oneself, and who does not simply reflect oneself back to oneself as if in a mirror. Later, in discussing the nature of 'you', I will be drawing upon Paul Weiss's (1980) book *You, I, and the Others*, both to elaborate this second aspect of my thesis – the importance of the second-person status – and at the same time to provide a case in point for its first aspect: the possible biases and partialities inherent in our own accounts of ourselves, even those like Weiss's avowedly aimed at correcting those self-same partialities. In particular, I shall be referring to Weiss's over-use of spatial language, and under-use of temporal language in his account, and how this leads him ultimately to undervalue the social and historical factors shaping people's experiences. Such incapacities – ones which are rooted in our own self-definitions, and hence in what we are to ourselves – are not easy to overcome. The social requirement of always attempting to be intelligible and legitimate necessitates making use of the self-same sense-making procedures one wishes to question.

Space-talk and Time-talk in Our Talk About Mental Processes

To alert you right from the start to the biases in our linguistic usages, let me remind you of the space-talk we all use and take for granted in talking about mental activities – and point out some time-talk alternatives.

Recently, both Jaynes (1979) and Lakoff and Johnson (1980) have documented the visual and spatial metaphors we all use in accounting for psychological phenomena (and they are rife, unavoidably so, in my account here). We 'see' solutions to problems, the best of which may be 'brilliant', and the person producing them 'bright' and 'clear-headed' as opposed to being 'dull' or 'dim'. These words are all metaphors, and the 'mind-space' to which they apply is a metaphor of actual space. 'In' our minds we can 'approach' a problem, perhaps from some 'viewpoint' within a 'perspective'; the problem may be in the 'back' or 'inner recesses' of our mind, 'private' and 'inaccessible', or 'unreachable' (Weiss talks about 'you' and 'me', etc. in these terms, as we shall see). Or perhaps we can 'point out' precisely what must be 'understood', i.e. exactly what the matter in question should 'stand under', and in doing so achieve a 'common ground' with other people. 'Introspecting', 'looking' at my ideas 'in my head', 'turning them over in my mind', I attempt to 'fit' or 'arrange' them to suit my circumstances. And so on. . . . As Lakoff and Johnson (1980, p. 5) say: 'The essence of metaphor is understanding and experiencing one thing in terms of another.' This was also essentially the description of the metaphorical offered by I. A. Richards (1936), in which he included all 'those processes in which we perceive or think or feel about one thing in terms of another'; or as Ryle (1963, p. 10) says about a myth: 'It is the presentation of facts belonging to one category in the idioms appropriate to another.'

There is both a superficial and a deep sense in which one can respond to these accounts of the metaphorical nature of descriptions of mental activities. (1) Superficially, one can respond as Lakoff and Johnson may at first seem to: they give examples of what they call structural metaphors – like TIME IS MONEY (Don't *waste* time; That will *save* time) – in which one concept is structured by another; orientational metaphors – like CONSCIOUS IS UP; UNCONSCIOUS IS DOWN (Wake *up*; He's *under* hypnosis; He *sank* into a coma) – in which whole systems of concepts are organized spatially; container metaphors – like MIND IS A CONTAINER (It's *in* my mind) – in which less clearly delineated concepts are brought within boundaries; and ontological metaphors – like THE MIND IS A MACHINE (My mind just isn't *operating* today) – which work to structure unbounded and non-material aspects of our experience as if they were entities or substances. In all these instances, a shifting or displacement of words from one context of usage to another works to give shape or form to experiences which they otherwise would lack.

(2) But Lakoff and Johnson make a deeper claim: 'that metaphor is pervasive in everyday life. Our ordinary conceptual system, in terms of which we both think and act, is fundamentally metaphorical in nature'

(1980, p. 3). So responding now more deeply to the definitions of the metaphorical given above, I think that we can in fact say that expressing anything linguistically involves metaphorical processes (and metonymical part-whole processes also – see later, and also note 3, chapter 6); for essentially what is involved is a process of ascribing or attributing shape or form to something (which is already partially specified) by specifying it further; by using in fact the sense-making procedures available to one in one's society to lend it intelligible and legitimate form. This is what happens, I suggest, when events, situations or states of affairs in the world are perceived, understood, described or accounted for in linguistic terms. Primarily vague, but not wholly unspecified states of affairs or processes, are specified further, in this or that particular way, within a medium of communication – according to the particular requirements of that medium of communication, which in the case of language is the reproduction of the dominant social order. This is the most important point in all that follows. It is the fact that a discourse constitutes in its conduct both a certain social order and a corresponding psychological make-up in those who are conducting it, which prevents them from fully describing the nature of the world in which they operate. For their purpose is not primarily to represent the world but to co-ordinate social action.

We can be empowered by being embedded in such discourses; we can be enabled both in controlling ourselves as well as the 'worlds' we make for ourselves to live in. But we can be entrapped and disabled by our immersion in them also. As Nelson Goodman (1972, p. 24) says in his justly celebrated paper 'The way the world is',

> Philosophers sometimes mistake features of the discourse for features of the subject of the discourse. We seldom conclude that the world consists of words just because a true description of it does, but we sometimes suppose that the structure of the world is the same as the structure of the description.

In other words, if we think that the metaphorical only exists where it is actually recognized as such – where there is a clear shifting or displacement in the use of words – then the metaphorical nature of *all* our descriptions of the world will remain hidden, and will work to mislead and bewilder us.

This is the case, I suggest, currently: for almost all our ways of communicating about mental events and processes are rooted in a wholly spatial conception of the nature of the world; and our talk about 'talk' is biased in this way also. Michael Reddy (1979) has discussed the 'conduit metaphor' – which still seems to inform a good deal of our talk about how talking works – suggesting that it works to transfer already well-formed objects of thought from one location to another. Now it is not to the fact that our talk about talk is metaphorical rather than literal that Reddy objects, for he also, like Lakoff and Johnson, accepts the all-pervasive metaphorical character of language. It is the current historical inappropriateness of the conduit metaphor that concerns him, and he offers as an alternative the 'toolmakers paradigm'; which is essentially the paradigm I have already been using above, i.e. that communication has an active formative function, working to specify further something already partially specified. What Reddy adds, which I have not yet made clear, is that, of course, such a specificatory procedure may still leave the situation open to yet further specification; in other words, leave it incompletely specified, and communication may fail because of that. In fact, in this paradigm, less than perfect communication is the normal state of affairs.

The 'conduit metaphor' may have been appropriate in more socially settled times, in which everyone knew their place and function, and 'success without an effort after meaning' (because all meanings could easily be clearly specified) was the usual or natural state of affairs in communication. Now, in our less socially settled times, when both people and their circumstances are changeable, the formative aspect of speech comes to the fore (and the degree to which it draws upon already structured forms retires into the background), and the making of less than complete sense and failures of communication, Reddy points out, are a much more common occurrence – the natural state of affairs in fact. Thus on this model the taken-for-granted nature of our communications becomes problematic, dependent upon certain conditions; if they do not obtain, communication breaks down.

In discussing language in this way, Reddy switches in fact from a spatially rooted metaphor to one rooted in an essentially temporal or 'form-producing' process. In such a temporalized scheme of things, concerned with activities rather than with things, described in terms of verbs rather than nouns, there can be no structures-at-an-instant, for there are in nature so conceived no instantaneous activities. One must speak of the regions and moments of a 'time–space' (see chapter 11 for an extended discussion of such processes).

I have mentioned such 'form-producing' processes here, because later, in talking of our experience of other persons, of us as second persons experiencing first persons, I want to refer to its 'developmental' nature, to the fact that although our knowledge of them is always open to further development, it nonetheless has a style to it. That is, although open to further specification, the specification it is open to is not unlimited; the ways in which it can be further specified are themselves already specified, there are only certain ways in which the structures can be developed further. Thus, as we shall see, our knowledge of others has a hermeneutical quality to it. Let me turn now, though, to the nature of our embedding in a social order, and to the nature of the requirement that we reproduce that order in all our transactions with one another.

Language and Social Orders

Many workers have argued, among them William James (1890), C. H. Cooley (1902) and G. H. Mead (1934), that if we are to study ourselves we must study the selves within us – as if it is not we as the whole persons we are who execute our own acts, but that there is an inner self or selves which cause us to act as we do. I think that this view is mistaken and misleading in many important ways: not least in the overly individualistic view of human self-development it promotes – a view I have come to as a result of attempting to conceptualize developmental processes in child develop-ment (see Part I). It suggests that not just adults, but children also can be 'developmentally self-sufficient' in the sense that the provenance for their development is to be found wholly within their selves, and that if they fail to develop, the failure is theirs. Thus it diverts attention away from the access they require to resources only available to them in their social environment – namely, to the different sense-making procedures it con-tains within its different regions, procedures they cannot learn unless they can actively participate in the social practices in which they are used.

It is thus that I want to claim that, in order to be me, I need you; all 'I's' need 'you's' if they are ever to appear in the world to themselves as 'me's', and to possess well-defined social identities, as well as acquiring what might be called the 'ontological skills' required to be first, second and third persons, to be speakers, listeners, spectators, etc., when appropriate. There is more to ourselves than just an 'I' and a 'me' (Mead, 1934). (Besides 'you's', we also need 'he's', 'she's' and 'they's', as well as 'we's', if we are to become self-conscious and able to discourse upon, and deliberate upon, our own situation in the world – as Weiss makes very clear.) 'I's' need 'you's'; I need you now as a reader of this text, because you now constitute for me an aspect of a social order into which I must 'direct' my activities, into which I must 'fit' what I write; for what I write depends upon the 'reality' I sense myself as writing into. 'You' afford me (in a Gibsonian sense) a set of structured barriers and opportunities, a set of constraints and enablements, which inform what I write. If I were to fail to honour them in an intelligible and legitimate way, then we could both (you and I) be placed in a difficult position; and someone's (an editor's) creative improvisation would be required to repair the situation and reinstitute a proper order, one in which once again routine procedures of sense-making were operative.

What this means is, I think, that if our experience and understanding of ourselves is something which is produced and reproduced (and possibly transformed) within the continuous flow of activity between us, and if the kinds of opportunities available to us for so acting are limited, then our experience and understanding of ourselves will be limited also. And such opportunities clearly *are* limited in at least two essential ways: (1) they are limited in the sense of being differentially distributed throughout a social order, so that certain 'places', 'positions' or statuses within it offer more opportunities for self-development than others – to such an extent that I do not think that it is going too far to suggest that there is a 'political economy of selfhood' at work here, differentially controlling the access to the 'developmental opportunities' people provide one another (as I have mentioned in chapter 7).

(2) Our oportunities are also limited, however, in a much more general way. They are limited by the fact that, within any social order, there is a style of being in common to everyone, for everyone must refer to the same 'vocabulary of motives' in accounting (when required to do so) for those of their actions 'situated' within that order; they must make sense of their actions in the taken-for-granted ways available to them in their social order. And the upshot of the view that I am proposing – that our 'commonsense' ideas of ourselves, of who and what 'we' *are*, are grounded in the activities required of us to reproduce our social order – is that our ideas about ourselves can all too easily be false. Or at least, they can be partial or biased ideas. We can come to perceive and experience ourselves as being quite other than what we actually are – i.e. we can face Goodman's problem at a very deep level: we can mistake features of the discourse about ourselves as being features truly of ourselves, simpliciter, rather than features of ourselves we constitute only within our discourses.

Let me illustrate the constitutive process at work by taking the current case in point: whether we do or do not have selves within us, as entities in some way distinct from ourselves as persons. If intuitively we feel it necessary in organizing and accounting for our experiences to refer to 'a self', that may very well be because we must, to repeat the formula, 'account for ourselves to ourselves in a way which is intelligible and legitimate within our dominant social order' – using the procedures of sense-making it allows. Now clearly, at the moment, the dominant order is an 'individualistic' and 'scientific' one: only talk about causal processes from a third-person, external-observer point of view is officially author-ized, and scant value is placed upon talk about people's meanings from a second-person audience position. That is 'subjective' whereas 'objectivity' is valued – the 'social accountability' view is neither, by the way, and treats both (subjectivity and objectivity) as simply 'ways of talking'. The individualistic, atomistic vision of reality implicit in our current accounting practices requires us to locate the causes of people's actions in space somewhere, in people themselves, or in their environment (rather than allowing such influences to be spread out in a 'non-locatable' way in their world at large, the view which implicitly I am arguing for here – and see also chapter 11). Thus within such an order, our current dominant order, our way of accounting for ourselves to ourselves does *not* suggest to us that it is we ourselves who act (because as agents we simply have the power to do so), nor does it suggest to us that we can act just as much to fit ourselves into the opportunities offered us by our situation as out of our own plans and desires to fit our situation to ourselves. We seem forced to postulate a mysterious other self which does things in us, for us, with us ourselves as its beneficiaries, so to speak. Our current modes of accountability are such that it seems we *must* to talk about ourselves in that way – we are entrapped; we cannot formulate within the categories of third-person, external-observer-causal-talk, a forceful and intelligible doubt about the source of our actions being in our 'self' or one of our 'selves'.

Just to reinforce this point, let me refer briefly to the description given by David Sudnow (1978) of his execution of a skilled activity, executed completely unselfconsciously. Sudnow, an ethnomethodologist, describes, after a seven-year effort to learn to play jazz-piano in a genuinely improvisatory way, his experience of himself thus:

> From an upright posture I look down and see my fingers, and my looking is so differently related to the work of my fingers, in contrast to former modes of 'hookup', that I see things I never saw before. . . .
> I see my hands for the first time now as 'jazz piano player's hands', and at times, when I expressly think about it, one sense I have from my vantage point looking down is that the fingers are making music all by themselves. (p. xiii)

It is a view that leaves Sudnow completely puzzled as to the nature of his 'self', for in genuine improvisation he says:

> I choose places to go, in what this speaking I finds as miraculous ways, miraculous merely against the background of my history with the piano, and a history of other speakings that seem to have little room for a conception that would not partionalize 'my' body in some way. (p. 152)

For it is as if he, so to speak (and one's manner of speaking is everything here), is inhabited by a new 'I' or 'self', a 'jazz-making-self' which performs while his 'speaking-self', so to speak, looks on as a spectator.

Our current ways of speaking – both about things in the world as well as about ourselves – are such that, given Sudnow's experiences, he is entrapped, not just into conceiving of himself as at least two selves in the same body – one which plays and another which watches and talks but which has no linguistic access to how he executes his performances – but into actually being for all practical purposes two such selves. For, to put my 'social accountability' point in a slightly different way, given that our language is not just for us a system within which to describe things, but is a medium for actually 'doing' things through communication with others, the linguistic reality within which Sudnow is embedded (along with ourselves) is such that 'he' (his speaking self) knows of no practical or socially intelligible way of formulating any doubt about such a conclusion – even though his failure to do so leaves him (and us) bewildered. That is how he must look upon himself if he is to be a competent member of his (and our) society – such an irrefutable, indubitable system of 'presuppositions' of this kind may still nonetheless be demonstrably misleading and inadequate, as we shall see, if we are prepared to treat them historically and anthropologically (Shotter, 1982).

Accounting

Our accounting practices are deeply embedded in our everyday activities. But people do not just happen, passively, to act in an accountable manner and to perceive events in accountable terms; their procedures of talking and listening are methodical. They act so as to make their behaviour accountable; it is, says Garfinkel (1967, p. 1), 'an endless, ongoing, contingent accomplishment'; and it is achieved by the use of certain methods and procedures which, says Garfinkel (p. 10), are experienced as 'unproblematic . . . and are known only in the doing which is done skilfully, reliably, uniformly, with enormous standardization and as an unaccountable matter'. We attend *from* the methods and procedures *to* the results they achieve, as Polanyi (1967) would put it in his 'structure of tacit knowing'; we become aware of the particulars of the procedures only to the extent that they work to specify an outcome.

People's normal behaviour is routinely 'accountable' in the sense that it is intelligible and legitimate without question. An 'account' as such is only required of someone if, for some reason, their behaviour is untoward. Then it must be excused or justified (Scott and Lyman, 1968), and the untoward action given a fitting place in the social order as a result. In other words, an account of an activity or state of affairs is itself a special kind of social activity which works, if it works at all, as an aid to perception, to render an otherwise indeterminate flow of activity recognizable as a sequence of commonplace events – the account may, of course, be retrospective, prospective or simultaneous (Harré and Secord, 1972). Whichever, to work in this way, as an aid to perception, the talk must have a certain function: it must instruct people in how to do something; it must instruct them in the method or procedure of doing it; and accounts which fail to do this will, literally, be 'pointless', and their content will be vacuous. As C. W. Mills (1940) put it, some years before Wittgenstein noted the same point: 'Rather than expressing something which is prior and in the person, language is taken by other persons as an indicator of future actions' (p. 162). And in particular, motive accounts, said Mills (p. 163), 'do not denote any elements 'in' individuals. They stand for anticipated situational consequences of questioned conduct.' Language is used to achieve concerted social action. And utterances indicate metonymically, as part to whole, what a person is trying to do in the activity they were observed as doing; they (the utterances) work to specify the larger whole (the 'world') in which such an activity can play its proper part. Accounting, then, in this account of it, is the activity in which people, methodically, by the use of established 'but as yet unaccounted for' accounting practices embedded in their everyday activities, actively *make* themselves accountable to one another. And it is a research activity, of course, to discover what these 'as yet unaccounted for' practices are – as Garfinkel points out.

Theories, Models and Accounts

Such accounting practices are constitutive of everyday life and of everything which goes on within it. As such, they are fundamental to the conduct of science itself. It will thus be instructive to contrast everyday accounting procedures with explanatory procedures in science.

Science, it is claimed, is concerned with achieving true knowledge of natural phenomena. It is generally taken as proceeding in terms of the formulation and empirical testing of theories or models, where a theory or model is taken as representing a true state of affairs to the extent that, by its use, one can predict or control an expected outcome. Knowledge arrived at in this way is often taken as a basic indubitable truth about the world in which we live, one upon which we should base our actions and our policy making. This view – as to the power of scientific modes of investigation – is clearly partial and limited, however. For the conduct of science rests upon the prior possession by all of us of a much more basic form of knowledge – let me call it simply 'practical common sense' knowledge – in terms of which scientific activities are conducted, and in terms of which they must make sense. Theories do not reach down and anchor themselves in a fundamentally neutral, physical reality (Stapp, 1972) – indeed, whenever we speak of atoms and molecules, and the laws of nature, we are speaking of what we mean, by the expressions 'atoms', 'molecules' and 'laws of nature' (Winch, 1958); they are all expressions associated with a particular way of 'seeing' the world and of manipulating it by the means it provides. Theories are grounded, as Kuhn (1962) makes clear, in the activities which give research practices their reproducability: namely, their accountability amongst those conducting them.

But notice how this accountability is achieved. Participants begin by appreciating how, given the practical phenomena confronting them, theoretical categories can be used to constitute them as events of a recognizable kind – the research practice provides an account as to how a theory should be used and applied (Stapp, 1972). Such categories are used as an unquestioned (and unquestionable) resource in organizing one's perception of events within the research paradigm (Hanson, 1958). And it is in this sense that one is entrapped: for by conducting all one's further activities in terms of a set of categories – grasped by, as Stolzenberg (1978) puts it, 'initial acts of acceptance as such in the domain of ordinary language use', and then suspended from all further doubt – necessitates one having to assimilate all further activities to a pre-established set of categories. There is no possibility of a hermeneutical development of new categories; the transformation of one's perceptual categories in the course of dialogue is denied. Consider, by comparison, the process of listening to an account: if the facts so far are unsatisfactory, incomplete or even bewildering, one waits for later facts and uses them in an attempt to decide the sense of the earlier ones; what sense there is to be found is not decided beforehand, but is discovered in the course of the exchange within which the account is offered.

In fact, to give a proper account of what something is, of what it is to be a person, say, neither a theory nor a model of persons will do: if we are to talk about persons as persons (which indeed *is* a part of what it is for human beings to be treated as persons), then we must not talk about them as really being something else, as really being entities requiring an unusual description in special theoretical terms; nor can we talk about persons as being to an extent *like* something else (information-processing devices, say) which, in other respects, are not actually like persons at all. For both these ways provide only partial views, ways of 'seeing' from within instrumental forms of activity, and our task is to talk about persons *as* persons. We must collect together in an orderly and systematic manner what people must already know as competent, autonomous members of their society – and to do this, they do not need to collect evidence as scientists, as competent persons, they should be a source of such evidence (Cavell, 1969). Drawing upon the knowledge we already possess, what we need is an account of personhood and selfhood in the ordinary sense of the term 'account': as simply a narration of a circumstance or a state of affairs. Something which in its telling 'moves' us this way and that through the current 'terrain' of personhood, so to speak, sufficiently for us to gain a conceptual grasp of the whole, even though we lack a vantage point from which to view it – it is a view 'from the inside', much as we get to know the street-plan of a city, by living within it, rather than from seeing it all at once from an external standpoint. It is a grasp which allows us to 'see' all the different aspects of a person as if arrayed within a 'landscape', all in relation to one another, from *all* the standpoints within it.

This illustrates another way in which our approach to our own self-understanding by use of theories is deficient: they lead to fragmentation, not integration. For at the moment there is a near chaos of different theories about ourselves all clamouring for survival. Could an all-embracing theory be developed to encompass them all? No, for it is in the very nature of what theories are that even if they were all 'good' theories (in the sense of producing when applied the results they predict) they still could not all be combined into *one* good theory. Because, as Marie Jahoda (1980, p. 185) has pointed out, 'each contains an extra theoretical element: the choice of the basic question the theory is meant to illuminate.' That is a non-rational matter: there being no single, basic question – such as 'Life, the Universe, and Everything?' – from which all other questions can be logically derived. In other words, as mentioned before, all properly scientific questions are rooted in a particular research tradition or 'paradigm' to use Kuhn's (1962) term, where the number of such paradigms is indeterminate, and where there is no possibility of a 'neutral' or 'superordinate' style of activity which includes in some simply logical sense all the rest. Living continually necessitates the making of value choices; it is here that the difference between theories and accounts becomes acute: accounts may depict value choices; theories suppress them.

Social Accountability and the Hermeneutical Nature of Selfhood

I hope that I have now said enough to warrant turning away from attempts to understand ourselves by references to theories or models of 'the self' or 'selves'. 'The self' is, as I have suggested, a scientific concept devised for scientific purposes: purposes to do with practical mastery, not with understanding; with the purposes one entertains as an 'outsider' to a social enterprise, but not as an 'insider'. In our attempts to understand ourselves, we have ignored the function of the second persons who are 'in contact' with us in a way in which third persons are not. But if we are truly to understand human beings and the nature of their existence, we must realize that they are the only creatures we know who have mastered a form of communication in which there is use of first-, second- and third-person talk. And this is not a mere 'linguistic' fact, as R. J. Bernstein (1981) points out, but an important ontological one too. If we are to understand fully the complex ways in which the words 'I', 'you', 'me' and the variety of other pronouns we have and use, then we must face the issues of (*a*) what we can *do* with such talk, and (*b*) to what we are referring when we use such words, i.e. what *is* the character of the I, the me, the you etc., in our society at this moment in history.

The comparison between the stance I am proposing – the 'social accountability' stance – and the Cartesian stance, with its radical division between subjectivity and objectivity, that we have inherited in our psychology in the present day, may be diagrammed as shown in figure 2.

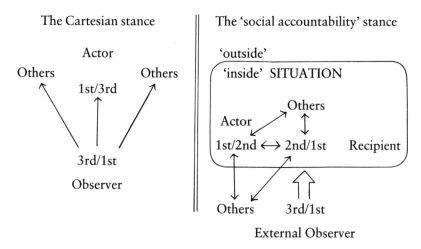

FIGURE 2   A comparison of accounting stances

The 'social accountability' diagram as it stands is, of course, inadequate. All the people depicted in it can switch between all three person statuses (first, second and third); and indeed they must be able to if they are to be able to indulge in deliberate action: for that requires them to know both

what to do and how to do it. Furthermore, the whole state of affairs
depicted may be itself a 'situation' for yet more observers 'external' to it.
All kinds of embeddings and structured organizations of 'situations' are no
doubt possible. And indeed, one must consider social life to consist in such
an ever changing 'landscape' or 'ecology' of action opportunities. Indeed,
if I were to be critical of my text, overall, I would criticize my inadequate
articulation of the notions of 'social order' and 'social ecology'. To talk of
them as consisting in different 'regions' and 'moments' is insufficient to say
what regions and moments are required; nothing is said about power,
about conflict and its resolution, about how a mass society is to be
maintained or not within such an ecology, and so on. My views rely upon
but fail to articulate these important issues.

Straightaway we may note that the drawing of a boundary around first/
second-person exchanges is entirely justified, as first and second persons
are 'in' a 'situation' – a CONTAINER metaphor – in relation to one another,
in a way in which first and third persons are not: an 'I' is surrounded by an
environment of 'you's', not like a subject surrounded by objects, but as an
agent surrounded by other agencies identifiably distinct from him- or
herself, but affording or offering him or her opportunities to act
meaningfully. Getting to know one's way around in such an environment
is, of course, a commonplace activity, but it involves some very strange
processes nonetheless.

In describing to someone my situation, in giving them an account of
what it is like to be me – of those things of which I am conscious and of
the ways in which I am conscious of them – I scan over my situation,
this way and that, distinguishing in it certain crucial 'features' or
'landmarks', so to speak. I can notice (and make) differences in my
surroundings, *and* notice (and make) them in different ways; and in my
accounts I can indicate both what those differences are and how they
can be noticed (or made), in sound, sight, touch or movement etc. These
differences can be used in a specificatory way progressively to specify or
determine a state of affairs. In other words, as many structuralist
writers such as Levi-Strauss and Lacan and psychologists such as
George Kelly, Gibson and Ossorio are doing, the intentionality of
mental activities can be described in terms of procedures working in
terms of systems of similar differences. Think of specifying an experience in terms of the following set of binary polarities: me/not-me;
inside/outside;   good/bad;   real/not-real;   here/there;   then/now;
pleasure/pain; wanted/unwanted; and so on. Others, on receipt of my
descriptive account, indicating the differences important to me in my
situation, can be 'instructed' by it to 'see', to discriminate their circum-

stances as I discriminate mine, thus to appreciate how I am placed: the opportunities and limitations my world affords me.

The process involved in appreciating such an account is a hermeneutical one; it is not induction, nor is it inference for the unique character of my situation cannot be understood by assimilating the details of my account to certain already established categories and premises – the task is to appreciate its unique meaning. As each 'part' of the description is supplied, a conceptual 'whole' has to be fashioned to accommodate it. Mentally, we have to 'construct' a context (a 'world') into which it can fit and play its part – where each new fact 'points to' or 'indicates' the 'world' in which they all have their place or function. And the hermeneutical process continues as each new fact is added to the account: the whole must be progressively transformed and articulated, metamorphosed in fact, in a back-and-forth process, from part to whole and back to part again, in such a way as to offer all the 'parts' of the whole, if possible, an undistorted accommodation – but sometimes, of course, there are some 'parts' which just will not 'fit' and then, perhaps, a number of distinct and possibly incompatible wholes must be formed.

And when is the process finished? Never, it would seem. Such formative processes are clearly always open to further specification . . . but only (and this is most important) of an already specified kind. In other words, at each point in the process, what has been specified so far is known in terms of its already specified further specifiability (Shotter, 1980a). Think here, say, of a plant growing from a seed: as a seedling, it works as a structured means mediating the further growth of the plant. In the same way, an intention is best thought of as related to an action, not as a script is related to a performance, but as a seed is related to the plant grown from it; with the awareness of what one has just said or done working as the structured means determining the possibilities available as to what one might go on to say or to do next. And just as it cannot be predicted how many leaves and blossoms a plant might have, because that is a matter of changeable local contingencies as the plant grows into the kind of plant it is, so the development of a mental structure cannot be predicted, though its style is such that only certain progressions can fit and be appropriate to it.

Weiss's Depiction of 'You'

Let me turn now to the hermeneutical grasp that second-person you's can achieve of first-person I's as they perform. The rights and duties of second persons in relation to first persons, which as I described in chapter 1 are quite different to those of third persons in relation to first persons, become important here: for it is only in relation to *you* that I exist as recognizably a person; to third-person, external observers with no duty to listen to 'me', and to let me develop myself, hermeneutically, in the 'situation' between us, I cannot recognizably be myself, for they are not present to me as second-person you's.

How does a you appear to an I? Paul Weiss (1980), in his attempt to understand the fundamental nature of human beings in relation to one another, begins his book with a systematic analysis of you's, and moves through an analysis of me's, to the self, and to I's. I want to give you the flavour of his analysis, and then to criticize it for its over-reliance upon spatial metaphors.

Here are some of the primary claims that Weiss makes about you: 'You are confrontable'; 'You have dense depth'; 'You are accountable'; 'You have a public and a private status'; 'You are perceivable'; 'what you *will* be is *now* indeterminate'; 'You are a free causal agent'; and 'You have a predominantly bodily role'. The key motif, as Bernstein points out, which helps to make sense of and to unify these (and many other related claims) is, in Weiss's lexicon, the dimension of publicness and privacy, or in my manner of speaking (and one's manner of speaking *is* everything here), a matter of specifiability and unspecifiability. For what is at issue is the fact that, while I can encounter, perceive and know you in many ways, you as such are never exhausted by what I perceive, encounter and know: 'What you will be is now indeterminate.' This does not mean that there is another you which stands hidden from me, behind the you I encounter, a you which is totally inaccessible to me (and perhaps to you). It means, as Weiss (1980, p. 5) puts it, clearly using Polyani's 'from–to' terminology of tacit knowing, that:

> No one of us is two people, one inside the other. Each is single. A man's privacy is continuous with what he is publicly. The pain he feels is expressed in his grimaces. The grimaces are the pain made public at the same time that they are distinguished from it. . . . When I attend to you, I attend directly *to* what is presented *from* a privacy which remains continuous with it. (my emphases)

The intentionality of your behaviour is such that *it can be said* to 'indicate' or to 'point to' or to specify the character of a 'privacy' from which it issues. I can thus come to know you and to 'penetrate' the privacy from which you operate – to use Weiss's way of talking. But this does not mean that I could ever *fully* penetrate your privacy, else it would not be a 'true privacy'; it would not be the 'dense depth' that Weiss means, one which can never be fully penetrated or violated. But 'though I never get beyond you, I do get beyond what I confront and beyond what is confrontable,' says Weiss (p. 6):

> When I confront you, and particularly when I confront you in sympathy, hate, fear or love I penetrate beyond what is confrontable. . . . I do not merely encounter you at those times; I move into you. On your side, what I reach is continued into a depth I never fully probe.

A human being's privacy is both continuous with but distinguishable from – by him- or herself and by others – what he or she is publicly. Human beings simply would not be human beings unless they each possessed a distinctive and unique privacy, a privacy *to* which one can attend, *from* their activities, a privacy 'indicated' or 'specified' in their actions, a privacy which, however, is never completely specified by their activities.

The power of Weiss's analysis is that this same approach – of attending *to* what is presented as if it issues *from* a privacy which remains continuous with it, but which is never completely penetrated – can be continued, he says, 'in depth into more powerful, free privacies' (p. 165). His analysis of the you leads directly on to the me, the I and the self; where the you is continuous with and grounded in the me, the me continuous with and grounded in the I, and the I finally presupposes a self, which, he says, 'encompasses an I and other distinguishable sources of privately initiated acts' (p. 174). While distinguishable, each phase mutually requires all the others, and together they constitute a unity. But Weiss extends his account even further: to encompass the we, the they and the others; and to show, of course, that the reference of first-, second- and third-person pronouns is dialectically related to the reference of 'we', thus as the nature of 'we' changes, so does the nature of all the other references. As our ways of accounting for ourselves to ourselves change – by the use of written rather than oral accounts, say (Ong, 1982; Vygotsky, 1962, 1978) – so *we* change, and I change too: perhaps by becoming more self-conscious and self-determining. Weiss's analysis is, I think, of great importance.

Yet, as R. J. Bernstein (1981) has pointed out, despite Weiss's 'official' stance in claiming to do justice to both the spatial and temporal dimensions of human being, his language is heavily weighted in favour of spatial and physical terms used metaphorically: he speaks of 'dense *depth*'; of something being presented '*from* a privacy'; of getting '*beyond* you'; of '*moving into* you'; of the self and the person as being '*adjacent* specializations'; of the self's role as 'more *central*'; and so on. Now the difficulty we face here is in saying what, practically it means to penetrate or move into your privacy? Can a procedure for doing it be specified? Is there a way in which such statements can be understood as instructing us in how actually to do something? In the case of you, the answer is probably yes: I have in fact been attempting to specify the kind of hermeneutical process required. But Weiss (p. 191) speaks of 'the self' as being 'forever private, beyond the reach of external observation', and goes on to say of it:

> Since it is not public, a self lacks extension and location. Still it makes sense to speak of it as being voluminous. Not only does the self provide a *domain* within whose compass the I and mind occur, but it is expressed as the living of *a responsibly governed body*. (p. 198, my emphases)

So we have to ask for further instructions. For the prefix 'self-(dash)' usually indicates a reflexive reference, but does not usually imply a reference to anything conceptually separable from the acting person. If it is to be separated, *is* it to designate an agency in its own right? If so, how can a 'domain' also be an 'agency'? Perhaps, say, in the sense that the 'United Kingdom' is both a 'domain' and 'a responsibly governed body'. Is, then, Weiss's notion of 'a self' modelled on a society? If so, then not only is it regressive but might it not be that the ultimate source of many of our 'privately initiated acts' should be sought, literally, in our society, rather than metaphorically within 'the selves' we are each supposed to possess? If so, their ultimate roots would not be inpenetrable so much because of their 'privacy' as because of their 'diffuseness', geographically and historically, because of their non-locatability (see chapter 11).

Weiss, it seems to me, in moving methodically from his initial acceptance of people's acts as all pointing back to a privacy from which they issue, into deeper, 'more powerful, free privacies', has entrapped himself: he has extended his initial formulation in terms of depth and privacy illegitimately into the domain of self-reference, in which it seems to me to cease to apply. At this point, rather than revealing the true nature of the relations between you, I and the others, it seems to me to begin to conceal them, to hide from us their origins in our social history.

Conclusions

If how we understand and experience our reality is constituted for us by the language we use in our attempts to account for it, and if the language distorts temporal and developmental processes, by providing only the resources to describe them metaphorically as spatial structures, then our understanding and experience of them will be distorted. Taking temporality seriously, from a social accountability stance, means not just detailing how we talk about I, you, me and ourselves *now*, but tracing the stages in history of not just their temporal unfolding, but also, of how the very notion or concept of community has changed in history. For as the notion of what *we* are changes, so do the conceptions of I, you and me – I might (as a result of reading Freud, say) come to treat you as less responsible for your own actions, for instance. As our ways of accounting to ourselves for ourselves change, so *we* change. Currently, we are coming to an increasing realization of the very different modes of being available to human beings, and the significant differences between what is being talked about – whether it is in different sub-cultures, historical communities or so-called 'primitive societies' – when expressions equivalent to our 'I', 'you', 'me' etc., are used (Geertz, 1973; Washabaugh, 1980; Heelas and Lock, 1981).

The problems and questions this raises, as Bernstein points out, are not just theoretical; they have enormous practical importance: in politics, education, psychotherapy and personal relations. We cannot determine what and who we are, and should be, unless we are clear as to what I's, me's and you's *can* be. Politically, we can only become what our developmental opportunities will allow us to be. Indeed, without an understanding of the developmental processes, the procedures and methods by which competent adults are produced from our newborns, and learn how to reproduce our social order in all their actions, the disturbances people suffer in their being would seem to be impossible to understand also. It is here especially that Weiss's kind of analysis fails us. Conducted from a single point of view, it prescribes *a* way of accounting for reality which proceeds in terms of a set of initially acceptable statements, which, because of their supposed self-evident nature, are indubitable. These ways are then extended methodically into domains beyond which they are legitimately applied – it's a common enough method. It is, as Descartes said, 'the method of properly conducting one's reason and of seeking the truth in the sciences' (see Epilogue). But it denies dialogue, and provides only a partial view: a 'positioned' or 'situated' view, not an understanding (sic) of a world containing (sic) many such positions. In the to-and-fro, back-and-forth movement of discourse, as long as genuine dialogue is *not* denied, a grasp of the whole person, ourselves, would seem to be possible 'from the inside', as long as no *one* vantage point is allowed to prevail over all others.

Part Four

Ecological Being: Being Ecological

11

'Duality of Structure' and 'Intentionality' in an Ecological Psychology

> There is, it seems to us,
> At best, only a limited value
> In the knowledge derived from experience.
> The knowledge imposes a pattern, and falsifies,
> For the pattern is new every moment
> And every moment is a new shocking
> Valuation of what we have been. . . .
> (T. S. Eliot, *East Coker*)

I want to explore below what it is for people to act in ways which are appropriate to their circumstances and how it is that they can do it. Clearly, in one sense, but in a not very well-articulated way, we must already know something of what is involved in such an activity – for here we all are in the middle of doing it. We have, however, little explicit idea as to the nature of worlds which allow of such modes of existence, worlds which work in terms of the individuals in them establishing relations of appropriateness or fittingness between themselves, in which the 'elements' comprising them are related meaningfully both to one another and their environments. We badly need a theory of such worlds, in which human phenomena can be seen as arising naturally, as an orderly consequence of the operation of their natural processes.

The concept of duality of structure is designed to play an important role in such a theory. It refers to the fact that all human action is doubly structured, for it is structured both as a product and as a process, or better, it is both structured and structuring. And the significance of this is that, when linked to the concept of intentionality, it explains how human action can, in the course of its own performance, provide itself with the conditions for its own continuation. In other words, by acting we can create the conditions for further action. Thus, although all actions may seem to require mediation by an 'idea', 'image' or 'representation', or at least seem to be directed by an inner reference to such entities as indicative of desired end states, the concept of duality of structure suggests something quite different. To be appropriate to its circumstances, an action need not be guided by an 'inner' representation of the 'outer' circumstances in question at all. Due to its ability to produce in its wake, so to speak, a structured context for its own continuation, an action can be informed, not so much by factors present in the source from which it issues, as by the context *into* which it is directed. It is this view which will be developed below.

Time, the Forgotten Dimension

My overall aim in this chapter is to contribute to the development of what is coming to be called an ecological approach to psychology and to social psychology, an approach proposed some time ago by Brunswick (1956), but currently attributed very largely to Gibson (1966, 1979). The account presented here however, though sympathetic in many respects to Gibson's approach, is not presented in Gibsonian terms. For although, as Gibson sees it, an ecological psychology is sensitive to the dynamic relations of mutuality and reciprocity between living entities and their environments, the beings in Gibson's world are depicted merely as observers, not as actors, i.e. not as beings able to provide for themselves, by their own action, conditions appropriate to support their action's continuation. They may move about, but they do not act; thus rather than 'makers', they are presented merely as 'finders' of what already exists. Such a view, I would argue, fails to recognize the peculiar form-producing character of activity in a biological and social world; it fails to assign a proper role to time and to processes of growth and development. It is in characterizing such a world as a world-in-the-making, rather than a world-already-made, that the concept of the duality of structure plays its part.

Given that the essence of an ecological approach is that it explores the relations constituting a totality, my coverage must of necessity be broad, thus many topics can only be given a brief treatment and sometimes only hinted at. Essentially, following Prigogine's (1980) discussion of processes of flow, and the account he presents of irreversible, evolutionary processes, I also want to argue for a thoroughgoing evolutionism

– orthodox evolutionists are to be criticized for not being evolutionary enough, for not extending the concept of evolutionary processes into the world at large, allowing for their operation at every moment, at every level. Rather than a world of merely functional entities, possessing static geometrical structures, an evolving world can be thought of as being full of agencies, as containing everywhere structurizing activities or formative causes (Bohm, 1973a), or as being constituted of what Giddens (1979) calls structuration. It is within the context of such formative processes that I shall explore the notions of duality of structure and intentionality.

Such processes are always in the process of becoming other than what at any moment they already are. Their growth is an essential and irreducible aspect of their nature; it cannot be partialled out and 'added in' later, when convenient. Temporal processes cannot be made up from parts themselves devoid of temporality. Truly temporal processes are continuous or indivisible in the sense that, the very process of differentiating them into phases of before and after serves, not to separate them into a 'patchwork of disjoined parts' as Dewey (1896) puts it, but on the contrary, to relate their phases as aspects of the same dynamic unity. It is a unity which is perceived as a unity, not in spite of its novelty in every moment, but because of it; for while clearly changing in one sense, like a swirl or eddy in a stream, it remains recognizable in another sense as continually the same.

Its unity is that of a stability within a flow rather than that of a static object. A static object can be said to be a unity of homogeneity made up of static parts, which all belong together in one sense because of their similarity to one another (like building blocks). A swirl or an eddy in a flowing stream, however, is a unity of heterogeneity, for it can only be seen as occurring within a flow (rather than as a static object) if its regions are at every moment, in some sense, different from what they were at a previous moment. But in what sense? The difference cannot be a change in configuration, a rearrangement, for unless the relations between its component regions all remain the same, or change in an orderly manner, an eddy is simply not recognizable as the same eddy from one moment to the next. There must be an irreducible, qualitative difference between its successive phases for it to be recognizable as a stability within a flow; each phase of it must be novel in some respect by contrast with the phase preceding it. But it would be incorrect to say that its phases were separated from one another by their novelty. On the contrary: it is their continual novelty which relates them to one another as perceptually distinguishable aspects (but not of course as physically isolatable parts) of the same flowing totality. It is by their genuine novelty, continuously renewed, that flowing processes are recognized as such.

Furthermore, if Prigogine is correct, the 'elements' flowing through such regions must themselves also be treated as flowing processes, existing as sub-systems within the larger whole (itself embedded in a similar super-systematic flow), and manifesting the same principles of organization and growth as those at other levels. This means that no matter how remarkable the 'static' geometrical structure of such flowing processes may appear to be, as structuring structures they cannot properly be thought of as *things* at all: they must be conceived of as *activities*, as regions of structurizing activity, within which not strictly localizable dynamic stabilities are continually reproduced by other activities . . . which depend in their turn, upon dynamic exchanges at lesser and greater levels (Prigogine, 1980).

In such a view – in contrast to the mechanistic view, in which complex behaviour is seen as arising out of the interrelated behaviour of simpler (often indistinguishable) objects – complexity cannot be explained in terms of simplicity at lower levels. For they also must be treated as equally complex. 'Belief in the "simplicity" of the microscopic level now belongs to the past,' claims Prigogine (p. xv). He concludes that,

> The elementary particles that we know are complex objects that can be produced and can decay. If there is simplicity somewhere in physics and chemistry, it is not in the microscopic models. It lies more in idealized macroscopic representations. . . . Once we no longer believe in the simplicity of the microscopic, we must reappraise the role of time. (p. xiii)

I want to suggest that this must be the case also with our 'objects' of interest in the social sciences. Rather than as static, geometrical structures subject only to changes of configuration and rearrangement, people's utterances and actions, their social institutions and practices, etc., must also be seen as dynamic stabilities produced and reproduced (and as decaying) within a continuous flow of conduct, i.e. within the structuration constitutive of social worlds.

In Prigogine's terms, such 'objects' appear within a flowing medium as 'dissipative structures'; they are dynamic equilibria produced in non-equilibrium, or far-from-equilibrium conditions. That is, in conditions of energy expenditure which ought, according to the second law of thermodynamics, to lead to increasing disorder, but which under some conditions do not! In such a view, the 'objects' of our interest develop (i.e. progressively differentiate or specify themselves) over time. Thus, the history of their development is just as important as the logic of their momentary structure, for their specification at one moment indicates the kind of further specification still open to them in the future (Shotter, 1980a). In other words, they are always indeterminate or incomplete in some degree, for as genuinely temporal processes there is always more of them to come; their structure is always becoming another structure. Indeed, if we are to take the reality of time seriously, there can be no logic of their structure-at-an-instant, for there are in nature no instantaneous activities, and hence no solely spatial organizations existing only at a timeless moment. All spatial relations must also stretch across or through time. Thus, following Giddens (1979, pp. 2–3), an organized flow is best seen as situated, not in 'space' *and* 'time', thought of as separate containers for 'position' and 'motion' respectively, but as existing in regions or moments of 'time–space' – where the distances between its separate regions are not wholly spatial (for all activities must take some time to execute), nor those between its moments wholly temporal (for all activities must occupy some space.

Prigogine (1980) talks of time as 'the forgotten dimension', and Giddens (1979, p. 3) of 'the repression of time in social theory'. The static view of the world, in which all distances are purely spatial, and the past and the future play the same role, has been deeply rooted in western thought since the Greeks. However, the introduction of a proper appreciation of time and the concept of a world evolving at every level – in which there are no solely spatial distances, and in which the future is always qualitatively different from the past (i.e. in which time is not wholly spatialized) – is not something which can be done easily, by simply attempting to insert another, temporal dimension into our thought. A proper appreciation seems to involve, strangely, almost an inversion of many of our most deeply held beliefs. The classical mechanistic or 'Galilean' view of the world in science suggests that we regard it as an object of analysis to which we do not belong (the as-if-a-Martian stance). As such it has a number of features: It is a place best characterized by number, in which everything of importance can be measured and quantified, with all the data relevant to its understanding being gained from the position of an external observer. It is not an incomplete world-in-the-making, but an already determined world, thus its nature as one's object of study is already essentially fixed and unchanging, and is thus also unchanged by any of the methods used to study it. Its structure is to be described by finding its simple elements and the relations between them, where these are regarded as essentially of a causal kind. Such a world is a 'timeless' world, in the sense that its elements could, by taking up again a previous configuration, eradicate from within itself any trace of the past; and thus also, in returning to its original state, appear subject to 'time' with a reversible flow.

But that conception of the world is now profoundly changing in all its details. And if Prigogine is correct – and there is every reason to believe that he is – then, as he himself says,

> We are in a period of scientific revolution – one in which the very position and meaning of the scientific approach are undergoing reappraisal – a period not unlike the birth of the scientific approach in ancient Greece or of its renaissance at the time of Galileo. (1980, p. xi)

Such a reappraisal is necessary, for as is now becoming increasingly clear to us our conception of the classical world has arisen from the illegitimate extension of principles, derived from imagery appropriate only to a world of 'solid bodies' and 'middle dimensions', into a metaphysical realm. We have forgotten that perception is selective, and we have claimed that the world is everywhere as we perceive it to be in our activities in our 'external world' (in which, of course, many of the results we produce *are* reversible). We need to explain not only the selectivity to which we have fallen victim, but also how such selectivity is possible and what its determinants are. The difficulty is that timeless, purely spatial imagery sneaks back in to influence unconsciously even those theorists who self-consciously attempt to avoid it.

The Ecological Approach and the Reality of Vagueness

The ecological approach currently developing is already beginning to reflect some of the reappraisals of which Prigogine speaks. It consists in treating everything within its purview as existing only in reciprocal relation to everything else; nothing is seen as existing in isolation. Furthermore, processes of flow play a central part in it also. Of central concern is the relation of an animal to its environment. As indicative of its fundamental stance on this point, a statement of Gibson's (1979, p. 8) may be taken as an example:

> the words *animal* and *environment* make an inseparable pair. Each term implies the other. No animal could exist without an environment surrounding it. Equally, although not so obvious, an environment implies an animal (or at least an organism) to be surrounded.

But as Noble (1981) has argued, there is much that is wrong with his exposition of it (wrong in fact in Gibson's own terms), for he often seems to forget that the reciprocal implication of animal and environment he emphasizes above only appears within a cycle of activity flowing between them. And he lapses back into a 'naive realist' position, claiming that an environment's 'affordances' – the opportunities for action afforded by an environment to the creatures in it – exist in 'the world' independently of any animal's activity. For example, in describing their nature, he states:

> The affordance of something does *not change* as the need of the observer changes. The observer may or may not perceive or attend to the affordance, according to his needs, but the affordance, being invariant, is always there to be perceived. An affordance is not bestowed upon an object by a need of an observer and his act of perceiving it. The object offers what it does because it is the object it is. To be sure, we define *what it is* in terms of ecological physics, instead of physical physics, and it therefore possesses meaning and value to begin with. (1979, p. 138–9)

It would be difficult to find a more explicit claim as to what the nature of the world is independently of our participation in it. Gibson acknowledges the relational character of an environment-for-activity in his theorizing, and then seens to abandon the notion in his methodology and metaphysics.

In criticizing Gibson, Noble recruits Dewey and the account he gives of the relation between an action and its environment in his 1896 paper *The Concept of the Reflex Arc in Psychology*. In arguing against mechanistic interpretations of mental activity, Dewey argued instead that only an evolutionary, organic approach could account for both of its major features: its continual change *and* its sensible continuity. But in terms of what units, or unities? In criticizing the proposed concept of the reflex arc – decades before it became psychology's central analytic unit, and manifested in fact all the faults Dewey ascribed to it – he first pointed out its advantages:

> It being admitted that the sensori-motor apparatus represents both the unit of nerve structure and the type of nerve function, the image of this relationship passed over psychology, and became an organizing principle to hold together the multiplicity of fact. (p. 355 – page numbers refer to reprint in Dennis, 1948)

In other words, it works as an organizing principle because it possesses duality of structure: in virtue of its recursive nature, and its ability as a 'forming co-ordination' progressively to reconstitute itself by feeding the results of its own activity back into itself, so to speak, it can represent both a product *and* a process. Which of the two one perceives depends in which 'direction' one looks: looking back, retrospectively, one sees structure, i.e. that which has been specified or determined to date; looking forward, prospectively, one sees function, i.e. the productive or formative process. And all moments in truly temporal processes possess such a duality of structure when viewed in this 'bidirectional' manner. Usually, however, the prospective view is forgotten, for the productive process involved is not easy to specify or determine. We must seemingly either be inaccurate or vague, for a process in progress is always essentially incomplete and its outcome uncertain; thus we must discover a way to describe the character of this vagueness clearly and accurately, without distortion.

Now all the 'parts' of continuously functioning feedback loops, whether forming co-ordinations or not, are (1) in operation simultaneously, yet the feedback function depends upon (2) the co-ordination of a temporal succession amongst them. In seizing upon the latter feature, Dewey pointed out, exponents of the reflex arc theory forgot the former. Preconceived ideas as to how the arc *must* operate supervened. It must consist in, first a stimulus, then some central activity, and then the motor discharge. But must it? For Dewey, such a conception,

> instead of being a case of plain science, is a survival of the metaphysical dualism, first formulated by Plato, according to which the sensation is an ambiguous dweller on the border land of soul and body, the idea (or central process) is purely psychical, and the act (or movement) purely physical. Thus the reflex arc formulation is neither physical (or physiological) nor psychological; it is a mixed materialistic-spiritualistic assumption. (p. 361)

It arises out of the very understandable but nonetheless misleading tendency to describe the nature of processes by their products. The fallacy produced, Dewey points out, is virtually the 'psychologist's fallacy', as described by William James (1890, p. 196): it occurs when terms, appropriate only to the description of an already completed outcome, are used wholly inappropriately to describe processes which might (or might not) be productive of it. Regarding the reflex arc, we are only able to describe a stimulus as a stimulus and a response as a response, by assuming their 'common reference to an inclusive end which marks each member off as stimulus and response' (1896, p. 361). If there is no such outcome, then the events occurring, however else they may be described, cannot legitimately be described as consisting in stimuli and responses. It is only within the interpretative framework provided by the reflex arc concept (as a complete circuit) that such terms are applicable. But if in reality the arc is incomplete, the proper conditions for their use do not exist. Persisting with their use, regardless of their applicability, leads to a distorted account of the proper nature of 'forming co-ordinations'; their formative or structur-izing quality is lost.

How then might formative processes, with both sequential and simultaneous properties, be properly described; what kind of interpreta-tive framework would allow us to capture their often incomplete nature? Rather than as a unity of homogeneity, Dewey describes a sensori-motor co-ordination as a unity of heterogeneity, as a comprehensive unity which holds together as a unity, not in spite of its continual transformation and reconstitution, but because of it. It is from within such an evolving or forming co-ordination that the nature of its perceptually distinguishable 'parts' should be described; this Dewey proceeds to do:

> The stimulus is that phase of the forming co-ordination which represents the conditions which have to be met in bringing it to a successful issue; the response is that phase of one and the same forming co-ordination which gives the key to meeting these condi-tions, which serves as instrument in effecting the successful co-ordination. They are therefore strictly correlative and contempor-aneous. (pp. 364–5)

A stimulus does not precede a response, but, as an aspect of a forming co-ordination, develops as the response develops, and is complete only when the response is complete. And at any one moment, to the extent that the response is still incomplete or uncertain, the stimulus is also incomplete or uncertain. This incompleteness or vagueness is real, for a stimulus is only completely specified as the stimulus it is when the response to which it has been the stimulus is complete.

In other words, an animal's responses select and constitute the very stimuli to which they are, within a forming co-ordination, the responses. But the selectivity is not just one-way. For, just as the animal's activity works (by making differences) to specify which of all the conditions in the environment at large (if any) constitute a response's proper stimulus, so the conditions selected will work back upon the animal to specify the response's value (i.e. by making a difference to the animal), thus to provide in a response's execution a basis for its own further appropriate modification. So an animal's response, as Dewey says, is not so much *to* a stimulus as *into* it (1896, p. 357). Responses only occur, in other words, if furthered by an environment providing or affording the means for them in each moment of their operation. If we hear a loud, unexpected sound and respond to it by running away in fright, then, says Dewey, the running and the fright 'enlarges' or 'transforms' the original auditory experience, and reconstitutes the sound as a basis for our continued response to it. We act *into* the sound, and,

> Just as the 'response' is necessary to constitute the stimulus, to determine it as sound and as this kind of sound, of wild beast or robber, so the sound experience must persist as a value in the running, to keep it up, to control it. (p. 359)

Dewey's image here clearly is not that of a world of static, 'timeless' objects and geometrical structures existing only in causal relation to one another; it is a world of living unities, maintaining themselves by their capacities to sense distinctions and their abilities to make differences in their surroundings. It is a world of temporal, flowing processes, very much as characterized in the first section of this chapter.

Returning now to Gibson and his claim that 'affordances' exist in an environment whether anyone there perceives or attends to them or not: Dewey would say that an affordance is only completely specified as the affordance it is when the activity it affords is complete. Thus although it may seem that affordances are 'there' in the environment irrespective of whether anyone is there in the environment to perceive them or not, this is not so. Prior to the performance of some further activity within it, the only clear and accurate description of an environment which can be given is one in terms of the actions so far taken within it. What further action it may afford must remain to a degree uncertain. Hence the need for intelligent selectivity in the performance of any such action. Gibson's ecological approach, however, is supposed to eradicate the need to refer to any mental activities mediating the relation between perception and action: he claims that, as a theory of 'direct perception', it explains perception without any reference to 'old-fashioned mental acts [such as] recognition, interpretation, inference, concepts' (1979, p. 238). But there is a hiccup in the Gibsonian cycle of activity flowing between an animal and its environment: for as he describes it, the animal perceives an affordance *first* as a moving observer, by 'resonating' to it, and *then* as an actor – as a result of some 'inner' process of looking at the perceived affordance – decides how to make use of it . . . thus to move and resonate again, and so on. It is within that hiccup that mental activity occurs. Gibson's hidden Platonism here is, I think, plain to see. As a theory of direct perception it fails in its own terms. To echo Guthrie's famous criticism of Tolman's sign-Gestalt theory, Gibson's theory leaves us buried in thought in the middle of our affordances; how we act in relation to the 'affordances' of the environment is our concern, not the concern of the theory. And many other theories of so-called cognitive processes leave important concerns to the users of the theories in the same way, demanding from them, as Dennett (1979, p. 12) very aptly puts it, 'a loan of intelligence'.

Intentionality and Duality of Structure

I now want to turn to a discussion of human action within the context of an ecological approach. Central to the account I want to give is the notion of intentionality. It manifests itself in two ways, or better, in two 'directions': in terms of people fitting themselves into their environment (in their responses), as well as their fitting their environment to themselves (by their actions). The intentional nature of mental activity is such that (to put it cryptically) it only ever occurs in relation to something other than itself. Since Brentano (1973, orig. pub. 1874), mental phenomena have often been characterized as being 'directed upon an object', 'as containing within themselves something as an object', as 'pointing to', 'meaning', or as being 'a means to' something other than themselves – whether that something exists or not. In other words, mental activity exhibits an intrinsic connectedness to, an interpenetration of, an appropriate fittedness (call it what you will), of itself to its surroundings or context.

A more dynamic way of characterizing how it 'points beyond itself', however, is in terms of attributing to it a specificatory function or aspect. As Gauld and I (Gauld and Shotter, 1977, p. 127) say, in discussing the fact that a thought is always a thought 'that something is the case or a supposal that something is the case':

> Now when one has such a thought it could always be said that one's thought has a specificatory function or aspect, or perhaps more truly that when one thinks one specifies; one exercises various of one's conceptual capacities so as to specify, as it were upon a grid, some state of affairs beyond the thought itself. The specificatory function does not exhaust the thought – there is, prima facie, a difference between thoughts in which the specified state of affairs is affirmed, and those in which it is merely supposed – but it is a *sine qua non* of there being any thought at all.

I shall take this view of all mental activity: that it is to do with making differences or noticing distinctions.

Implicit in such a view is the idea that mental activity in progress has duality of structure in the following sense: in any one moment, the activity will have functioned to specify or differentiate a state of affairs into a set of distinct regions – the product of the process when viewed retrospectively. However, such regions will clearly still be open to further specification or differentiation, but only in terms of what they already are. Thus when viewed prospectively, it is not just that they are further specifiable, it is that they are further specifiable in an already specified manner. Thus, for instance, a sentence presents, at every moment in the course of its production, a content already specified to a degree, but that content also specifies the possible further specification which may then be introduced into it. In other words, it presents at any one moment, as an aspect of its duality of structure, both its meaning so far, as well as the means for its own continuation. In this sense, the production of a sentence is hardly different in character from the growth of a plant. And it will often be useful to bear this image in mind: for the relation of, say, a person's intention of saying something to their saying it is much more like the relation of seed to plant (as I have said in chapter 10) than that suggested by the currently more popular image of a script to its performance. For rather than being the outer expression of something already specified internally, the expression of an intention is, as a process of temporal unfolding, a passage from an indeterminate to a better-articulated state of affairs.

In such a passage something is formed, or perhaps better, forming occurs; momentary 'product forms' are continuously created in the flow of activity in question. This idea is captured, Bohm (1980) maintains – Bohm is a theoretical physicist concerned like Prigogine to construct an evolutionary theory of microphysical processes – in the original meaning of the word 'form' in ancient Greek philosophy; as a verb it meant, he says, an inner forming activity, which is the cause of the growth of things, and of the development of their various essential forms. He (1973a, p. 95) illustrates what he means as follows:

> For example in the case of an oak tree, what is indicated by the term 'formal cause' is the whole inner movement of the sap, leaves, etc., which is characteristic of that kind of tree, and different from that taking place in other kinds of trees. In more modern language, it would be better to describe this as the *formative cause*, to emphasize that what is involved is not a mere form imposed from without, but rather *an ordered and structured inner movement that is essential to what things are.*

Just as an intention may be said to 'contain' or 'point to' its object, so an acorn may be said to 'contain' or 'point to' an oak tree. But an acorn certainly does not contain an oak tree, or anything like it, even in miniature (preformationism is not true). It is best seen as the structured medium or means through which, in interaction with its surroundings, an oak tree forms, developing itself through its own progressive self-specification. Furthermore, although an acorn specifies the production of an oak tree, and not any other kind of tree, it does not specify the tree that grows from it exactly (not the number of branches, twigs, leaves, etc.), for the tree grows in a quite predictable manner, sensitive to local contingencies. Similarly, an intention may specify a whole range of possible expressions, the actual one realized being formulated (progressively) in interaction with its circumstances.

The similarities between the expression of an intention and the growth of a seed were also noted by Wittgenstein (1981). In a marginal note he remarked: '((Remembering a thought, an intention.)) A *seed*.' (no. 656). In another remark he questions whether a correlation could be found between one's brain-processes and the system or order in one's spoken or written thoughts, and says,

> But why should the *system* continue further in the direction of the centre? Why should this order not proceed, so to speak, out of chaos? The case would be like the following – certain kinds of plants multiply by seed, so that a seed always produces a plant of the same kind as that from which it was produced – but *nothing* in the seed corresponds to the plant which comes from it; so that it is impossible to infer the properties or structure of the plant from those of the seed that it comes out of – this can only be done from the *history* of the seed. (no. 608)

Here Wittgenstein is wrestling with the essential vagueness or indeterminacy of mental activities. In *Philosophical Investigations*, in attempting to say what it is one knows when one knows how to perform an activity (e.g. doing mathematics), he again notes its indeterminacy, saying: 'What is most difficult here is to put this indefinitness, correctly and unfalsified, into words' (Wittgenstein, 1953, p. 227), rather than describing an essentially incomplete process by a completed product, by the outcome towards which it was tending at the time – when a proper account ought to describe it simply as a tendency or power (Harré and Madden, 1975; Bhaskar, 1979).

But is reference to seeds and plants and to their growth, once again to run the risk of misleading ourselves by use of an inappropriate metaphor? Is it wrong to see intentionality – as an intrinsic property of a world of form-producing processes – in the same terms as the relation of seeds to plants? No, not at all, not initially at least. For all such form-producing processes must, in the evolutionary view I am putting forward, be described as transformations of one another,[1] with the stage reached at each moment providing the means for progress to a more highly differentiated stage. In other words, there is no point at which intentionality makes its appearance in such a world as a product of essentially non-intentional processes; it is present at least in proto-typical form even at the most crude and primitive levels of activity. Its better-articulated manifestations simply have their origins in less well-articulated processes of the same kind; not in some other kind of phenomena altogether. It is to be found in what Bergson (1911) called the 'mnemic or temporal span' of the present moment, that is, in the extent to which the past is 'condensed' in the present. Or in the extent to which, as I have put it, the present is 'already specified', its already specified further specifiability determines 'lines of intentionality which trace out in advance at least the style of what is to come' (Merleau-Ponty, 1962, p. 416). In other words, memories come to be embodied in the very structure of the present.

Thus it is memory – not as the process of 'retrieving' something 'stored', but as the process by which past specificatory activities are linked to current specifiability – which makes for intentionality, and give a 'directionality' to mental activities. Thus, although eddies and vortices in a stream of water are dissipative structures or dynamic stabilities, and one may liken mental entities to them because of that (cf. William James, 1890, p. 239 – 'the stream of thought'), they lack any appreciable mnemic span, and thus do not accumulate within themselves the conditions for their own further self-development.

Whilst our ordinary language may embody something better than the metaphysics of the Stone Age (Austin), it nonetheless clearly embodies a misleading 'official' dualistic metaphysics which suggests to us that our 'minds' are 'in our heads', and that often it is not us but 'our minds' which do our thinking for us. Thus, in this idiom, it may seem that reference to the growth of seeds and plants is misleading, in so much that such growth involves the whole individual, while our 'official' metaphysics suggests a separation between ourselves and our mental activities – and indeed, up till now I have talked in the same way of mental activities, actions and intentions as 'pointing beyond' themselves. But as Gauld and I (Gauld and Shotter, 1977, p. 115) say about a thought, for instance:

> It would perhaps be better to say that in thinking the thinker points beyond his momentary self, his self as engaged in thinking *that* thought. For to talk of thoughts 'pointing beyond' themselves is to make them sound like momentary agents in their own right. Furthermore, the object of a thought is not thought of as set over

against that thought; it is thought of as set over against the thinker as he now is.

In other words, we mislead ourselves if we think of ourselves as already fixed and unchanging beings possessing like receptacles an 'inside' and an 'outside', and furthermore having 'inner selves' set over against our 'inner' thoughts, etc., in such a way that we ourselves are one thing and our thoughts quite another. If that really were the case, then it would be difficult to see how people's thoughts, intentions etc., could be accounted as *theirs*, as something they themselves were committed to, which mattered to them, which if inappropriate in one way or another would produce suffering or despair. While our thought, etc., may be 'in' us, it is not in us like a pea is in a pod, but like a swirl or eddy is in a stream, as a phase or aspect of what the stream *is*; our thought is inseparable from what we *are*.

Reference to the growth of plants (and the flow of streams) can help to explicate some of the concepts relevant to the proper description of truly temporal processes. All exhibit duality of structure in so much that, at any moment, the continuously produced product of the process is the ever-present means (the formative cause) of its continuation as the process it is; they are all in that sense continuously self-reproducing. They are also 'rooted' within a medium, so to speak, from which they emerge, and to which they may return. However, living processes (plants and organisms) as distinct from non-living ones (streams) also seem able to accumulate in some way their past in their present. Thus,

> the present moment of a living body does not find its explanation in the moment immediately before . . . [but] *all* the past of the organism must be added to that moment, its heredity – in fact the whole of a very long history. (Bergson, 1922, p. 21)

In other words, duality of structure, although necessary, is not sufficient for agency; the prolongation of the past into the present (i.e. memory, but not as a process of storage) is necessary also, for it is that which gives a 'line of intentionality' into the future determining the style of what is to come.

These conditions are, however, as we shall see, still insufficient for human agency: human beings seem to accumulate within themselves, not just a history, but a sense of their 'position' in their world in relation to all the others with whom they share it. As persons they must be not just conscious but self-conscious, that is, aware of the function of their own actions in relation to the social order at large in which they are 'rooted'. Their action is thus mediated in some way by a sense of who and what, and of where they are. Before discussing people's reflexive sense of themselves, however, I shall turn to an examination of those human activities which have a 'mediatory' function.

Mediation and Representation

As presented here human action is that aspect of human activity in which people make a difference in their environments. To talk of the world of human action immediately after talk of streams and plants may seem to entail something of a 'jump'. But with the resources at our disposal, it is possible to see that no essential discontinuity in our way of talking is involved; only transformations, i.e. the further articulation and differentiation of notions already introduced, should be necessary.

Earlier, in discussing forming co-ordinations, little distinction was made between a response to a stimulus, and an action. That distinction must now be drawn. Mead (1934, p. 305) describes well the relation between stimuli and responses:

> The two fit into each other and mutually determine each other, for it is the instinct-seeking-expression that determines the sensitivity of the animal to the stimulus, and it is the presence of the stimulus which sets the instinct free.

A response only occurs, in other words, if the *means* for its continuation is present in the animal's environment. The essence of human action is such, however, that individuals may project themselves forward without the support of the environment, towards a future state of affairs which need not yet exist. People find the means for the continuation of their actions within themselves. Instead of fitting themselves to their circumstances (a themselves-to-world direction of fit), they can also fit their circumstances to themselves (a world-to-themselves direction of fit) – to modify Searle's (1979) useful direction-of-fit terminology. Thus an action, even as it occurs, reciprocally implies a context into which it fits, a momentary 'world' differentiated into different regions. But more than that: due to its duality of structure, it posits in effect a whole realm of other possible next actions as appropriate continuations.

The concept of duality of structure serves to link these two 'directionalities', to link what has already been done to what might be done next. It emphasizes that the structure evident in human action is only produced or articulated as the action unfolds in time-space; that it is not the simple translation of a pre-existing, inner structure ordered in space into an outer one, ordered in time. It thus, in fact, provides a representation-free theory of intentionality (which is not to say that representations may play no part in informing action; on occasions they clearly do). It suggests that the moment of my control of my action can be informed – not by my consulting an 'inner representation' or 'plan' in a stop-refer-act-stop-refer process (cf. Miller, Galanter and Pribram, 1960) – but by what I have just specified in my action remaining 'on hand', so to speak, as a structured context into which I can act further. In passing out of my agency to control it further it becomes, strictly speaking, a region of my own immediate environment, the perceived context for the next phase of my action. But it is not at all a passive context; what is specified at any moment acts back upon the actor to make a difference in the value of the act, and its value unfolds as the action unfolds. Thus, just as in the growth of an oak tree, a point is reached when the next appropriate phase of growth is the production of acorns, so in the progress of human action, at each moment only certain further actions fit and are appropriate. Not just any action is possible, for the action's context must have its 'say' also.

Thus, in the course of their actions, agents seem at every moment to sense from within a 'shape' – '*feelings* of *tendency*, often so vague that we are unable to name them at all' (James, 1890, p. 254) – into which they must make their actions and expressions fit. James describes the experience eloquently. He asks (pp. 252–3): 'What then is the meaning of the words we think we understand when we read? What makes that meaning different in one phase from what it is in the other?' He replies:

> The truth is that large tracts of human speech are nothing but *signs of direction* in thought, of which direction we nevertheless have an acutely discriminative sense, though no definite sensorial image plays any part in it whatsoever. Sensorial images are stable psychic facts; we can hold them still and look at them as long as we like. These bare images of logical movement, on the contrary, are psychic transitions, always on the wing, so to speak, and not to be glimpsed except in flight. Their function is to lead from one set of images to another. As they pass, we feel both the waxing and the waning images in a way altogether peculiar and a way quite different from the way of their full presence. If we try to hold the feeling of direction, the full presence comes and the feeling of direction is lost.

Such a feeling of direction, as he goes on to say (p. 256), 'shoots its perspective far before it, irradiating in advance the regions in which lie the thoughts as yet unborn'. If the word 'man' is used in a sentence, for instance: 'It casts its influence over the whole of the sentence, both before and after the spot in which the word *man* is used' (p. 256). As moments in a progressively unfolding process, such feelings of tendency or direction are, as James points out, intrinsically vague – necessarily so if, as intentions, they are to afford predictable realization. Yet their vagueness is not at all of a disorderly kind; they are, in their duality of structure, already specified as to their further specifiability.

Mead (1934, p. 140) also provides an excellent account of the self-specifying nature of human action:

> That process . . . of responding to one's self as another responds to it, taking part in one's own conversation with others, being aware of what one is saying and using that awareness of what one is saying to determine what one is going to say thereafter – that is a process with which we are all familiar.

In fact, the process of using one's own past experience in structuring one's own further actions could hardly after all be more familiar. But what is perhaps not quite so obvious is that the relation between oneself and one's own past experience is, both logically and phenomenologically, similar to the relation between oneself and the tools one uses. Both our own past experience and our tools may be experienced as a-part-of-us as well as distinct from us in some way, i.e. experienced as mediators in between ourselves and the world; but also, as being on our-side of the relationship. The relation may be depicted as below:

$$\{\text{agency}\longleftrightarrow\text{mediator (as tool-like means)}\}\longleftrightarrow\text{world}$$

We 'dwell in' (Polanyi, 1967) such mediators, embodying them as means through which to achieve our ends (e.g. not only as the blind man uses his stick, but as we use words in influencing other people).

On the other hand, we can also experience the relation between ourselves and a mediator as being text-like, with the mediator as being more on-the-side-of-the-world. Such a relationship may be depicted thus:

$$\text{agency}\longleftrightarrow\{\text{mediator (as text-like meaning)}\longleftrightarrow\text{world}\}$$

Here, instead of the mediator being somewhat 'transparent' when used as a means – remember, for instance, that the blind man does not experience his stick as vibrating in the palm of his hand, but through his use of it, the roughness of the terrain at its tip – in contrast, the mediational instrument appears to an extent 'opaque'. It exists as a 'text' to be interpreted rather than as a 'tool' to be used (e.g. as with the pointer of the dial of an instrument, or an utterance depicting a state of affairs). It presents a meaning rather than affording a means. As a means we may say that a mediator exists in an 'embodiment-relation' with an agent, whereas, as a meaning, its relation can be said to be a 'hermeneutical' one. But if the mediator is itself another agency (or an aspect of one's own), then its duality of structure may be ambiguously of a tool-text kind, and it may function both as a continually developing means as well as a source of (also developing) meanings, oscillating between the two, as directed. In the relationship depicted below:

agency⟷mediational agency⟷world (also as agency)

it may 'side' with either side.

There is not space here to explore further the complex permutations of the relationships depicted above. One final comment, however, is important: all mediators work both as enablements and as constraints. While telescopes and microscopes, say, work to *reveal* features invisible to the naked eye, they do so at the cost of restricting both one's field of view and one's movement within it. In other words, they do so at the cost of *concealing* other features, the more large scale, overall features, among others. All mediators would seem to be equivocal in this respect. However, it is especially the way that our linguistic practices mediate in everything that we do which should give us most pause for thought here (see chapter 10). For clearly a version of reality is implicit in a practice whether it appears as an idea, as a sensorial image (James), in consciousness or not. Indeed, we have already met the dualistic metaphysics currently enshrined in our talk about ourselves which seems to suggest to us, misleadingly, that thinking goes on 'in our minds'. Such usages work to conceal from us the possibility that thought is not in fact located in some deep centre, privately within us, but may be immanent in everything we do. But the implications of such a view, the properties of its 'logical grammar', are hard to express. It is as if in some circumstances our window on the world is itself so highly patterned and framed that we can see nothing through it which is not itself 'coloured' and 'shaped' by the window itself. Making explicit the actual version or versions of reality implicit in our practical (i.e. not idle, not speculative) usages is clearly a project for much further research.

Social Orders and Self-Consciousness

To be creatures of intelligence rather than instinct, agents must be able to project themselves into the future, to act not as their circumstances require, but as they themselves require. Thus for them, there cannot be a *direct* relation between their environment and their behaviour; stimulus and response cannot simply fit into each other and mutually determine one another. The actions of intelligent agents must continually be mediated by mental activity, activity which must link their present action both to its possible future consequences and their own past experience. In other words, unlike instinctual organisms, they must show both foresight and memory, for they have to act without the support of their environment, but in a way appropriate to it nonetheless. Rather than relying upon their external environment to give directionality to their behaviour, they must carry an equivalent or equivalents to it within themselves; they must sense themselves as 'situated'.

But for human beings as persons, as socially autonomous members of a society, the requirements are even more demanding. More than simply a sense of their 'position' in their immediate environment, their 'situation', they must also be conscious of their own momentary 'position' in their society, a sense of the part they themselves might play in relation to the parts played by other people's actions in maintaining or progressing their society's aims. They thus have a duty: i.e. to act responsibly, in terms of their social 'position'. However, along with that duty goes a right: that of having most of what one says or does accepted as meaning what one intends it to mean without question, and taken seriously as such, with other people being prepared to base *their* actions upon it in fact. People only have their conduct questioned and have to account for it (to justify it) if it is puzzling or enigmatic to others in some way (Peters, 1958; Scott and Lyman, 1968) – for only if the normal process by which an activity is seen as appropriate in everyday social life fails must repairs be done.

Persons then, also possess a duality of structure; people experience themselves both as a 'me' and as an 'I' (James, 1890). Looking back upon their experience they see their place in society, who they are, their 'me'; looking forward as 'I's', they sense their own freedom to act – but not in every which way – but in terms of the vague 'feelings of tendency' afforded them also by their experience up to and including their present moment. It is at this point that we make contact with the discussions of duality of structure in Bhaskar (1979) and Giddens (1979):

> it is easy to see that both society and human praxis possess a *dual character*. Society is both the ever-present *condition* (material cause) and the continually reproduced *outcome* of human agency. And praxis is both work, that is *conscious* production, and (normally unconscious) *reproduction* of the conditions of production, that is, society. One could refer to the former as the duality of structure

[Giddens, 1976] and the latter as the duality of praxis. (Bhaskar, 1979, pp. 43–4)

In other words, society – social institutions and social practices – are continually reproduced by all members of a society in *all* their actions.

The duality of structure relates the smallest item of day-to-day behaviour to attributes of far more inclusive social systems: when I utter a grammatical English sentence in a casual conversation, I contribute to the reproduction of the English language as a whole. This is an unintended consequence of my speaking the sentence, but one that is bound indirectly to the recursiveness of the duality of structure. (Giddens, 1979, pp. 77–8)

Thus, paradoxical though it may seem, although my sentences are my own free products of myself alone, if I wish to maintain my autonomous status and to be seen as making sense, I must reproduce a version (albeit a transformed version) of an already established social reality in what I say. Such a reproduction is an unintended result of people trying to make themselves understood; their social reality does not directly determine their actions in any way. Prospectively, people are free to project themselves forward; and not only have they every right to do so, they *must* do so if human societies are to endure (see chapter 8). For to the extent that human societies are not maintained instinctually, they must be maintained by the individuals in them acting intelligently, i.e. on detecting transgressions and departures from the established social order, they must act to reinstitute it – and such repairs, although accountable as such, cannot *of necessity* be simply rule-governed actions, as they must occur in all kinds of predictable ways. Thus, only if individuals have freedom of action – to act in the service of the continual reproduction of 'a' social order, motivated by a desire for continued intelligibility to others – can such an order be automatically self-reproducing, i.e. be continually reproduced and transformed as an unintended consequence of everyone's actions. Without such a freedom, a social order requires somewhere in its ecology authorities, and they must see to it, intentionally, that transgressions and departures from 'their' social order are prevented and repaired. Clearly, most actual social orders are both unintentionally *and* intentionally reproduced in some respects.

As living totalities, social institutions must be self-reproducing over the long term as well as in the short term. In other words, they must contain, spread throughout their ecology, processes for the 'manufacture' from its newborns of persons, new members to replace older members as they die. In becoming a person, activity which at first occurs spontaneously, required by the child's socially arranged circumstances, must be transformed into activity done deliberately, when children *themselves* require. The process is described at length in the chapters in Part II.

Things which are at first spread out in the spontaneous, unintended (playful), non-localizable activities going on between people become localized within them. Consciousness thus seems to develop in a gradual passage from the less realized to the more realized, from the intensive to the extensive, from a reciprocal implication of parts to their juxtaposition – as Bergson (1920, p. 188) said of the very operation of life itself. Thus, rather than developing out of nothing, out of non-consciousness, or from total chaos, consciousness seems to develop by a series of transformations, each making a difference, each producing a new differentiation into the totality produced so far – all from a totality already in some sense partially conscious; and already in some sense partially ordered (i.e. not a chaos as Descartes imagined). It is a process in which what is spread out everywhere is accumulated or condensed into locatable foci. Elsewhere (in chapter 6), I have related the description of such processes to Bohm's (1980) account of a holonomic, implicate order. In such a process in a social world, practices always precede the theory of them, at every stage and every level.

Final Remarks

There can be no final conclusions to a discussion of duality of structure for,

> to make an end is to make a beginning.
> The end is where we start from.
> (T. S. Eliot, *Little Gidding*)

And it is this quality – of being both an end and a new beginning; of being both specified but further specifiable; of both relating past and future together in the present while differentiating them into qualitatively distinct moments – which many ways of talking in the social and behavioural sciences lack. The problem is to express in a clear and determinate fashion the character of intrinsically vague and incomplete processes without distorting their actual natures; i.e. to express the true character of their vagueness without being vague ourselves. Many concepts emphasize the retrospective, structural aspects of social institutions and practices. But structuration, their prospective structurizing activity, is often neglected, and thus they have little to say about how, not just social change, but processes of transformation might take place. The concept of duality of structure (with its associated images and paradigms), however, suggests to us how an activity, as something coherent and ordered, may continue to be recognizable as the activity it is while also being continuously transformed. Indeed, only if it *is* continuously transformed to meet new contingencies as they arise can it retain its identity as such. Furthermore, the concept of duality of structure relates the minor and seemingly trivial forms of daily social activity – the smiles, nods and frowns, the utterances of individuals, their tones of voice and bodily postures – both to the structural properties of large-scale social movements, to social history (moments) and social class (regions), as well as to the general evolutionary nature of the micro- and macrophysical world. In other words, it may serve to bring theoretical physics, biology and the social sciences together in a deep and fundamental way, within the general confines of an ecological approach.

Ecologically, we can see a social world as an evolving, dynamic system of ordered activities, all existing (when active) only in mutual relation to one another – not just in spite of one another, but also because of one another, i.e. owing their character and their existence to their differences. But the conflicting tendencies produced by living processes, operating just as much *off* as *for* one another, would be prone to disrupt each other unless assigned their own regions or moments of expression, and the boundaries between them maintained (M. Douglas, 1966). Within such bounded regions and moments, there can be social orders, but it is a society's ecology which provides the more large-scale context for their operation. But that further investigation – of our society's social ecology – is work for another day. Suffice it here simply to remark that, given an ecological approach, the idea that there *must* be some fundamental building blocks, some indistinguishable atomic elements whose different configurations constitute the distinguishable entities in such a world, is unnecessary. There need be no fundamental elements at all, only ways of, procedures for, methods by which, etc., distinguishing and describing one activity in terms which make it recognizably distinct from another, each way of talking existing in terms of its differences from the others – for it is the dance not the dancers which is important.

Epilogue: Mastery and Entrapment

A part of what it is to be a person is to be a member of a social order, experiencing oneself as embedded within its associated reality. And its nature is such that, as I put it in chapter 1, our understanding and experience of it is constituted very largely by the ways in which we must talk in our attempts to account for everything which occurs within it – i.e. *must* talk if we want still to be accounted competent members of our social order and assigned a status as an autonomous individual. For in general, the function of our ways of talking about occurrences in our everyday social lives, our accounting practices, is to ensure that we continuously and intelligibly reproduce our social order in all of our actions. Thus, in being concerned to act accountably, no matter what the diversity of the activities we engage in, we conform ourselves, so to speak, to our society's ways of sense-making. In other words, our systems of accountability 'speak' us more than we speak them, for they determine what, in all our activities, we can intelligibly understand and experience, and the communicative influences to which we are open.

Such forms of talk or ways of sense-making can be said to provide in a society a set of enabling-constraints, working both to put limitiations upon acceptable ways of talking, perceiving, acting, etc., while at the same time indicating what can follow from what, i.e. what the intelligible connections between things are. They are thus clearly selective and in no way all-inclusive. However, they cannot be 'refuted'; they cannot, like scientific theories, be called in question by, for example, expected outcomes failing to occur, etc. Indeed, failures, enigmas, puzzlements, etc., must all, sooner or later, be made sense of by use of the same procedures for making sense which have currency within one's society. So, although 'outsiders', members of other social orders, may find certain accounts of occurrences given by 'insiders' to be ridiculous, unbelievable, or demonstrably incorrect, to 'insiders' things look different. Evans-Pritchard

(1976, p. 150) describes the situation when he tried to confront the Azande with what seemed to him at least to be obvious failures of the chicken-oracle in which they believed:

> I was met sometimes by point-blank assertions, sometimes by one of the evasive secondary elaborations of belief that provide for any particular situation provoking scepticism, sometimes by polite pity, but always by an entanglement of linguistic obstacles, for one cannot well express in its language objections not formulated by a culture.

For quite literally insiders do not know how to formulate an intelligible doubt about their ways of accounting for occurrences in their world, without at least tending to give those self-same ways further currency in their formulations – for what other ways of talking, of making sense, do they have available? And to an extent, if this book is 'successful', the result could be similar: an unintended consequence of its success could be, in arguing against 'theory relevant' research in favour of a 'practical descriptive' alternative to it, the reinforcement of the current 'mind- and self-talk' which I have criticized in chapter 10 (i.e. the way of talking which assumes that we have 'minds in our heads', that they 'contain' such things as 'beliefs' and 'memories', etc.).

That kind of over-spatialized talk, which seems to refer to 'things' located 'somewhere', has been criticized by Wittgenstein (1980, 1981) thus:

> Where do you feel grief? – In the mind – What kind of consequences do we draw from this assignment of place? (1981, no. 497)

> But here the thought is: 'After all, you *feel* sadness – so you must feel it *somewhere*; otherwise it would be a chimera'. (1981, no. 510)

In other words, he is suggesting that our current way of understanding our own current 'mind-talk' may be wrong, that it is based upon a misleading paradigm; we cannot simply take it that in talking about mental activities thus, we are talking about certain things, and simply proceed to investigate what their characters seem to be. We must examine the roles, the functions, the parts that different terms play in all the various accounting practices we use in different activities in the hurly-burly of everyday life.

> Try not to think of understanding as a 'mental process' at all. For *that* is the way of speaking that is confusing you. Rather ask yourself:

in what kind of case, under what circumstances do we say 'Now I can
go on'. (1981, no. 446)

So what is the method Wittgenstein is suggesting here? Surely, it is the
method of what I have called a practical hermeneutics: the abandoning of
the attempt to 'picture', as if in immediate perception, the nature of human
activities (for as activities they cannot in any case be pictured), and the
taking up of the attempt to understand them 'in' their doing – for in this
case: 'to be is not to be perceived, but rather . . . just to be able to do'
(Bhaskar, 1979 – see note 1, chapter 8). Ultimately, to know about
ourselves in theory, we must first know of ourselves in practice. Only by
comparing our ways of talking in one activity with how we use the same
words in others, drawn from different regions and moments in the ecology
of everyday life, can we hope to break out of the 'entanglement of linguistic
obstacles' of which Evans-Pritchard speaks. Such investigations are work
for the future.

But why should we be so easily bewitched, entangled and ultimately
disabled by the devices which enable us to do so much? The answer seems
to be in our search for *mastery*; it is that which, paradoxically, seems to
lead to its own opposite: i.e. to our entrapment (Stolzenberg, 1978).
Mastery, we feel, will be ours if we possess, as Descartes put it, the right
kind of 'practical philosophy'. And as we know – following Descartes,
Galileo, Newton, etc. – that was thought to be of a 'geometrical' kind: a
procedure which involves constructing a system within which one can first
reason before acting. And we have taken this as a model for all intelligent
action: having an 'inner' logical 'plan', or 'script', 'theory' or 'representation' to consult in our acting is, for many, what intelligence *is* (Boden,
1977; Dennett, 1979). One's capacity to act intelligently is thus thought to
be enhanced if one can formulate a logical plan or theory, etc., *before*
embarking upon any activity. To do this, how should one proceed?

Stolzenberg, in discussing how the process of entrapment (as he calls it)
works, suggests that the first step people take in attempting to formulate
logical systems is 'an act of acceptance as such in the domain of ordinary
language use'; i.e. one begins by accepting a set of principles, claims,
assertions,   axioms,   etc.,   as   indubitable,   self-evident,   as   unquestionable – indeed, they may be such that as presented in their simple
form, one quite literally does not know *how* to doubt them. The next step
is to combine these statements, etc., with one another using agreed rules
(of combination, substitutions, deletion, etc.) to form new statements . . .
without further questioning of the initial, self-evident 'assumptions'. 'The
basic evil of Russell's logic, as also of mine in the *Tractatus*,' says
Wittgenstein (no. 38, 1980), 'is that what a proposition is is illustrated

by a few commonplace examples, and then pre-supposed as understood in full generality'. In other words, everything else one encounters is treated as recognizable within the initial categories *already accepted* as indubitable. Such a procedure, of course, takes no account at all of the usually 'situated' usage of ordinary language. Since Descartes, this 'geometrical' mode of thought has enjoyed wide currency; but it entraps us in demonstrably incorrect systems of thought which we cannot refute. For instance, about 'both metaphysical and methodological variants of behaviourism . . . the following', claims Koch (1975, p. 5, to give now the statement partially quoted in chapter 1), 'can be said':

> These are essentially irrational positions (like, e.g. solipsism) which start with a denial of something much like a foundation-tenet of common sense, which *can* in the abstract, be 'rationally' defended for however long one wishes to persist in one's superordinate irrationality, but which cannot be *implemented* without brooking self-contradiction.

In our attempts to produce a single, coherent system of description for a diverse collection of activities, we have entrapped ourselves; we can account for, justify, the attempt to discover logical systems describing their character to anyone who questions our endeavour to do so. But we cannot *live* according to any such system. For the living of our lives consists in the doing of many activities, with no one of which on its own constituting a livable life – for in life we switch from one activity (with one intention) to another (with another intention) for reasons we find within the context of our choice. We have to choose activities appropriate to how we are 'situated'; the responsibility is ours, and it weighs upon us. We would like ourselves not to have to choose. Surely there must be an authoritative system (of laws? of rules?) somewhere to which we could appeal? The belief that one exists *somewhere* to be discovered is reinforced by the fact that just one language seems to be required to describe our reality, our ordinary language. But, says Wittgenstein (1953, p. 224):

> We remain unconscious of the prodigious diversity of all the everyday language-games because the clothing of our language makes everything alike.

That is, it makes everything look alike if we work in terms only of visual forms (Galileo); if we take a more temporal (or time–space) view, and ask whether such forms in fact *do* the same thing, then the answers are very different. To escape from the entanglements, bewitchments, the entrapments occasioned by the paradigms embedded within our everyday accounting practices, is one of our major tasks in a practical-descriptive psychology; for our problem with ourselves (and others) is rooted in our own self-definitions.

How then exactly should we define ourselves? Currently, as I have been trying to argue, we are very much as we exemplify ourselves as being in the ecology of our everyday social lives. And that is what I have been attempting to describe above. But such forms, exemplary though they may be, cannot be definitive, for life is not yet finished or complete. There is more of it to come. Hence the answer to the question as to what we are is evidently still in the making.

Notes

Chapter 2 A Science of Psychology: Theoretical or Practical?

1 An account of the hermeneutical approach can be found in chapter 5. See also Palmer (1969) and Gadamer (1975). Gauld and Shotter (1977) set out some of the properties of an hermeneutical psychology; and Shotter (in press) surveys the numerous different positions within hermeneutical theory itself.

2 See chapters 8 and 11, and Searle (1979a, b and c), for an account of the intentionality of intention and action, and for a description of the way in which human activity can be said to 'point to' or to 'contain' something beyond itself. It is in this sense that, by perceiving *from* people's expressions in relation to their circumstances, *to* whatever it is that they 'indicate' (to use Polanyi's (1967) useful terminology of 'tacit knowing'), that one is able to perceive *what* they are doing – in the sense of being able, in the circumstances, to see its point, to see what they are committing themselves to in the future by what they are doing now. For people do not always have to break off their actions to say what their actions *are*: the intrinsic intentionality of action is such that, what a person says or does is a pointer to what he or she is saying and doing (see chapter 11). The point of their behaviour is not 'contained' simply within their behaviour, however, but is in their-behaviour-in-their-'situation' (see Mills (1940) and chapter 1 for a discussion of the necessarily 'situated' character of our accounts of psychological phenomena).

3 Ossorio (in Davis, 1981, pp. 88–96) gives a very clear account of the powerful nature of paradigm cases as devices, instruments or resources, for use as canonical forms, in constructing accounting practices. For paradigm case formulations are possible in circumstances where definitions, as such, are not; for a definition already presupposes the existence of an appropriate accounting practice. Although lengthy, the importance of this account justifies its inclusion here. To quote him: 'A paradigm case formulation is accomplished in two major steps:

    1   Introduce a Paradigm Case (of X)
    2   Introduce one or more transformations of the Paradigm Case

As in the case of definition, the Paradigm Case must be either directly intelligible or finitely explainable in order for communication to be successful. The Paradigm Case will directly identify some portion of the cases which are to be picked out. Each transformation will pick out additional cases. Each transformation may be considered to be a constructional instruction or an indirect description: 'Change the Paradigm Case in this way (the transformation) and the result will still (also) be a case of X.' Thus, if the PCF is successful, the Paradigm Case and the transformations will, collectively, pick out all and only those cases that one wants to pick out, even if there is no second thing that those cases have in common. Therefore, a PCF will accomplish the identification of a subject matter (a range of possible cases) no less effectively than would a definition.

A standard example of a paradigm case formulation is the following PCF for the concept of a family.

1 Paradigm Case: A husband and his wife living with their natural children, who are a seventeen-year-old son, a ten-year-old daughter, and a five-year-old daughter.

2 Transformations:

   T1 Eliminate one parent.
   T2 Change the number of children to N, N > 0.
   T3 Change the sex distribution of the children to any distribution other than zero boys and zero girls.
   T4 Change the ages of the children to any values compatible with the ages of the parents.
   T5 Add any number of additional parents.
   T6 Add adopted and other legally defined sons and daughters.
   T7 Eliminate the requirement of living together.
   T8 Add zero children if husband and wife are living together.
   T9 Eliminate the requirement that the parents have the legal status of 'married.'

Note that constructing a PCF has a good deal in common with constructing a definition . . . what someone approves as a 'good' definition someone else will disapprove as misleading, defective, or wrong. . . . [To] give a definition of a term already in use, e.g. 'behaviour', 'emotion', or 'family' is to run the risk of violating the existing use and hence to run the risk of degrading the language and misleading or manipulating one's audience. All of these possibilities are the case for paradigm case formulations, though the danger is not as great.

There are also important differences between a definition and a paradigm case formulation. First, of course, we have noted that a PCF will do the job of identifying a subject matter in circumstances where a definition would fail because there is no second set of necessary and sufficient conditions for the use of the term in question. . . .

Considered as a formal device, i.e. a device type, rather than as a substantive construction, the paradigm case formulation has a reflexive use as well as a recursive logic. That is, not only is it the case that some element of a PCF can be given by means of a PCF, but also the very notion of a paradigm case formulation as given above can be handled in PCF fashion. Let us construct an example. I introduced the paradigm case formulation by specifying a two-step procedure, namely, (*a*) first, introduce a Paradigm case of X, then (*b*) introduce some number of transformations of the Paradigm Case such that when the Paradigm Case of X is transformed in that way the result will also (still) be a case of X. Let us designate this as PCF1. Now consider the following paradigm case formulation, which is designated as PCF2:

1 Paradigm Case: PCF1 i.e. A Introduce a Paradigm Case of X
                                      B Introduce transformations of Paradigm Case.

2 Transformations:

T1 Change the number of Paradigm Cases to N, N > one
T2 Eliminate the requirement that the Paradigm Case is a case of X. (It will be sufficient if the transformations generate cases of X.)
T3 Replace 'transformation' with any functional equivalent thereof.
T4 Allow transformations not only of the Paradigm Case, but also of the results of a previous transformation.

Here, we accomplish a bit of bootstrapping. The paradigm case formulation, as previously presented, can now be assigned the status of a Paradigm Case in a new PCF and the letter gives us a more complex and adequate representation of what a paradigm case formulation (what the range of instances of a PCF is).'

Ossorio here, of course, discusses PFC formulations for use by those who are already to a degree socially competent. The imaginative task required is to understand their use in the very early stages of life, in the initial building up of that competence.

4 If I were to claim that '13 × 31 = 403' and some one were to ask 'How do you know?' I could show them my 'workings', i.e. how within the rules of arithmetic: 3 × 3 = 9; 3 × 1 = 3; and 1 × 1 = 1, and so on. But if they were then to ask 'How do you know that 1 × 1 = 1?', I could only say 'That is what multiplying is, that's what its based on, to doubt those basic forms is not to doubt a particular arithmetic result, but the very practice of multiplying itself.' They are the basic paradigmatic 'moves' we learn to make in learning a 'language-game'. As Wittgenstein (1969, no. 139) says, 'Not only rules, but also examples are needed for establishing a practice. Our rules leave loop-holes open, and the practice has to speak for itself.' Indeed, As Garfinkel (1967, p. 22) says in reference to what he calls the *ad hocing* practices required if rules are to be applied intelligently and critically: 'It is not the case that the "necessary and sufficient" criteria are procedurally defined by [rules]. Nor is it the case that *ad hoc* practices . . . are eliminated . . . by making [rules] as definite as possible. Instead *ad hocing* practices are *used in order to recognize what the instructions* [rules] *are definitely talking about.*'

Chapter 3 What is it to be Human?

1 The OED defines 'possessor' as: 'one who holds something as property or in actual control . . . an owner, proprietor . . . one who takes, occupies, or holds something without ownership, or as dist[inct] from the owner.' In other words, to be in the relation of only a possessor to parts of myself means that they are parts which are alienable; being capable of ownership, their ownership is transferable; others may come to own them or control them instead of myself. They can be put on the market as commodities and given a price. While originally offered me as a gift of nature, my possession of them has to be earned; they become mine only through my mastery of them. Failing to master and control my own powers, I may find parts of myself under the control of others; they may appropriate the natural resources available in my person to their own ends. The alternative to only 'having' myself, so to speak is to 'be' myself: this, however, is a mode of existence easier to name than to analyse.

2 When I use the terms man, men, 'man-made', etc., here, I now use them (unlike four or five years ago) consciously, to mean that just men or a man did something, and not a woman or women. Recently, I have been made acutely aware that the literature of exploitation, mastery and domination is the literature of a culture dominated by (some) men – although not by *all* men by any means. Thus my reasons now for attempting to avoid the seemingly sexist terminology of men, mankind, etc., are not all just to avoid sexism; I am also concerned to avoid misleading generalities: for it was not 'mankind' as a mystic being over and above individual and select groups of men who fashioned the currently dominant mode of rationality. To talk as if it was is to obfuscate the possibility of a proper historical understanding of the undemocratic origins of our current dominant social practices, and how they might be changed.

3 Cf. the discussion distinguishing theories from accounts in chapter 2. Although in Aristotle's terms, psychology clearly can intend an existence as a 'theoretical science', and has done so for the last hundred years, it is not my intention here to attempt to further that goal by producing a speculative theory for empirical test; it is to attempt to describe the accountable context within which all speculative theories must be formulated and tested (and their meaning evaluated).

Chapter 4 The Development of Personal Powers

1 In reproducing Shotter (1974), this chapter contains some small but important revisions: I have tried to suggest now that individuals do not draw their personal powers from natural powers solely from within themselves, but from natural powers available to 'them' as persons in 'their' surroundings, in whatever is 'other than' themselves, where often such powers are only available in the circumstances between themselves and persons. In the original version of this article, the impression given was definitely that babies were born with their natural powers already within them in some way – I now think that this 'innatist' position is quite wrong, and that children can only develop the capacities that they are offered the 'developmental opportunities' to develop. I

have also eradicated all reference to 'unconscious inferences' as being involved in perception. I now think that all perception is essentially 'direct', and I have offered a 'hermeneutical model' to account for it.

2   It was Franz Brentano who was responsible for introducing the concept of intentionality into modern philosophy. In attempting to clarify the distinction between mental and physical phenomena he suggested that every mental phenomenon is characterized by what the Schoolmen of the Middle Ages called the 'intentional inexistence' of the object. In other words, mental activity is 'directed upon an end or object', it 'points to' or 'contains' something other than itself – whether that something exists or not. And it is this, its intention, which distinguishes an act from other acts, not anything in the temporal order of basic event-episodes, or suchlike, in the behaviour.

3   These two different views define two different spheres of study: the natural and the artificial or humanly 'constructed'. And it would be surprising if the same frameworks of thought and techniques of investigation were appropriate to both, a point Vico first made in 1744. Not that the word 'natural' is the best word to use here, for it is used not in any physical or organic sense, but simply to mean unselfconscious and impersonal activity.

4   By this he does not mean intended, for although the smile may be 'directed', in the sense of being something the baby him- or herself 'did', it could not be said at this stage to have a specific 'content'; it can only be vaguely directed (see chapter 11). Babies' activities, however, must be considered to be intentional from the start; intentionality as such cannot have a 'birthday' or else we create for ourselves the problems Stout (1938) discusses – see quotation later in the chapter.

5   See chapter 7 for a critical account ·of the 'object relations' school's developmental psychoanalysis.

6   Strictly, we should say that all our experiences are derived from 'outside' *us* as individual personalities responsible for our own actions etc.; from 'outside' ourselves that is. For often we want to talk about our experience of the motions of our own bodies as well as our experience of the motions of other people's.

7   A distinction not of existence but in intention (see Macmurray, 1957, for the nature of this most important distinction).

8   Rules specify possibilities, and not all the possibilities they specify are necessarily realizable. That is why, of course, we have to test theories, and why also mistakes are often intelligible.

9   While organic behaviour may indeed by directed or regulated it need not be rule-regulated. Regulation as such is a characteristic of all processes in 'open systems' maintained in a 'steady state' according to 'system parameters' (v. Bertalanffy, 1968); rules involve agreements between people.

Chapter 5   Developmental Practices: Practical Hermeneutics and Implication

1   Hermeneutics: 'The Greek word *Hermeois* referred to the priest at the Delphic oracle. This word and the more common verb *hermenuein* and the noun *hermeneia* point back to the wing-footed messenger-god Hermes from whose name the words are apparently derived (or vice versa?) Significantly, Hermes is

associated with the function of transmuting what is beyond human understanding into a form that human intelligence can grasp. The various forms of the word suggest the process of bringing a thing or situation from unintelligibility to understanding. The Greeks accredited Hermes with the discovery of language and writing – the tools which human understanding employs to grasp meaning and to convey it to others' (Palmer, 1969, p. 13). See also Shotter (in press).

Chapter 6 The Ecological Setting for Development: Implicate Orders, Joint Action and Intentionality

1 See chapter 11 for my objections to Gibson's use of the word 'affordances' (as a noun): essentially, the situation is one of people affording (verb) one another developmental opportunities in their actions. No affordance is there, in the environment, completely specified as the affordance it is, before the activity it affords is complete.

2 Furthermore, how does one know if what one is doing is correct? Especially when it comes to remembering or imagining something. Does one check out what one is doing by reference to an inner criterion, a copy or image of what is required? Wittgenstein would argue not:

> Our problem is analogous to the following:
>
> If I give someone the order 'fetch me a red flower from that meadow,' how is he to know what sort of flower to bring, as I have only given him a *word*?
>
> Now the answer one might suggest first is that he went to look for a red flower carrying a red image in his mind, and comparing it with the flowers to see which of them had the colour of the image. Now there is such a way of searching, and it is not at all essential that the image we use be a mental one. In fact the process may be this: I carry a chart co-ordinating names and coloured squares. When I hear the order 'fetch me etc.' I draw my finger across the chart from the word 'red' to a certain square, and I go and look for a flower which has the same colour as the square. But this is not the only way of searching and it is not the usual way. We go, look about us, walk up to a flower and pick it, without comparing it to anything. To see that the process of obeying an order can be of this kind, consider the order '*imagine* a red patch.' You are not tempted in this case to think that *before* obeying you must have imagined a red patch to serve you as the pattern for the red patch you were ordered to imagine. (Wittgenstein, 1965, p. 3)

'An "inner process" stands in need of outer criteria,' as Wittgenstein says elsewhere (1953, no. 508); its correctness cannot be tested by comparison with yet another inner process – for how could the correctness of *that* process be tested? At some point, reference to activities in daily life at large is necessary, for that is where judgements as to what is right and wrong take place. Such judgements are not made for one by one's biology or neurology; they operate just as effectively whether one is acting correctly or mistakenly.

3   The mode of 'representation' meant here is, to use the language of tropes, of a metonymical rather than of a metaphorical kind: it is a matter of a part (or sub-whole) indicating or evoking the whole to which it belongs, and within which it has its being as the kind of thing it is; rather than a relational- structure being used to indicate that a structure in question is one of like form. The (metaphorical) example of metonymy usually cited is that of the way in which a crown denotes the whole constitution of kingship, or a sceptre that of authority; but another example might be that of how in Proust, the taste of the madeleine evokes a whole earlier world. This form of 'representation' is not that of one structure of relations paralleling another, but is of an intentional kind, in which something 'points to', or 'indicates' or 'evokes' the larger whole or context within which it has its being as what it is. To the extent that the use of a word as a word in a language requires the user to have a knowledge of the language within which the word functions linguistically, a word must be considered as functioning metonymically, rather than metaphorically, in its use. For enfolded (or implicated) in the use of a word *as a word* is a knowledge, not just of a language, but of what a form of life it is which makes the use of speech as a form of communication possible. Such a form of implicate-representation is of quite a different kind to that currently discussed as 'representation' in cognitive psychology.

Chapter 7 Models of Childhood in Developmental Research

1   In chapter 11 I have argued that the term 'affordances' (noun) is unfortunate as it assumes that affordances are 'there' in the environment whether anyone is there to make use of them or not. Whereas I would want to say that an 'affordance' is only *specified* as the affordance it is when the activity it affords is complete. The two are correlative: the structure of the environment and the action within it are specified together as constituting the act done.
2   Inner here is presumed to be really internal, and is not indicative of just 'a way of talking'. Elsewhere in this book I have put 'inner' and 'outer' in quote marks to denote their generally metaphorical use – see chapter 10 and note 3.
3   I put the words 'self' and 'selves' in quote marks as I do not now see, contrary to my previous usage, any compelling reason to postulate a 'self' as an entity conceptually separable in any way from the person, him- or herself. I use the prefix (self-) or suffix (-self) to indicate reflexive reference; not to stand for any thing hidden 'within' the person.

Chapter 8 Vico, Joint Action, Moral Worlds and Personhood

1   As Bhaskar (1979, pp. 15–16) points out, science does not always require something to appear as an object in immediate perception to ascribe it reality. 'On this criterion, to be is not to be [immediately] perceived, but rather . . . just to be able to do' (my addition). Indeed, as I pointed out in chapter 4, people *show* their psychological states in the temporal organization (or 'directing') of their actions; they 'point to' *what* they are saying or doing in their saying and doing.

Chapter 9 Telling and Reporting: Prospective and Retrospective Uses of Self-Descriptions

1 At some point, as Wittgenstein (1969, no. 164) says, 'Doesn't testing come to an end?' Our procedures and practices, no matter how rigorous, no matter how 'scientific', rest upon foundations which themselves cannot be tested in the same way (see note 4, chapter 2). 'At some point one has to pass from explanation to mere description' (no. 189), and at that point 'justification comes to an end' (no. 192). The fact is: 'If I don't trust *this* evidence why should I trust any evidence?' (no. 672). Here: 'We might speak of fundamental principles of human enquiry' (no. 670). And the difficulty Nisbett and his associates raise is with our understanding of *what* in everyday life our valid forms of inquiry are, not with any of the particular findings we make by their use.

2 Levi-Strauss (1963, ch. 10) discusses the song used by the shaman of the Cuna tribe (who live in the Panama Republic) to aid a difficult childbirth. It is a song of an epic quest to restore order: in which animals represent the different 'souls' of the different organs of the body, where a rabbit, representing *Muu*, the 'soul' of the uterus, the power responsible for the formation of the foetus, gets 'above' itself and has to be 'put back' in its place, thus restoring Muu to her rightful place in relation to all the other 'souls' belonging to other parts of the body. The sick woman becomes enthralled in the story of how, after many vicissitudes and the overcoming of great obstacles, order is restored, and in the course of listening to the story she gets well. 'The song constitutes,' Levi-Strauss suggests, 'a purely psychological treatment, for the shaman does not touch the body of the sick woman and administers no remedy. . . . In our view, the song constitutes a *psychological manipulation* of the sick organ, and it is precisely from this manipulation that a cure is expected' (pp. 191–2). Her very being is constituted in such a way that, due to the 'embodied presuppositions' she acquired in her socialization, she can be affected in a way that is (probably) unavailable to us. 'Once the sick woman understands [the song],' claims Levi-Strauss,

> she gets well. But no such thing happens to our sick when the causes of their diseases have been explained to them in terms of secretions, germs or viruses. We shall perhaps be accused of paradox if we answer that the reason lies in the fact that microbes exist and monsters do not. And yet, the relationship between germ and disease is external to the mind of the patient, for it is a cause-and-effect relationship; whereas the relationship between monster and disease is internal to his mind, whether conscious or unconscious . . . . The shaman provides the sick woman with a *language*, by means of which unexpressed, and otherwise inexpressible, psychic states can be immediately expressed. (p. 197)

Chapter 11 'Duality of Structure' and 'Intentionality' in an Ecological Psychology

1 The point to remember here is that we are never simply describing the world as

it *is*; we are always describing the nature of our own accountable behaviour in it. And this is Stapp's (1972) point concerning the use of quantum theory in practice:

> The essential points are that attention is focused upon some system that is first prepared in a specified manner and later examined in a specified manner. Quantum theory is a procedure for calculating the predicted probability that the specified type of examination will yield some specified result. . . .
>
> The wave functions used in these calculations are functions of a set of variables characteristic of the prepared and measured systems. These systems are often microscopic and not directly measurable . . . . They are described in terms of things that can be recognized and/or acted upon by technicians. These descriptions refer to the macroscopic properties of the preparing and measuring devices. (p. 1100)

It is in this sense that quantum theory, Stapp maintains, is not anchored in space–time realities, but is 'turned back and anchored in the concrete sense realities that form the basis of social life' (p. 1098). The trouble with the quantum theory, as many physicists such as Bohm (1980) maintain, is that it does not provide an image of the physical reality it purports to describe; it allows one to predict results, but not to say *why* they occurred in the way that they did. It does not, in other words, seem to *refer* actually to things in the world. Thus, in the sense of the terms I am using, rather than a 'theory', it collapses into an 'accounting practice'. Because of this, physicists, in talking in their discussions of 'wave functions', etc., cannot be said to be talking about real objects in the real world – although they do, and it leads them to posit some very weird happenings in the world when the wave function 'collapses'. In fact, they are talking about their ways of talking about what they can do in their 'world'.

And it would be no surprise if their contact with their 'world' had a practical hermeneutical quality to it: i.e. that they like psychologists had to accept that as a result of their 'dialogues' with the 'things' (activities?) in their surroundings, they had to change their way of talking about them as what they were talking about changed – changed in their whatness – as a result of their activities in interaction with them: a paradigm here, being, perhaps, the way one must change one's way of talking to and about one's children as they grow up, as a result of the developmental opportunities one has offered them – after certain 'rites de passage', a Barmitzvah, for instance, the change can be quite drastic.

Here, the point of Ossorio's boot-strapped paradigm case formulation [see note 3, chapter 2] comes to the fore. It provides for transformations in the paradigms in terms of which accounting practices work. And when what is being talked about are form-producing processes, which are themselves, in fact, ways of accounting or of making sense (and which are all in the process of transformation anyway), then the claim that they can all be seen as related to one another in terms of intelligible, i.e. specifiable, differences is, I think, a very powerful claim indeed. A fitting speculative note upon which to end.

References

Abelson, R. (1977) *Persons: A Study in Philosophical Psychology*. Basingstoke: Macmillan.

Allport, D. A. (1975) The state of cognitive psychology: a critical notice of W. G. Chase (ed.) *Visual Information Processing*. New York: Academic Press. *Quarterly Journal of Experimental Psychology, 27*, 141–52.

Anscombe, G. E. M. (1957) *Intention*. Oxford: Blackwell.

Antacki, C. (1981) *The Psychology of Ordinary Explanations of Behaviour*. London and New York: Academic Press.

Argyle, M. (1969) *Social Interaction*. London: Methuen.

Argyle, M. (1973) *Social Encounters: Readings in Social Interaction*. Harmondsworth: Penguin.

Ariès, P. (1973) *Centuries of Childhood*. Harmondsworth: Penguin.

Ariès, P. (1976) *Western Attitudes Toward Death from the Middle Ages to the Present*. London: Boyars.

Aristotle (1928) *The Works of Aristotle*: vol. VIII, *Metaphysica*. (ed. and trans. W. D. Ross, 2nd ed.) Oxford: Clarendon Press.

Austin, J. (1962) *How to do Things with Words* (ed. J. O. Urmson). London: Oxford University Press.

Ayers, M. R. (1968) *The Refutation of Determinism*. London: Methuen.

Bar-Hillel, Y. (1954) Indexical expressions. *Mind, 63*, 359–79.

Bem, D. J. (1967) Self-perception: an alternative interpretation of cognitive dissonance phenomena. *Psych. Rev., 74*, 183–200.

Berger, J. (1973) *G: a Novel*. Harmondsworth: Penguin.

Berger, P. and Luckman, T. (1967) *The Social Construction of Reality*. Harmondsworth: Penguin.

Bergson, H. (1911) *Matter and Memory*. London: George Allen & Unwin.

Bergson, H. (1920) *Mind-Energy*. London: Macmillan.

Bergson, H. (1922) *Creative Evolution*. London: Macmillan.

Berlin, I. (1969) A note on Vico's concept of knowledge. In G. Tagliacozzo (ed.) and H. V. White (co-ed.) *Giambatista Vico: an International Symposium*. Baltimore: Johns Hopkins.

Berlin, I. (1976) *Vico and Herder*. London: The Hogarth Press.

Bernstein, B. (1971) *Class, Codes and Control*, vol. 1. London: Routledge & Kegan Paul.

Bernstein, B. (1972) *Class, Codes and Control*, vol. 2. London: Routledge & Kegan Paul.

Bernstein, R. J. (1972) *Praxis and Action*. London: Duckworth.

Bernstein, R. J. (1981) Critical study: Human beings: plurality and togetherness. *Review of Metaphysics, 35*, 349–66.

Bertalanffy, L. v. (1968) *General System Theory*. New York: George Braziller.

Bhaskar, R. (1975) *A Realist Theory of Science*. Leeds: Leeds Books.

Bhaskar, R. (1979) *The Possibility of Naturalism*. Sussex: Harvester Press.

Blum, A. (1974) *Theorizing*. London: Routledge & Kegan Paul.

Boden, M. (1977) *Artificial Intelligence and Natural Man*. Sussex: Harvester Press.

Bohm, D. (1965) *The Special Theory of Relativity*. New York: Benjamin.

Bohm, D. (1969) Some remarks upon the notion of order. In C. H. Waddington (ed.) *Towards a Theoretical Biology*, vol. 2: *Sketches*. Edinburgh: Edinburgh University Press.

Bohm, D. (1973a) Human nature as a product of our mental models. In J. Bentall (ed.) *The Limits of Human Nature*. London: Allen Lane.

Bohm, D. (1973b) Quantum theory as an indication of a new order in physics. Part B. Implicate and explicate order in physical law. *Fouindations of Physics, 3*, 139–68.

Bohm, D. (1980) *Wholeness and the Implicate Order*. London: Routledge & Kegan Paul.

Bower, T. R. G. (1966) The visual world of infants. *Scientific American, 215*, 80–92.

Bower, T. R. G. (1971) The object in the world of the infant. *Scientific American, 225*, 31–8.

Bower, T. R. G. (1974) *Development if Infancy*. San Francisco: Freeman.

Bowlby, J. (1940) The influence of early environment in the development of neurosis and neurotic character. *International J. of PsychoAnalysis, 21*, 154–78.

Bowlby, J. (1944) Forty-four juvenile thieves: their character and their home life. *International J. of PsychoAnalysis, 25*, 15–52; 107–27.

Bowlby, J. (1953) *Child Care and the Growth of Love*. Harmondsworth: Penguin.

Brentano, F. (1973) *Psychology from an Empirical Standpoint* (trans. A. C. Rancurello, D. B. Terrell and L. L. McAlister). London: Routledge & Kegan Paul (orig. pub. 1874).

Bruner, J. S. (1966) *Toward a Theory of Instruction*. New York: W. W. Norton.

Bruner, J. S. (1969) On voluntary action and its hierarchical structure. In A. Koestler and J. R. Symthies (eds) *Beyond Reductionism*. London: Hutchinson.

Bruner, J. S. (1972) Address to Developmental Section of British Psychological Society, London, December 1972.

Bruner, J. S. (1976) From communication to language: a psychological perspective. *Cognition, 3,* 255–87.

Bruner, J. S. and Sherwood, V. (1975) Early rule structure: the case of peekaboo. In J. S. Bruner and K. Sylva (eds) *Play: its Role in Evolution and Development.* Harmondsworth: Penguin.

Brunswick, E. (1956) *Perception and the Representative Design of Psychological Experiments.* Berkeley: University of California Press.

Bryant, P. E. (1974) *Perception and Understanding in Young Children.* London: Methuen.

Bryant, P. E. and Trabasso, T. (1971) Transitive inferences and memory in young children. *Nature, 232,* 456–8.

Busfield, J. (1974) Family ideology and family pathology. In N. Armistead (ed.) *Reconstructing Social Psychology.* Harmondsworth: Penguin.

Buss, A. R. (1978) Causes and reasons in attribution theory: a conceptual critique. *J. of Pers. and Soc. Psychol., 36,* 1311–21.

Butterworth, G. and Light, P. (eds) (1982) *Social Cognition: Studies of the Development of Understanding.* Sussex: Harvester Press.

Čapek, M. (1965) *The Philosophical Impact of Contemporary Physics.* New York: Van Nostrand.

Cassirer, E. (1950) *The Problem of Knowledge: Philosophy, Science, and History since Hegel.* New Haven: Yale University Press.

Cassirer, E. (1953) *Philosophy of Symbolic Forms,* vol. 1. New Haven: Yale University Press.

Cassirer, E. (1957) *The Philosophy of Symbolic Forms,* vol. 3. New Haven: Yale University Press.

Cavell, S. (1969) *Must We Mean What We Say?* London: Cambridge University Press.

Chein, I. (1972) *The Image of Man and the Science of Behaviour.* London: Routledge & Kegan Paul.

Chomsky, N. (1957) *Syntactic Structures.* Hague: Mouton.

Chomsky, N. (1965) *Aspects of the Theory of Syntax.* Cambridge, Mass.: MIT Press.

Chomsky, N. (1966) *Current Issues in Linguistic Theory.* The Hague: Mouton.

Chomsky, N. (1968) *Language and Mind.* New York: Harcourt, Brace & World.

Chomsky, N. (1972) *Problems of Knowledge and Freedom.* London: Fontana.

Cicourel, A. (1973) *Cognitive Sociology.* Harmondsworth: Penguin.

Clark, H. H. and Haviland, S. E. (1977) Comprehension and the given-new contract. In R. O. Freedle (ed.) *Production and Comprehension.* Norwood, N. J.: Ablex Publishing.

Cohen, G. (1977) *The Psychology of Cognition.* London: Academic Press.

Condon, W. S. and Sander, L. S. (1974) Neonate movement is synchronized with adult speech. *Science, 183,* 99.

Cooley, C. H. (1902) *Human Nature and the Social Order.* New York: Scribner's.

Craik, K. J. W. (1943) *The Nature of Explanation*. Cambridge: Cambridge University Press.

Davis, K. E. (ed.) (1981) *Advances in Descriptive Psychology*, vol. 1. Connecticut: JAI Press.

Davis, K. E. and Mitchell, T. (eds) (1982) *Advances in Descriptive Psychology*, vol. 2. Greenwich: JAI Press.

Dawkins, R. (1978) *The Selfish Gene*. St Albans: Paladin Books.

Dennett, D. (1979) *Brainstorms: Philosophical Essays on Mind and Psychology*. Sussex: Harvester Press.

Dennis, W. (ed.) *Readings in the History of Psychology*. New York: Appleton-Century-Crofts.

Denzin, N. K. (1977) *Childhood Socialization: Studies in the Development of Language, Social Behaviour and Identity*. San Francisco: Jossey-Bass.

Descartes, R. (1968) *Discourse on Method and Other Writings* (trans. with intro. by F. E. Sutcliffe). Harmondsworth: Penguin.

Dewey, J. (1896) The concept of the reflex arc in psychology. *Psychol. Rev., 3*, 13–32. Reprinted in W. Dennis (ed.) *Readings in the History of Psychology*. New York: Appleton-Century-Crofts, 1948.

Donaldson, M. (1977) *Children's Minds*. London: Fontana.

Douglas, J. (1971) *Understanding Everyday Life*. London: Routledge & Kegan Paul.

Douglas, M. (1966) *Purity and Danger*. Harmondsworth: Penguin.

Dreyfus, H. L. (1965) Why computers must have bodies in order to be intelligent. *Review of Metaphysics, 21*, 13–22.

Dreyfus, H. L. (1972) *What Computers Can't Do: A Critique of Artificial Reason*. New York: Harper & Row.

Dunn, J. and Kendrick, C. (1982) *Siblings: Love, Envy and Understanding*. London: Grant MacIntyre.

Duval, S. and Wicklund, R. V. (1972) *A Theory of Objective Self-Awareness*. New York: Academic Press.

Elias, N. (1978) *The Civilising Process: the History of Manners*. Oxford: Blackwell.

Elms, A. C. (1975) The crisis of confidence in social psychology. *Amer. Psych., 30*, 967–76.

Evans-Pritchard, E. E. (1976) *Witchcraft, Oracles and Magic among the Azande*. London: Oxford University Press.

Fantz, R. L. (1976) The origin of form perception. *Scientific American, 204*, 66–72.

Feyerabend, P. (1975) *Against Method: Outline of an Anarchist Theory of Knowledge*. London: New Left Books.

Freud, S. (1961) *Civilization and its Discontents*. New York: W. W. Norton.

Gadamer, H. G. (1975) *Truth and Method* London: Sheed & Ward.

Gallwey, T. (1974) *The Inner Game of Tennis*. London: Cape.

Garfinkel, H. (1956) conditions of successful degradation ceremonies. *Amer. J. Sociol., 61*, 420–4.

Garfinkel, H. (1967) *Studies in Ethnomethodology*. Englewood Cliffs:

Prentice-Hall.

Gauld, A. and Shotter, J. (1977) *Human Action and its Psychological Investigation*. London: Routledge & Kegan Paul.

Geertz, C. (1973) *The Interpretation of Cultures*. New York: Basic Books.

Gergen, K. J. (1973) Social psychology as history. *J. of Pers. and Soc. Psychol.*, 26, 309–20.

Gergen, K. J. (1978) Toward generative theory. *J. of Pers. and Soc. Psychol.*, 36, 1344–60.

Gergen, K. J. (1980) Towards intellectual audacity in social psychology. In R. Gilmore and S. Duck (eds) *The Development of Social Psychology*. New York: Academic Press.

Gergen, K. J. (1982) *Toward Transformation in Social Knowledge*. New York: Springer.

Gergen, K. J. and Davis, K. E. (in press) *The Social Construction of the Person*. New York: Springer.

Gibson, J. J. (1966) *The Senses Considered as Perceptual Systems*. Boston: Houghton Mifflin.

Gibson, J. J. (1979) *The Ecological Approach to Visual Perception*. London: Houghton Mifflin.

Giddens, A. (1976) *New Rules of Sociological Method*. London: Heinemann.

Giddens, A. (1979) *Central Problems in Social Theory: Action, Structure and Contradiction in Social Analysis*. London: Macmillan.

Goffman, E. (1959) *The Presentation of Self in Everyday Life*. New York: Doubleday & Co., Penguin, 1971.

Goffman, E. (1968) *Asylums*. Harmondsworth: Penguin.

Goffman, E. (1971) *Relations in Public*. London: Allen Lane, The Penguin Press.

Goodman, N. (1972) The way the world is. In *Problems and Projects*. New York: Bobbs-Merrill.

Goodman, N. (1978) *Ways of Worldmaking*. Sussex: Harvester Press.

Grice, H. P. (1975) Logic and conversation. In P. Cole and J. L. Morgan (eds) *Syntax and Semantics*, vol. 3. New York: Academic Press.

Habermas, J. (1970a) On systematically distorted communication. *Inquiry*, 13, 205–18.

Habermas, J. (1970b) Towards a theory of communicative competence. *Inquiry*, 13, 360–75.

Habermas, J. (1972) *Knowledge and Human Interests*. London: Heinemann.

Halliday, M. A. K. (1975) *Learning How to Mean*. London: Arnold.

Hampshire, S. (1959) *Thought and Action*. London: Chatto & Windus.

Hanson, N. R. (1958) *Patterns of Discovery*. Cambridge: Cambridge University Press.

Harré, R. (1970a) Powers. *Brit. J. Philos. Sci.*, 21, 81–101.

Harré, R. (1970b) *The Principles of Scientific Thinking*. London: Macmillan.

Harré, R. (1974) The conditions for a social psychology of childhood. In M. P. M. Richards (ed.) *The Integration of a Child into a Social World*. London: Cambridge University Press.

Harré, R. (1979) *Social Being: a Theory for Social Psychology*. Oxford: Blackwell.

Harré, R. (1981) Expressive aspects of descriptions of others. In C. Antacki (ed.) *The Psychology of Ordinary Explanations of Social Behaviour*. London and New York: Academic Press.

Harré, R. and Secord, P. F. (1972) *The Explanation of Social Behaviour*. Oxford: Blackwell.

Harré, R. and Madden, E. H. (1975) *Causal Powers: a Theory of Natural Necessity*. Oxford: Blackwell.

Harvey, J. H. and Tucker, J. A. (1979) On problems with the cause-reason distinction in attribution theory. *J. of Pers. and Soc. Psychol.*, 37, 1441–6.

Heaton, J. (1976) Theoretical practice: the place of theory in psychotherapy. *J. of the Brit. Soc. for Phenomenology*, 7, 73–85.

Heelas, P. and Lock, A. (1981) *Indigenous Psychologies: the Anthropology of the Self*. London: Academic Press.

Hegel, G. W. F. (1966) *The Phenomenology of Mind*. London: George Allen and Unwin, first pub. 1807.

Heidegger, M. (1967) *Being and Time*. Oxford: Blackwell.

Heider, F. (1958) *The Psychology of Interpersonal Relations*. New York: Wiley.

Hertz, H. H. (1956) *The Principles of Mechanics*. New York: Dover.

Hollis, M. (1977) *Models of Man*. London: Cambridge University Press.

Huizinga, J. (1949) *Homo Ludens*. London: Routledge & Kegan Paul.

Hunter, I. M. L. (1979) Memory in everyday life. In M. M. Grunberg and P. E. Morris (eds) *Applied Problems in Memory*. London: Academic Press.

Jacoby, R. (1975) *Social Amnesia: a Critique of Conformist Psychology from Adler to R. D. Laing*. Sussex: Harvester Press.

Jahoda, M. (1977) *Freud and the Dilemmas of Psychology*. London: Hogarth.

Jahoda, M. (1980) Work, employment and unemployment. *Amer. Psych.*, 36, 184–91.

Jakobson, R., Fant, G. and Halle, M. (1951) *Preliminaries to Speech Analysis: the Distinctive Features and Their Correlates*. Cambridge, Mass.: MIT Press.

James, W. (1890) *Principles of Psychology*, vol. 2. London: Macmillan.

James, W. (1917) The dilemma of determinism. In *The Will to Believe and Other Essays in Popular Philosophy*. New York: Dover, 1956.

James, W. (1956) *The Will to Believe*. New York, Dover.

Jaynes, J. (1979) *The Origins of Consciousness in the Breakdown of the Bicameral Mind*. London: Allen Lane.

Joachim, H. H. (1951) *Aristotle: the Nicomachean Ethics* (ed.) D. A. Rees. Oxford: Clarendon Press.

Johnson-Laird, P. N. and Wason, P. C. (1977) *Thinking: Readings in Cognitive Science*. London: Cambridge University Press.

Jones, E. E. and Davis, K. E. (1965) From acts to dispositions: the attribution process in person perception. In L. Berkowitz (ed.) *Advances in Experimental Social Psychology*, vol. 2. New York: Academic Press.

Jones, E. E. and Nisbett, R. E. (1972) The actor and the observer: divergent perceptions of the causes of behaviour. In E. E. Jones, D. E. Kanouse, H. H. Kelley, R. E. Nisbett, S. Valins and B. Weiner *Attribution: Perceiving the Causes of Behaviour*. Morristown: General Learning Press.

Jones, E. E., Kanouse, D. E., Kelley, H. H., Nisbett, R. E., Valins, S. and Weiner, B. (1972) *Attribution: Perceiving the Causes of Behaviour*. New Jersey: General Learning Press.

Jong, E. (1978) *How to Save Your Own Life*. London: Panther Books.

Joynson, R. B. (1974) *Psychology and Common Sense*. London: Routledge & Kegan Paul.

Kelley, H. H. (1967) Attribution theory in social psychology. In D. Levine (ed.) *Nebraska Symposium on Motivation*. Lincoln: University of Nebraska Press.

Kelly, G. A. (1955) *The Psychology of Personal Constructs* (2 vols.) New York, W. W. Norton.

Klein, M. (1932) *The Psycho-Analysis of Children* (rev. edn). London: Hogarth Press and the Institute of PsychoAnalysis.

Kline, M. (1980) *Mathematics: the Loss of Certainty*. Oxford: Oxford University Press.

Koch, S. (1959) Epilogue. In S. Koch (ed.) *Psychology: A Study of a Science*, vol. 3, 729–88. New York: McGraw-Hill.

Koch, S. (1964) Psychology and emerging conceptions of knowledge as unitary. In T. W. Wann (ed.) *Behaviourism and Phenomenology*. Chicago: University of Chicago Press.

Koch, S. (1975) Psychology as science. In S. C. Brown (ed.) *Philosophy of Psychology*. London: Macmillan.

Koffka, K. (1921) Die Grundlagen der Psychischen Entwicklung Osterwieck am Harz, quoted in E. Cassirer (1957) *The Philosophy of Symbolic Forms*, vol. 3, pp. 64–5. New Haven: Yale University Press.

Kuhn, T. S. (1962) *The Structure of Scientific Revolutions*. Chicago: University of Chicago Press.

Labov, W. (1969) The logic of non-standard English. *Georgetown Monographs on Language and Linguistics, 22*, 1–31.

Lacan, J. (1977) *Ecrits* (trans. A. Sheridan). London: Allen Lane.

Laguna, G. A. de (1963) *Speech: its Function and Development*. Bloomington: University of Indiana Press.

Laing, R. D. (1962) *The Politics of Experience and The Bird of Paradise*. Harmondsworth: Penguin.

Laing, R. D. (1971) *Knots*. Harmondsworth: Penguin.

Lakatos, I. (1970) Falsification and the methodology of scientific research programmes. In I. Lakatos and A. Musgrave (eds) *Criticism and the Growth of Knowledge*. London: Cambridge University Press.

Lakoff, G. and Johnson, M. (1980) *Metaphors We Live By*. Chicago: University of Chicago Press.

Langer, E. J. (1978) Rethinking the role of thought in social interaction. In J. H. Harvey, W. J. Ickes and R. F. Kidd (eds) *New Directions in Attribution*

Research, vol. 2. New Jersey: Erlbaum Associates.

Laplace, P. S. (1886) *Introduction à la théorie analytique des probabilités*. Paris.

Lashley, K. S. (1951) The problem of serial order in behaviour. In L. P. Jeffress (ed.) *Cerebral Mechanisms in Behaviour*. New York: Wiley.

Leith, E. N. and Upatnieks, J. (1965) Photography by laser. *Scientific American, 212*, 24—35.

Lemert, C. C. (1979) *Sociology and the Twiglight of Man: Homocentrism and Discource in Sociological Theory*. Carbondale: Southern Illinois University Press.

Levi-Strauss, C. (1963) *Structural Anthropology*. New York: Basic Books.

Levi-Strauss, C. (1966) *The Savage Mind*. London: Routledge & Kegan Paul.

Lewin, K. (1944) Constructs in psychology and psychological ecology. *Univ. Iowa Stud. Child Welf., 20*, 1–29.

Lewis, C. S. (1943) *The Abolition of Man*. Oxford: Oxford University Press; reissued London: Collins, Fount Paperback, 1978.

Lock, A. (1980) *The GuidedReinvention of Language*. London: Academic Press.

Lyons, J. (1968) *Introduction to Theoretical Linguistics*. London: Cambridge University Press.

Macfarlane, A. (1974) If a smile is so important. *New Scientist*, 25 April 1974.

Machiavelli, N. (1961) *The Prince* (trans. by G. Bull). Harmondsworth: Penguin.

Macmurray, J. (1957) *The Self as Agent*. London: Faber & Faber.

Macmurray, J. (1961) *Persons in Relation*. London: Faber & Faber.

Manicas, P. T. and Secord, P. F. (1983) Implications for psychology of the new philosophy of science. *Amer. Psych., 38*, 399–413.

McGuire, W. J. (1973) The yin and yang of progress in social psychology. *J. of Pers. and Soc. Psychol., 26*, 446–56.

McHugh, P., Raffel, S., Foss, D. C., and Blum, A. (1974) *On Beginning Social Inquiry*. London: Routledge & Kegan Paul.

Mead, G. H. (1934) *Mind, Self and Society*. Chicago: University of Chicago Press.

Merchant, C. (1980) *The Death of Nature: Women, Ecology, and the Scientific Revolution*. New York: Harper & Row.

Merleau-Ponty, M. (1962) *Phenomenology of Perception* (trans. C. Smith). London: Routledge & Kegan Paul.

Merleau-Ponty, M. (1970) *Themes from the Lectures at the College de France* (trans. John O'Neill). Evanston: Northwestern University Press.

Miller, G. A., Galanter, E. and Pribram, K. H. (1960) *Plans and the Structure of Behaviour*. New York: Holt, Rinehart & Winston.

Mills, C. W. (1940) Situated actions and vocabularies of motive. *Amer. Socio. Review, 5*, 904–13.

Minsky, M. (1977) Frame-system theory. In P. N. Johnson-Laird and P. C. Wason (eds) *Thinking: Readings in Cognitive Science*. London: Cambridge University Press.

Mumford, L. (1967) *The Myth of the Machine*, London: Secker & Warburg.

Neisser, U. (1967) *Cognitive Psychology*. New York: Appleton-Century-Crofts.

Neisser, U. (1976) *Cognition and Reality*. San Francisco: Freeman.

Newell, A. (1973) You can't play twenty questions with nature and win. In W. G. Chase (ed.) *Visual Information Processing*. New York: Academic Press.

Newson, J. and Newson, E. (1968) *Four Years Old in an Urban Community*. London, Allen & Unwin.

Newson, J. and Newson, E. (1974) Cultural aspects of child rearing in the English-speaking world. In M. P. M. Richards (ed.) *The Integration of a Child into a Social World*. London: Cambridge University Press.

Newson, J. and Newson, E. (1975) Intersubjectivity and the transmission of culture; on the social origins of symbolic functioning. *Bull. Br. Psychol. Soc., 28*, 437–46.

Newson, J. and Pawlby, S. (1972) Imitation and pre-verbal behaviour. Dept. of Psychol., Nottingham.

Nisbett, R. E. and Bellows, N. (1977) Verbal reports about causal influences on social judgements: private access versus public theories. *J. of Pers. and Soc. Psychol., 35*, 613–24.

Nisbett, R. E. and Wilson, T. D. (1977) Telling more than we can know: verbal reports on mental processes. *Psych. Rev., 84*, 231–59.

Noble, W. G. (1981) Gibsonian theory and the pragmatist perspective. *J. Theory Soc. Behav., 11*, 65–85.

Ong, W. J. (1982) *Orality and Literacy*. London: Methuen.

Ossorio, P. G. (1973) Never smile at a crocodile. *J. Theory Soc. Behav., 3*, 121–40.

Ossorio, P. G. (1978) *What Actually Happens*. Columbia, South Carolina: University of South Carolina Press.

Ossorio, P. G. and Davis, K. E. (1968) The self, intentionality, and reactions to evaluations of the self. In C. Gordon and K. J. Gergen (eds) *The Self in Social Interaction*. New York: Wiley.

Palmer, R. E. (1969) *Hermeneutics*. Evanston: Northwestern University Press.

Peters, R. S. (1958) *The Concept of Motivation*. London: Routledge & Kegan Paul.

Piaget, J. (1950) *Introduction à l'épistémologie génétique*, vol. III Paris: Presses Universitaires France.

Piaget, J. (1971) *Structuralism*. London: Routledge & Kegan Paul.

Piaget, J. (1972) *Principles of Genetic Epistemology*. London, Routledge & Kegan Paul.

Piaget, J. and Inhelder, B. (1969) *The Psychology of the Child*. London: Routledge & Kegan Paul.

Polanyi, M. (1967) *The Tacit Dimension*. London: Routledge & Kegan Paul.

Pompa, L. (1975) *Vico: a Study of the 'New Science'*. Cambridge: Cambridge University Press.

Popper, Sir K. (1963) *Conjectures and Refutations*. London: Routledge & Kegan Paul.

Popper, Sir K. (1972) *Objective Knowledge*. Oxford: Oxford University Press.

Prigogine, I. (1980) *From Being to Becoming: Time and Complexity in the Physical Sciences*. San Francisco: Freeman.

Quine, W. V. (1953) Two dogmas of empiricism. In W. V. Quine, *From a Logical Point of View*. Cambridge, Mass.: Harvard University Press.

Reddy, M. (1979) The conduit metaphor. In A. Ortony (ed.) *Metaphor and Thought*. London: Cambridge University Press.

Richards, I. A. (1936) *The Philosophy of Rhetoric*. London: Oxford University Press.

Richards, M. P. M. (1974a) First steps in becoming social. In M. P. M. Richards (ed.) *The Integration of a Child into a Social World*. Cambridge: Cambridge University Press.

Richards, M. P. M. (1974b) The development of communication in the first year of life. In K. Connolly and J. S. Bruner (eds) *The Early Growth of Competence*. London: Academic Press.

Ricoeur, P. (1970) *Freud and Philosophy: an Essay on Interpretation*. New Haven: Yale University Press.

Rommetveit, R. (1976) The architecture of intersubjectivity. In L. Strickland, F. Aboud and K. J. Gergen (eds) *Social Psychology in Transition*. New York: Plenum Press.

Rosch, E. (1973) Natural categories. *Cognitive Psychology, 4*, 328–50.

Ross, L. (1977) The intuitive psychologist and his shortcomings. In L. Berkowitz (ed.) *Advances in Experimental Social Psychology*, vol. 10. New York: Academic Press.

Russell, B. (1914) *Our Knowledge of the External World*. London: Allen & Unwin.

Russell, B. (1948) *Human Knowledge: Its Scope and Limits*. London: Allen & Unwin.

Ryle, G. (1963) *The Concept of Mind*. Harmondsworth: Peregrine.

Saussure, F. de (1960) *Course in General Linguistics* (ed. C. Bally and A. Sechehaye). London: Peter Owen.

Schaffer, H. R. (1971) *The Growth of Sociability*. Harmondsworth: Penguin.

Schaffer, H. R. (1977) *Mothering*. London: Fontana.

Schank, R. C. and Abelson, R. P. (1977) *Scripts, Plans, Goals and Understanding*. New York: Lawrence Erlbaum.

Scheibe, K. E. (1978) The psychologist's advantage and its nullification: the limits of predictability. *Amer. Psych., 33*, 869–81.

Schutz, A. (1953) Common-sense and scientific interpretation of human action. *Philosophy and Phenomenological Research, 14*, 1–38.

Schutz, A. (1962) *Collected Papers I: The Problem of Social Reality*. The Hague: Marinus Nijhoff.

Schutz, A. (1964) *Collected Papers II: Studies in Social Theory*. The Hague: Marinus Nijhoff.

Schutz, A. (1966) *Collected Papers III: Studies in Phenomenological Philosophy*. The Hague: Martinus Nijhoff.

Schutz, A. (1967) *The Phenomenology of the Social World*. Evanston, Ill.: Northwestern University Press.

242   *References*

Schutz, A. (1972) *The Phenomenology of the Social World*. London: Heinemann.

Scott, M. D. and Lyman, S. (1968) Accounts. *Amer. Sociol. Review.*, *33*, 46–62.

Searle, J. R. (1969) *Speech Acts*. Cambridge: Cambridge University Press.

Searle, J. R. (1979a) The intentionality of intention and action. *Inquiry*, *22*, 253–80.

Searle, J. R. (1979b) Intentionality and the use of language. In A. Margalit (ed.) *Meaning and Use*. Dordrecht: Reidel.

Searle, J. R. (1979c) What is an intentional state? *Mind*, *88*, 74–92.

Shorter, E. (1977) *The Making of the Modern Family*. London: Fontana.

Shotter, J. (1973a) Acquired powers: the transformation of natural into personal powers. *J. Theory Soc. Behav.*, *3*, 141–56.

Shotter, J. (1973b) Prolegomena to an understanding of play. *J. Theory Soc. Behav.*, *3*, 47–89.

Shotter, J. (1974a) What is it to be human? In N. Armistead (ed.) *Reconstructing Social Psychology*. Harmondsworth: Penguin.

Shotter, J. (1974b) The development of personal powers. In M. P. M. Richards (ed.) *The Integration of a Child into a Social World*. London: Cambridge University Press.

Shotter, J. (1975) *Images of Man in Psychological Research*. London: Methuen.

Shotter, J. (1978) The cultural context of communication studies: methodological and theoretical issues. In A. Lock (ed.) *Action, Gesture and Symbol*. London: Academic Press.

Shotter, J. (1980a) Action, joint action, and intentionality. In M. Brenner (ed.) *The Structure of Action*. Oxford: Blackwell.

Shotter, J. (1980b) Men the magicians: the duality of social being and the structure of moral worlds. In A. J. Chapman and D. Jones (eds) *Models of Man*. Leicester: British Psychological Society.

Shotter, J. (1981a) Vico, moral worlds, accountability, and personhood. In P. Heelas and A. Lock (eds) *Indigenous Psychologies: the Anthropology of the Self*. London: Academic Press.

Shotter, J. (1981b) Telling and reporting: prospective and retrospective uses of self-ascriptions. In C. Antaki (ed.) *The Psychology of Ordinary Explanations of Social Behaviour*. London: Academic Press.

Shotter, J. (1982) Consciousness, self-consciousness, inner games, and alternative realities. In G. Underwood (ed.) *Aspects of Consciousness*, vol. 3. London and New York: Academic Press.

Shotter, J. (1983) 'Duality of structure' and 'intentionality' in an ecological psychology. *J. Theory Soc. Behav.*, *13*, 19–43.

Shotter, J. (in press) Hermeneutical interpretive theory. In R. Harré and R. Lamb (eds) *The Encyclopedic Dictionary of Psychology*. Blackwell: Oxford.

Shotter, J. and Gregory, S. (1976) On first gaining the idea of oneself as a person. In R. Harré (ed.) *Life Sentences*. Chichester: Wiley.

Shotter, J. and Newson, J. (1982) An ecological approach to cognitive development: implicate orders, joint action, and intentionality. In G. Butterworth and P. Light (eds) *Social Cognition: Studies of the Development of Understanding*. Sussex: Harvester Press.

Shotter, J. and Burton, M. (1983) Common sense accounts of human action: the descriptive formulations of Heider, Smedslund, and Ossorio. In L. Wheeler (ed.) *Review of Personality and Social Psychology*, vol. 4 Beverly Hills, Ca: Sage.

Skinner, B. F. (1953) *Science and Human Behaviour*. New York, Macmillan.

Skinner, B. F. (1972) *Beyond Freedom and Dignity*. London: Cape; Harmondsworth: Penguin, 1973.

Smedslund, J. (1969) Meanings, implications and universals: towards a psychology of man. *Scand. J. Psychol.*, 10, 1–15.

Smedslund, J. (1970) Circular relations between understanding and logic, *Scand. J. Psychol.*, 11, 217–19.

Smedslund, J. (1977) Piaget's psychology in practice, *Brit. J. Educ. Psychol.*, 47, 1–6.

Smedslund, J. (1978) Bandura's theory of self-efficacy: a set of common sense theorems, *Scand. J. Psychol.*, 19, 1–14.

Smedslund, J. (1979) Between the analytic and the arbitrary: a case study in psychological research. *Scand. J. Psychol.*, 19, 1–14.

Smedslund, J. (1980) Analysing the primary code. In D. Olson (ed.) *The Social Foundations of Language: Essays in Honour of J. S. Bruner*. New York: Norton.

Smedslund, J. (1981) The logic of psychological treatment. *Scand. J. Psychol.*, 22, 65–77.

Smith, M. B. (1972) Is experimental social psychology advancing? *J. of Exp. Soc. Psychol.*, 8, 86–96.

Spitz, R. (1965) *The First Year of Life*. New York: International University Press.

Stapp, H. P. (1972) The Copenhagen interpretation. *American Journal of Physics*, 40, 1098–1116.

Stolzenberg, G. (1978) Can an inquiry into the foundations of mathematics tell us anything interesting about mind? In G. A. Miller and E. Lenneberg (eds) *Psychology and Biology of Language and Thought: Essays in Honour of Eric Lenneberg*. New York: Academic Press.

Storms, M. D. and Nisbett, R. E. (1970) Insomnia and the attribution process. *J. of Pers. and Soc. Psychol.*, 16, 319–28.

Stout, G. F. (1938) *A Manual of Psychology*. London: University Tutorial Press.

Sudnow, D. (1978) *Ways of the Hand*. London: Routledge & Kegan Paul.

Sutherland, N. S. (1970) Is the brain a physical system? In R. Borger and F. Cioffi (eds) *Explanation in the Behavioural Sciences*. London: Cambridge University Press.

Tajfel, H. and Fraser C. (1978) *Introducing Social Psychology*. Harmondsworth: Penguin.

Taylor, A. E. (1955) *Aristotle*. New York: Dover.

Taylor, C. (1971) Interpretation and the sciences of man. *Rev. Metaphysics,* 25, 3–51.

Taylor, C. (1980) Understanding in human science. *Rev. Metaphysics, 34,* 3–23.

Taylor, R. (1966) *Action and Purpose.* Englewood Cliffs: Prentice-Hall.

Thompson, E. P. (1982) Beyond the cold war. In *Zero Option.* London: Merlin Books.

Tinbergen, N. (1951) *The Study of Instinct.* London, Oxford University Press.

Trevarthen, C. (1974) Conversations with a one-month-old. *New Scientist,* 2 May 1974.

Trevarthen, C. (1975a) Early attempts at speech. In R. Lewin (ed.) *Child Alive: New Insights into the Development of Young Children.* London: Maurice Temple Smith.

Trevarthen, C. (1975b) Psychological actions in early infancy. *La Récherche, 6,* 447–58.

Trevarthen, C. (1980) The foundations of intersubjectivity: development of interpersonal and co-operative understanding in infants. In D. Olson (ed.) *The Social Foundations of Language: Essays in Honour of J. S. Bruner.* New York: Norton.

Trevarthen, C. (1982) Origins of social cognition in infancy. In G. Butterworth and P. Light (eds) *Social Cognition: Studies in the Development of Understanding.* Sussex: Harvester Press.

Turnbull, C. M. (1973) *The Mountain People.* London: Cape.

Uexküll, J. (1957) A stroll through the world of animals and men. In C. H. Schiller (ed.) *Instinctive Behaviour.* London: Methuen.

Valins, S. and Ray, A. A. (1967) Effects of cognitive desensitization on avoidance behaviour. *J. of Pers. and Soc. Psychol., 7,* 345–50.

Vico, G. (1975) *The New Science of Giambattista Vico,* (ed. and trans. T. G. Bergin and M. H. Fisch). Ithaca, N.Y.: Cornell University Press (3rd edn orig. pub. 1744).

Vygotsky, L. S. (1962) *Thought and Language.* Cambridge, Mass.: MIT Press.

Vygotsky, L. S. (1966a) Play and its role in the mental development of the child. *Soviet Psychology, 12,* 6–18.

Vygotsky, L. S. (1966b) Development of the higher mental functions. In *Psychological Research in the USSR.* Moscow: Progress Publishers.

Vygotsky, L. S. (1978) *Mind in Society: the Development of Higher Psychological Processes.* Boston: Harvard University Press.

Walkerdine, V. (1982) From context to text: a psychosemiotic approach. In M. Beveridge (ed.) *Children Thinking Through Language.* London: Edward Arnold.

Washabaugh, W. (1980) The role of speech in the construction of reality. *Semiotica, 31,* 197–214.

Weir, R. H. (1962) *Language in the Crib.* New York: Humanities.

Weiss, P. (1980) *You, I, and the Others.* Carbondale: University of Southern

Illinois Press.

Wilson, W. O. (1975) *Sociobiology: the New Synthesis*. New Haven: Harvard University Press.

Winch, P. (1958) *The Idea of a Social Science and its Relations to Philosophy*. London: Routledge & Kegan Paul.

Winnicott, D. M. (1974) *Playing and Reality*. Harmondsworth: Penguin.

Wittgenstein, L. (1922) *Tractatus-Logico-Philosophicus*. London: Routledge & Kegan Paul.

Wittgenstein, L. (1953) *Philosophical Investigations*. Oxford: Blackwell.

Wittgenstein, L. (1961) *Tractatus-Logico-Philosophicus*. London: Routledge & Kegan Paul.

Wittgenstein, L. (1965) *The Blue and Brown Books*. New York: Harper Torch Books.

Wittgenstein, L. (1969) *On Certainty*. Oxford: Blackwell.

Wittgenstein, L. (1980) *Remarks on the Philosophy of Psychology*, vol. I. Oxford: Blackwell.

Wittgenstein, L. (1981) *Zettel* (2nd edn) (ed. G. E. M. Anscombe and G. H. V. Wright). Oxford: Blackwell.

Wolff, P. (1969) The natural history of crying and other vocalizations in early infancy. In B. Foss (ed.) *Determinants of Infant Behaviour*, vol. 4. London: Methuen.

Index of Subjects

Index of Names